ENGAGED JOURNALISM

COLUMBIA JOURNALISM REVIEW BOOKS

COLUMBIA JOURNALISM REVIEW BOOKS

Series Editors: Victor Navasky, Evan Cornog, Elizabeth Spayd, and the editors of the *Columbia Journalism Review*

For more than fifty years, the *Columbia Journalism Review* has been the gold standard for media criticism, holding the profession to the highest standards and exploring where journalism is headed, for good and for ill.

Columbia Journalism Review Books expands upon this mission, seeking to publish titles that allow for greater depth in exploring key issues confronting journalism, both past and present, and pointing to new ways of thinking about the field's impact and potential.

Drawing on the expertise of the editorial staff at the *Columbia Journalism Review* as well as the Columbia Journalism School, the series of books will seek out innovative voices as well as reclaim important works, traditions, and standards. In doing this, the series will also incorporate new ways of publishing made available by the Web and e-books.

Engaged Journalism

CONNECTING WITH DIGITALLY EMPOWERED NEWS AUDIENCES

Jake Batsell

Columbia University Press   New York

Columbia University Press
Publishers Since 1893
New York   Chichester, West Sussex
cup.columbia.edu

Library of Congress Cataloging-in-Publication Data

Batsell, Jake.
Engaged Journalism : connecting with digitally empowered
news audiences / Jake Batsell.
pages cm. — (Columbia journalism review books)
Includes bibliographical references and index.
ISBN 978-0-231-16834-2 (cloth : alk. paper) —
ISBN 978-0-231-16835-9 (pbk. : alk. paper) —
ISBN 978-0-231-53867-1 (e-book)
1. Journalism—United States—History—21st century.   2. News audiences—
United States—History—21st century.   3. Online journalism—United
States—History—21st century.   4. Social media—United States.   I. Title.

PN4867.2.B38   2015
071'.3—dc23   2014011950

Columbia University Press books are printed on permanent and durable
acid-free paper.
This book is printed on paper with recycled content.
Printed in the United States of America

Cover design by Martin Hinze

To Tracy, the most engaging person I know

CONTENTS

FOREWORD

As someone who has encouraged, inspired, cajoled, begged, and pleaded with journalists to engage with audiences for the better part of my twenty-year career in journalism, I'm honored to have the first word on Jake Batsell's book about how and—more important—*why* engaged journalism is so crucial in today's digital age.

"Why?" is a question I've been asked countless times since I started working on the digital side of news in 2000. Why should journalism change? Why should reporters listen to, and connect with, their audience? Why should the one-way lecture become a conversation? Why should anyone in a newsroom spend precious time reading comments on Facebook instead of, you know, reporting? After all, the journalist is the one with the college degree, the experience, and the wherewithal to contribute reporting to a world that needs it now more than ever.

As you will learn through the examples and lessons Batsell has collected, these questions have dozens of answers. In this foreword I'm going to attempt to answer a different one: Why not?

If we can learn why journalists (and journalism) have taken so long to adapt to the era of engagement brought on by digital and social media, we can identify the tools to assist those who still do not believe in the wisdom of the crowd. In my opinion journalists have resisted this movement because they are resistant to vulnerability. Journalists pride themselves on authority, credibility, and influence. These traits run directly counter to vulnerability, which many (both within and outside journalism) have seen as weakness. But as Brené Brown explains, the opposite actually is true. That is the cornerstone of her 2012 book, *Daring Greatly: How the Courage to Be Vulnerable Transforms the Way We Live, Love, Parent, and Lead*, and her popular TED talk (Brown 2010), which had more than fourteen million views as of early 2014.

"Vulnerability is no weakness, and the uncertainty, risk, and emotional exposure we face every day are not optional," Brown argues. "Our only choice is a question of engagement. Our willingness to own and engage with our vulnerability determines the depth of our courage and the clarity of our purpose" (2012:2).

Those journalists who have risked engaging with their audiences are courageous. They have exposed themselves to criticism and skepticism, and, as you will read in this book, their journalism and their audiences have reaped the rewards.

"Perfect and bulletproof are seductive, but they don't exist in the human experience," Brown writes in *Daring Greatly* (2). Newsrooms have long been known to demand perfection. But as we all should know by now, there is no such thing as perfection in journalism (or anything else, for that matter).

Another trait of many newsrooms is a "can't-do" culture. This is not by design, of course. It developed as traditional news companies went from positions of dominance to shaky ground. A significant aversion to risk is why entrenched companies fail to innovate fast enough to stay ahead of—or keep up with—more nimble start-ups, as Clayton Christensen (1997) powerfully demonstrates in his pathbreaking book *The Innovator's Dilemma: When New Technologies Cause Great Firms to Fail*.

The influential Silicon Valley investor Ben Horowitz (2014) describes the difference between a start-up and a big company by noting that, in a big company, a whole hierarchy of people needs to agree that a new idea is good in order to pursue it. "If one smart person figures out some-

thing wrong with an idea—often to show off or to consolidate power—
that's usually enough to kill it," Horowitz writes.

In every newsroom there lurks a Dr. No, the person who can quickly
find fault with any new idea and kill it with a litany of reasons why it
won't work. If you've ever worked in a newsroom, are you picturing that
person right now? (Or are there too many to count?)

Horowitz supports his point with a priceless passage about a Western Union report from an internal committee about why a new technology called the telephone was not worth paying $100,000 to its inventor,
Alexander Graham Bell, and his colleague, G. G. Hubbard: "Hubbard
and Bell want to install one of their 'telephone devices' in every city.
The idea is idiotic on the face of it. Furthermore, why would any person
want to use this ungainly and impractical device when he can send a
messenger to the telegraph office and have a clear written message sent
to any large city in the United States?"(2014).

Countless journalists originally regarded websites, blogs, and social
media to be as idiotic as this Western Union committee saw the telephone. For practicing journalism in today's digital age, engagement is
just as critical and indispensable as the telephone. And engagement will
be even more important tomorrow, making this book essential to surviving and thriving in the digital age.

What I really like about the book is how it provides a framework
for thinking about engagement in journalism, which can be a rather
vague concept. (It's more than updating your Facebook page and tweeting a handful of updates every day.) The book's five key principles—
face-to-face engagement, social media, niche/hyperlocal journalism, interactive platforms, and measuring engagement and making
it pay—provide a clear picture of the different facets and how they
tie together.

Journalism is about people, not technology. The tools, technologies,
and platforms we use today for engagement will inevitably change and
so will our need to change with them—and adapt again.

This book is about people, not technology. It's about journalists who
are using new methods (and some new tools) to do better journalism
than was possible just a few years ago.

As Benjamin Franklin famously said, "When you're finished changing, you're finished."

Mark Briggs

Mark Briggs is the author of *Journalism 2.0: How to Survive and Thrive, Journalism Next: A Practical Guide to Digital Reporting and Publishing,* and *Entrepreneurial Journalism: How to Build What's Next for News.* He also is a former Ford Fellow for Entrepreneurial Journalism at the Poynter Institute. He is currently the director of digital media at KING, the NBC affiliate in Seattle.

PREFACE

One early Monday morning in late June 1998, I bounded up the stairs to my third-floor desk at the *Seattle Times*. The little red light on my office phone greeted me ominously.

Time to sift through reader voice mail.

I picked up the receiver, pushed the touch-tone buttons, and braced for the unpredictable. Occasionally some kind soul called to praise a story I had written or to ask where to find more information. But more often than I might have preferred, readers called to nitpick. Or complain. Or vent. Or, in one bizarre case, sing about the actress Jennifer Connelly until the voice mail cut him off.

Just two years out of college, I was hitting my groove and finding my voice as a general assignment reporter for the *Times*'s business desk. The *Times* was then an afternoon paper, so I reported for duty at 5 A.M., turned out a few quick stories and briefs for the P.M. street editions, then worked on features and enterprise stories until my shift ended in midafternoon.

Toward the end of my shift on the previous Friday, the local Kroger-owned supermarket chain, QFC, had sent out a press release announcing it had acquired Art's, a grocery store in the Ballard neighborhood in northwest Seattle. More than a little eager to begin my weekend, I had banged out an unspectacular 344-word story with a formulaic lede: "Art's Food Center, a Ballard institution whose wide-ranging merchandise and low prices earned customer loyalty for more than 50 years, has been acquired by the Quality Food Centers chain" (Batsell 1998).

The ensuing weekend's voice-mail messages were brutal and unforgiving. Readers pointed out that Art's wasn't just any neighborhood grocery store; it was the unofficial hub of Crown Hill, a proud (and apparently feisty) subneighborhood within the larger Ballard area. My story had failed to note this distinction. Phone nestled against my ear, I cringed as a series of irritated Crown Hill readers branded me as a carpetbagger who obviously had not grown up in Seattle, a clueless cub reporter who had failed to capture the store's rich history as the linchpin of a neighborhood.[1] One reader asked if I had received my journalism degree from a Cracker Jack box.

The readers, I now realize, were right. (Well, except for the Cracker Jack comment.) But after I had absorbed the flurry of voice-mail zingers, my reaction was defensive. I groused to my editors: "Don't they realize I'm writing for a wider audience?"[2] I certainly didn't update the online version of my story to reflect the store's Crown Hill history. And I came to dread that little red voice-mail light even more. In so doing I lost the goodwill of those passionate Crown Hill readers. After all, their only recourse was to cancel their *Times* subscription and take the morning *Post-Intelligencer*, which paid equally scant attention to small neighborhoods like Crown Hill.

If the same story happened today, *MyBallard.com*, an award-winning hyperlocal news blog that partners with the *Seattle Times*, would cover it from every angle. By the time Kroger got around to issuing a press release, *MyBallard.com* likely would have been buzzing for weeks about the store's future, with Crown Hill readers debating at length what the change in ownership would mean for their neighborhood.[3]

But too often back then I considered readers—my paying audience—to be an afterthought. Like many newspaper reporters, for much of my career I wanted to hear from readers only when they had a scoop or tip to offer or perhaps some kudos I could share with my editor. Sure, I aggressively sought out sources of all stripes while reporting a story, but it didn't occur to me to make a habit of proactively engaging the readers who consumed my journalism. As a graduate of Arizona State University's Walter Cronkite School of Journalism (not a Cracker Jack box, by the way), I took comfort in the certainty of Uncle Walter's mantra: "And that's the way it is." Perhaps to a fault, I idealized the role of the journalist as a beacon for American society. *I* was the reporter. *I* was the expert. Readers were merely the people who had the privilege of beholding my brilliant informative prose. And most readers who called or e-mailed were crackpots anyway, right?

About a decade later, while reporting for the *Dallas Morning News*, I began to understand how interacting with readers could actually add value, purpose, and authenticity to my journalism. As I covered controversial toll road proposals during the 2007 Texas legislative session, I learned that breaking news on the web and blogging about my beat could elicit valuable real-time reactions from readers and sources, better informing my coverage for the next day's paper. A few months later, when I blogged from a fan's perspective about a quix-otic quest to upgrade my nosebleed seat for a sold-out Dallas Cowboys game, readers rooted me on and offered tips and suggestions about how to navigate the sea of eBay hawkers, Craigslist scammers, and game-day scalpers. Over time I realized that having an ongoing dia-logue with readers could be both practical and fun while helping me to build trust and better connect me as a journalist with the community I covered.[4]

During my decade-plus as a reporter, I saw the journalistic process evolve from a one-way lecture to two-way conversation. The impor-tance of interacting with readers became even more evident when I left the *Morning News* in 2008 and started a student news site at Southern Methodist University, where I also teach digital journalism classes. I worked with my students to create the online-only *SMUDailyMustang. com*, building a readership from scratch that grew to forty-three thou-sand monthly page views and attracted more than three thousand Twitter followers. Our small student news site partnered with media organizations both large (*Yahoo! News*, the *Dallas Morning News*) and small (*Dallas South News*) and won a First Amendment Award from the Society of Professional Journalists for a campus crime project that combined public records with Google Fusion Tables to create a series of interactive maps. My experiences as both a reporter and professor have taught me that if news providers hope to stay relevant, useful, and, perhaps most important, financially viable in an ever-connected world, they must embrace an interactive mind-set and constantly find new ways to effectively engage their audiences.

For newsroom leaders like Kathy Best, engagement isn't a buzzword; it's a matter of survival. Best, editor of the *Seattle Times*, started her career as a reporter at the *Quad-City Times*, which covers eastern Iowa and western Illinois, and the *St. Louis Post-Dispatch* in the early 1980s, a golden era of newspapering she recalls now with both nostalgia and contempt.[5] "That's when we got to say, 'We're just going to put it out there, and you're going to read it,'" Best told me. "We're paying for that now." Before I interviewed her, I had sent Best a summary of my ideas for this book, which I had tentatively titled Ready to Engage. "I think you're being too kind," she said. "I think it's Engage or Die" (pers. comm.).

Around the time that Best was beginning her newspaper career, a semiretired Walter Cronkite was penning vignettes about his love of sailing for a trilogy of illustrated coffee-table books. Admirers lined up for hours at bookstores to meet the former anchorman still widely known as "the most trusted man in America." At one signing he told his coauthor: "I've been broadcasting for years, and this is the first time I met my audience. It's a treat for people to walk up and say, 'You've been in my bedroom every night for decades'" (Brinkley 2012:580).

Cronkite was a personal hero of mine; as an undergraduate I had the rare chance to meet him and ask his advice about the profession I was entering. I know that single confession he jokingly made at the 1980s book signing doesn't sum up his overall attitude toward journalistic engagement. During the nineteen years he anchored the *CBS Evening News*, Cronkite often personally fielded viewers' phone calls, courteously replied to scores of letters, and warmly received face-to-face admirers.

Still, I was surprised to learn from the biography by Brinkley that Cronkite had left the anchor's chair before he ever proactively sought to interact with his audience. For all his incalculable contributions to journalism, Cronkite's legendary sign-off—"And that's the way it is"—typified the one-way lecture, an attitude about news delivery that reigned for decades among legacy (mainstream) news outlets and the journalists who worked for them. The Cronkite-caliber journalists of today and tomorrow will be engaged in a two-way conversation with their audience, and that constant dynamic interaction will make their journalism more inclusive and relevant than ever.

The pages that follow describe and analyze examples of more than two dozen news organizations that are experimenting with new ways to engage their audiences. The book is based on field research gathered through observation and interviews at traditional and start-up newsrooms across the United States and United Kingdom between June 2012 and July 2013. I decided to visit these organizations because each has structured or restructured its news operations around an engagement-focused mission.

At the *Seattle Times*, the city's sole surviving daily newspaper, daily front-page meetings begin with news producers' providing up-to-the-minute web traffic updates. Editors discuss how to adjust the website to reflect what's trending and promote the day's real-time chats and live blogs.[6] Flat-screen monitors throughout the newsroom show real-time traffic for the top ten stories of the moment. In mid-2011 the *Times* combined its print and online operations into one reorganized newsroom structured around the premise of constant interaction with its audience. Suki Dardarian, a top *Times* editor from 2000 to 2014, said that when deciding how to play stories, a central factor is "How are we going to have a conversation around it and help the story become more three-dimensional?" (pers. comm.).[7] Even before the reorganization, the *Times* was named the Associated Press Managing Editors' Innovator of the Year in 2010 for its experimental use of social networks during its Pulitzer-winning breaking news coverage of a police manhunt, and for partnering with dozens of hyperlocal blogs as part of the

Networked Journalism Project of J-Lab: The Institute for Interactive Journalism. (A sign of the times: APME has since changed its name to Associated Press Media Editors.)

Also in Seattle the tech news start-up *GeekWire*, national news hub *NBCNews.com*, hyperlocal darling *West Seattle Blog*, and the *Puget Sound Business Journal* all practice engagement in compelling ways that generate revenue.

Election night 2012 was a landmark occasion for *Yahoo! News* in Manhattan as its interactive portal, the Election Control Room, set an all-time record with 4.2 million live streams. The Control Room put users in charge of their own experience, offering video streams, live blogging, and real-time interactive electoral maps. "It all comes back to handing the control of the experience to the user, and having them decide what's important to them," explained E. J. Liao, senior product manager, as the state-by-state voting tallies came in (pers. comm.).

The *Texas Tribune* in Austin, a political news site that launched in November 2009, has drawn national attention for its leading-edge journalism and fund-raising prowess (Batsell 2010; C. W. Anderson 2012; Ellis 2013b).[8] During a spring 2012 membership drive, Evan Smith, editor-in-chief and CEO, proclaimed in an e-mail: "From public education and criminal justice, to border affairs and everything in between, The Texas Tribune engages citizens unlike ever before." All fund-raising pitches aside, the *Tribune* has broken ground in the arena of audience engagement through its rich interactive databases; its competitive games and contests; and such popular and profitable events as its Trib-Live interview series and annual Texas Tribune Festival. In the world of nonprofit news start-ups, the *Tribune* has found more success figuring out the engagement riddle than many of its peers.

The *Christian Science Monitor* in Boston abandoned its daily print edition in 2009 and now operates as a web-first newsroom and weekly print magazine. The *Monitor's* metamorphosis was one of the earlier and more radical digital-first experiments among traditional news outlets, so its successes and missteps are especially valuable for those that may be contemplating a similar move (see Groves and Brown-Smith 2011, 2013). Three years into the web-first experiment, John Yemma, editor of the *Monitor*, reported that the engagement-focused strategy had propelled the *Monitor* to its best fiscal year since 1963, cutting in half the subsidy the newsroom receives from its parent church (2012a).

WBEZ-FM, KTVK-3TV, and KING-TV are broadcast stations that take sophisticated approaches to engaging their digital audiences. KTVK, an independent station in Phoenix, calculates an engagement rate for each of the station's more than forty Twitter accounts and twenty Facebook pages and sums up the results on a "Social Media Scorecard," identifying which are leaders and laggards and comparing them with their counterparts at rival stations. KING, the NBC affiliate in Seattle, crowdsources soft-news photos on Facebook, Twitter, and Instagram in the hope that viewers will do the same when breaking news hits. WBEZ, the flagship station of Chicago Public Media, tracks engagement through a collection of individual metrics, from event attendance to social media shares to the number of call-ins to radio shows. Together the three stations are deploying audience engagement strategies that can provide lessons for U.S. broadcast outlets.

The *CNN Belief Blog*, run out of the network's Washington bureau, drew two million page views and thousands of comments in July 2012 by asking its readers a simple provocative question in the aftermath of the Colorado movie theater shootings: "Where was God in Aurora?" Instead of following the conventional one-and-done story format, Dan Gilgoff, the religion editor, channeled his readers' responses into an ongoing conversation that produced several follow-up posts. In this instructive case Gilgoff's role was to serve as a convener of an impassioned community rather than act as a traditional fact-gathering reporter. "Before, you would think a story has come and gone," Gilgoff said. "What the Internet allows you to see is that people are still talking about it . . . as opposed to you're the master, you've said what you want to say, and you're moving on" (pers. comm.).

The *Daily Post* in Llandudno Junction, Wales, reorganized its editorial workflow in late 2012 around a permanent live blog that is continuously updated with what editors call "snackable" nuggets of breaking news, weather, and traffic. Dan Owen, the *Daily Post*'s executive editor for digital, said the live blog "has really helped move the day forward" while boosting the site's engagement statistics (pers. comm.). The live blog is part of a larger "Newsroom 3.0" strategy that the *Daily Post*'s corporate parent has expanded across the United Kingdom (McAthy 2013).

Digital First Media reaches more than sixty million Americans each month across eighteen states with more than eight hundred digital and print products, including newspapers, websites, and mobile apps. John Paton, the CEO and a hard-core digital evangelist, is a renegade among the *Editor & Publisher* crowd, having preached for years to put "digital first, print last" (Kirchner 2011). The company's engagement efforts made a national splash with the Open Newsroom Project at the *Register Citizen* in Torrington, Connecticut; the project includes a cafe, free public wi-fi, workstations for local bloggers, and a community classroom and meeting space. But newsrooms throughout the Digital First chain are aggressively experimenting with reader engagement. The *New Haven (CT) Register* uses live public web chats to conduct its morning news meetings; the *Morning Sun* in Mount Pleasant, Michigan, set up a satellite newsroom downtown during the monthlong Art Walk in August 2012; and the *Oakland Press* runs training sessions for community bloggers in suburban Detroit. "It's part of building partnership," said Glenn Gilbert, who recently retired as executive editor of the *Press* in Pontiac. "It's part of bringing the outside in, so we really become a voice of the people" (pers. comm.). Digital First is the newest incarnation of the Journal Register newspaper chain, which declared bankruptcy amid staff cuts in 2009 and again in 2012, earning skepticism from critics who said the company was, as one put it, "in a hurry to jettison American newspaper business's most valuable traditions in favor of vague pronouncements about reader engagement and the use of social media" (Chittum 2012). The company proclaimed in April 2013 that it had exited bankruptcy, and Paton later told a crowd of media executives in France that the company's bold new strategies had helped Digital First achieve an operating profit of more than 40 percent (Beaujon 2013). However, Digital First experienced another setback in early 2014 when it folded a two-year experiment called Project Thunderdome, the chain's centralized digital news desk based in Manhattan.

The *Las Vegas Sun* used aggressive engagement strategies to grow its digital audience during a turbulent four-year run by the since-departed new media guru Rob Curley; the paper won a slew of national awards but also rang up some costly failures (Kingsley 2010). Curley left the *Sun* in mid-2012 and later joined the *Orange County Register*, but many of his ideas about audience engagement live on in Las Vegas, including an emphasis on new forms of storytelling and intensive coverage of niche topics like the Ultimate Fighting Championship (UFC). *Sun* staffers say they are connecting with readers like never before, but it has hardly been a seamless journey. "We have an international city where people are coming and going all the time—engaging that type of population has been difficult, to say the least," said Matt Hufman, the *Sun's* editorial and opinion editor. "This is a tough town to crack into" (pers. comm.).

MLive Media Group, owned by Advance Publications, combined its eight Michigan newspapers into a digitally centered news operation in February 2012. The chain reduced home delivery to three days a week, laid off hundreds of employees, and refocused newsgathering efforts around its flagship website, *MLive*. Advance would later follow this formula with its newspapers in New Orleans, Syracuse, Alabama, and Pennsylvania, drawing sharp criticism from legions of readers, employees, community leaders, and critics who called it "hamster wheel" journalism (see Starkman 2012; Chittum 2013a). But the leaner operation that survived in Michigan is an undeniably audacious experiment, built conspicuously around the idea of reader engagement. In downtown Kalamazoo reporters and editors now work out of a brand-new street-level office just a block from the historic but forbidding *Kalamazoo Gazette* building that had been the paper's home since 1925. The chic window-filled office, outfitted with hip furniture and a corner interview room, is designed to invite audience interaction, and it wasn't long before the mayor himself walked into the newsroom to complain about a story. *Gazette* reporters and editors constantly file updates to the real-time, breaking news blog that dominates the *MLive* home page, and they routinely jump into their stories' comment streams to mediate and interact.

Started in 2005 by the editor and publisher Paul Bass, the *New Haven Independent* is a pioneering web-only hyperlocal site that has won national acclaim for its interactive journalism. On the back cover of his book *The Wired City*, Dan Kennedy hails the *Independent* as "a promising model of how to provide the public with the information it needs in a self-governing society" (2013a). When the *Independent* broke a story in late 2012 about human skeletons unearthed by Superstorm Sandy, its journalists demonstrated how running-blog–style story forms can serve readers' needs better than the inverted pyramid. But even a hyperlocal stalwart like the *Independent* has struggled mightily with how to handle reader comments, and Bass freely acknowledges the site's long-term survival is anything but certain.

The news application teams at *ProPublica* and NPR are among the best in the business at creating interactive data platforms that empower readers and listeners to dig deeper and find information themselves. *ProPublica*'s Free the Files project rallied more than a thousand volunteers to sift through nearly eighteen thousand campaign-finance files in search of "dark money"—undisclosed donations—during the 2012 elections (Zamora 2013). NPR's Fire Forecast App pulls data from the U.S. Forest Service into a mobile app that informs users of their fire danger based on their location. NPR's Matt Stiles says the goal of any news app is to engage users to the point that they keep coming back for more: "What is someone going to bookmark and use again? What is someone really going to want?" (pers. comm.).

Politico started a premium service in 2010 called *Politico Pro* to cover niche topics ranging from defense to health care to transportation. For nearly $9,000 per institutional subscription, subscribers to *Pro* can tailor their own news experience with customized mobile alerts and daily e-mail newsletters about their topic of choice, as well as access to exclusive events. In late 2012 editors crowed in an internal memo that *Pro* "has exceeded the high business and editorial expectations we have set" and validated the site's strategy to place niche subscriptions "at the heart of the hybrid newsroom that we are building" (Rothstein 2012).

At Telegraph Media Group in London the interactive news and social media teams seek to engage readers with tactics ranging from news games to quizzes to polls. For the *Telegraph*, which adopted a metered subscription plan in 2013, part of the motivation is deepening loyalty among subscribers. "It's a useful way to keep [subscribers] feeling as though they're getting value from the site," said Kate Day, social media and engagement editor of the paper with one of the biggest circulations in the United Kingdom. "Because if each time they're interacting in some way, spending a little bit longer, that will encourage them to subscribe again next month" (pers. comm.).

The *Washington Post* developed an interactive video tool during the 2012 election campaign that matched the most tweeted moments of political speeches and debates with the corresponding video clip, allowing users to scan, select, and view their own highlights. "We try to put ourselves in the shoes of the reader and say, 'Hey, what are they looking for?'" explained Ryan Kellett, the *Post*'s national digital editor. "It's solving a fundamental problem. That simplicity is what makes it sing" (pers. comm.).

As Kellett and other forward-thinking journalists understand, solving a problem and filling a need are essential components for building a valuable engaged audience that can in turn support a news organization's future financially. In this book I will explore how the news organizations mentioned here (and others) are urgently seeking to fill that need.

ACKNOWLEDGMENTS

This book is the product of several years of research and creative work examining the changing relationship between journalists and the audiences they serve. I initially immersed myself in this subject while reporting and writing a pair of articles for *Columbia Journalism Review* from 2009 to 2011, under the deft editorial guidance of Mike Hoyt and Brent Cunningham. I am particularly indebted to Mike Hoyt for his encouragement when I first proposed a new contribution to the Columbia Journalism Review Books series and for his challenging feedback as I developed the proposal.

Southern Methodist University's Meadows School of the Arts generously supported this project by furnishing me a one-semester sabbatical, as well as several research grants, that enabled me to travel to more than two dozen newsrooms. For this I am grateful to former Meadows Dean José Bowen, as well as Kevin Hofeditz, associate dean for academic affairs, and his predecessor, Greg Warden.

I also owe considerable thanks to Tony Pederson, chair of SMU's Division of Journalism, who allowed me the time and freedom to pursue this project, as well as to my journalism faculty colleagues and staff members who helped cover my campus responsibilities while I was absent. I also am grateful for the enthusiastic and engaged feedback from my students, who reacted to nuggets of this book as I shared some of my early findings in my Digital Journalism, Media Entrepreneurship, and Technology Reporting classes.

Mark Briggs, a digital journalism pioneer and author who graciously agreed to write the foreword for this book, provided crucial early guidance for this first-time author. I also appreciate those who took the time to discuss the themes of the book, read chapter drafts, or invited me to speak to their classes—a distinguished group that includes Joshua Benton of Nieman Journalism Lab, Jayne Suhler of Southern Methodist University, Matt Goodman of WFAA-TV in Dallas, Amber Willard Hinsley of Saint Louis University, Theodore Kim of the *Washington Post*, Yolette Garcia of Southern Methodist University, Jim Stovall of the University of Tennessee, and many others.

I had the privilege of conducting more than one hundred interviews for this book. I did most interviews in newsrooms or the cities in which they are located, but I did some at industry conferences and, in a few cases, by phone or e-mail. Many people I interviewed have since been promoted or moved on to positions with other organizations, reflecting their considerable talents and skill sets.

I had a series of valuable opportunities to discuss my project and present early findings at industry conferences hosted by UNITY: Journalists for Diversity, the Association for Education in Journalism and Mass Communication, and the International Symposium on Online Journalism. My sincere thanks to the colleagues and attendees at these conferences who asked questions, offered encouragement, and pushed me to make this book better.

I also am grateful for the guidance and encouragement of Philip Leventhal and Whitney Johnson at Columbia University Press, the masterful copyediting of Polly Kummel, and the thoughtful critiques provided by several anonymous reviewers. The book benefited enormously from their feedback; any shortcomings that remain are mine alone.

A disclosure: In mid-2013, after I had completed the majority of work on this book, I was named one of two Texas Tribune Fellows. The fellowships, generously funded by the John S. and James L. Knight Foundation, were established to study and help refine the *Tribune*'s business model and to collect and disseminate best practices in the business of digital news. By the time I began work as a Tribune Fellow in August 2013, I had already completed all fieldwork for *Engaged Journalism* and had written most of the manuscript. That said, the *Tribune*'s newsroom was a wonderfully welcoming setting in which to complete the book, which dovetailed naturally with my fellowship activities. For this I am especially grateful to Evan Smith, John Thornton, Emily Ramshaw, Ross Ramsey, and Tim Griggs.

Many thanks to my parents, siblings, and other family members who constantly offered their support, encouragement, and understanding. And finally, I owe supreme thanks to Tracy Everbach, my wife, whose constant professional suggestions and personal faith in my ability to complete this project made me believe it could be done, and to our three dogs, Hildy, Griffey, and Henry, for their entertainment and companionship.

INTERVIEWS

Here is a full list of my interviews, along with the job title each participant held at the time of the interview.

AUSTIN AMERICAN-STATESMAN

Omar Gallaga, technology columnist
Maira Garcia, social media editor

THE CENTER FOR INVESTIGATIVE REPORTING

Meghann Farnsworth, senior manager, distribution and engagement

CHICAGO NEWS COOPERATIVE

Jim O'Shea, founder and editor

CHRISTIAN SCIENCE MONITOR

Lane Brown, social media manager
Molly Driscoll, staff writer
Marshall Ingwerson, managing editor

Marjorie Kehe, books editor
Amelia Newcomb, foreign editor
Eoin O'Carroll, online news editor
David Clark Scott, online director
John Yemma, editor

CNN DIGITAL

Meredith Artley, managing editor
Dan Gilgoff, religion editor

DALLAS MORNING NEWS

Rich Alfano, general manager
Mark Francescutti, senior managing digital editor
Kyle Whitfield, assistant sports editor, digital

DIGITAL FIRST MEDIA

Steve Buttry, digital transformation editor

GEEKWIRE

Todd Bishop, cofounder
John Cook, cofounder
Rebecca Lovell, chief business officer

GREAT LAKES ECHO

David Poulson, editor

KING-5 TV (SEATTLE)

Evonne Benedict, social media manager

KTVK-3TV (PHOENIX)

Lori Santa Maria, social media manager

LAS VEGAS CITYLIFE

Amy Kingsley, staff writer

LAS VEGAS SUN

Ray Brewer, sports editor
Tom Gorman, executive editor
Matt Hufman, opinion editor
Donn Jersey, publisher for digital
Case Keefer, mixed martial arts and gambling reporter

MLIVE MEDIA GROUP (MICHIGAN)

Mickey Ciokajlo, editor, *Kalamazoo Gazette*
Kelly Adrian Frick, director of community news, *MLive*
John Hiner, vice president of content, *MLive*
Fritz Klug, staff writer, *Kalamazoo Gazette*
Linda Mah, community engagement specialist, *Kalamazoo Gazette*
Colleen Stone, director of digital operations, *MLive*

MOUNT PLEASANT (MI) MORNING SUN

Holly Mahaffey, community engagement producer
Rick Mills, editor
Lisa Yanick-Jonaitis, photojournalist and community engagement
    editor

NBCNEWS.COM (FORMERLY MSNBC.COM)

Allison Linn, senior economics reporter
Michael Wann, managing editor

NEW HAVEN (CT) INDEPENDENT

Paul Bass, editor

NEW HAVEN (CT) REGISTER

Helen Bennett, city editor
Ed Stannard, community engagement editor

NORTH WALES DAILY POST

Alison Gow, editor
Helen Harper, head of audience engagement
Dan Owen, executive editor for digital

NPR

Elise Hu, digital editorial coordinator
Matt Stiles, data editor
Matt Thompson, editorial product manager

OAKLAND PRESS (PONTIAC, MI)

Monica Drake, community engagement editor
Steve Frye, online editor
Glenn Gilbert, executive editor
Julie Jacobson-Hines, local news editor
Karen Workman, community engagement editor

POLITICO

Tim Grieve, editor-in-chief, *Politico Pro*
Dave Levinthal, reporter and coauthor of *Politico Influence*, a daily
    newsletter
Patrick Reis, reporter
Alexis Williams, events coordinator

PROPUBLICA

Jennifer LaFleur, director of computer-assisted reporting
Amanda Zamora, senior engagement editor

PUBLIC EYE NORTHWEST

Matt Rosenberg, founder and executive director

PUGET SOUND BUSINESS JOURNAL

Michele Matassa Flores, managing editor

SEATTLE TIMES

Kathy Best, managing editor
Frank Blethen, publisher
Ryan Blethen, associate publisher
David Boardman, executive editor
Sharon Pian Chan, associate opinions editor
Suki Dardarian, managing editor
Danny O'Neil, Seattle Seahawks reporter
Sona Patel, social media producer
Bob Payne, editor for partnerships and audience engagement
Cheryl Phillips, data enterprise editor
Brian M. Rosenthal, staff writer
Jim Simon, assistant managing editor
Eric Ulken, assistant managing editor

TELEGRAPH MEDIA GROUP (LONDON)

Kate Day, social media and engagement editor
Joe Jenkins, mobile editor
Mark Oliver, online graphics editor
Conrad Quilty-Harper, interactive news editor

TEXAS TRIBUNE

Aman Batheja, staff writer
Tanya Erlach, events director
Rodney Gibbs, chief innovation officer
Reeve Hamilton, staff writer
April Hinkle, chief revenue officer
Ryan Murphy, news apps developer
Ross Ramsey, executive editor
Emily Ramshaw, editor
Evan Smith, editor-in-chief and CEO

TORRINGTON (CT) REGISTER CITIZEN

Matt DeRienzo, Connecticut group editor
Emily Olson, managing editor

TWITTER

Mark Luckie, manager of journalism and news

WALL STREET JOURNAL

David Ho, editor for mobile, tablets, and emerging technology

WASHINGTON POST

David Beard, director of digital content
Ryan Kellett, national digital editor

WBEZ-FM

Daniel Ash, vice president of strategic communications

WEST SEATTLE BLOG

Tracy Record, editor and cofounder

YAHOO! NEWS

Carolyn Clark, senior consumer communications manager
Sheigh Crabtree, senior editor
E. J. Liao, senior product manager
Jason Sickles, staff reporter

INDIVIDUAL INTERVIEWS

Kevin Anderson, freelance journalist and digital consultant, London
Romeo Arrieta, attendee, Texas Tribune Festival, Austin
David Barmore, attendee, Politico Pro Trivia Night, Washington, D.C.
Kristen Carrillo, attendee, Texas Tribune Festival, Austin
Rebecca Kohler, attendee, community blogger workshop, Pontiac, Michigan
Haresh Sangani, attendee, GeekWire Summer Bash, Seattle
Jaycee Taylor, visitor to the Register Citizen Open Newsroom, Torrington, Connecticut

ENGAGED JOURNALISM

Introduction

Why Engagement Matters

The deeper we journey into the digital age, the more the term *engagement* is bandied about in newsrooms, classrooms, journalism conferences, blogs, and social media. The ever-growing imperative for news media to interact with their audiences has been drummed relentlessly into journalists' heads, sometimes to the point of satire. In a video spoof created for the Lone Star Emmy Awards ceremony by the local Fox affiliate in Dallas, the anchor Clarice Tinsley alerts viewers to a fictional shooting at city hall, where the intrepid reporter Matt Grubs is on camera "tweeting details to his eighty-seven followers," as Tinsley dryly quips (figure o.1) (see Axon 2010). As fake sirens wail and faux shots ring out, Grubs fixates on his smartphone, typing furiously with his thumbs before declaring: "Clarice, it is now eighty-eight followers, and I have just been re-tweeted. Sweet."

In a BBC skit (2008) of similar spirit, the comedian David Mitchell portrays an anchor who desperately begs his viewers to e-mail their

Figure 0.1 Clarice Tinsley, anchor, concludes a FOX4 social media spoof. Dallas, Texas, October 2010. © Copyright KDFW-TV, produced for the Lone Star Emmy® Awards. Image: KDFW-TV, Dallas.

thoughts. "You may not know anything about the issue, but I bet you *reckon* something," Mitchell implores. "So why not tell us what you reckon? Let us enjoy the full majesty of your uninformed, ad-hoc reckon . . . and keep those e-mails coming. It is, for some reason, apparently vital that you do."

Journalists always have been prone to dark humor, especially when it comes to trendy buzzwords that carry a whiff of the latest bright idea from some consulting firm. However, at a time when digitally empowered audiences have infinite options for getting their news, engagement isn't just a buzzword; it's a puzzle, and solving it is more urgent than ever.[1] For news outlets in the twenty-first century, engagement means somehow getting audiences invested enough in the outlets' journalism to make a habit of coming back—and converting that attention into revenue that pays the bills. But in an era when fickle, harried, impatient smartphone owners can get news simply by thumbing through their Facebook and Twitter feeds, how can today's journalists find new ways to attract and maintain the loyal audiences they once took for granted? What does engagement really mean, and to what end and for what purpose? These questions are at the heart of this book.

The last half of the twentieth century was an era of disengaged journalism, at least when it came to audience interaction. During this heyday of one-way mass media, journalists did plenty of important work to inform the public but still maintained a comfortable distance from their customers, an aloof detachment that carried a certain unacknowledged arrogance. Advertisers seeking a sizable daily audience had few options beyond the newspapers, television stations, and radio stations that dominated their market. Readers, viewers, and listeners were welcome to send letters to the editor or to occasionally sound off on audience feedback segments at the end of news broadcasts. But reporters, editors, producers, anchors, and news directors were the professionals who selected, shaped, and crafted the news—the gatekeepers, as labeled by several generations of journalism scholars (see White 1950; Tuchman 1978; Gans 1979; Shoemaker and Vos 2009). Decades of mass communication research examined the causes and effects of a media system predicated on professionals' preparing and delivering news to mass audiences that did not have much of a voice in shaping the content they received (see Shoemaker and Reese 1996; Baran and Davis 2009; DeFleur 2010). And that same media system was based on faulty but entrenched assumptions that news audiences cared mostly about the daily escapades of politicians, celebrities, and sports figures, even though studies repeatedly have shown that the public craves more substantive news, as Thomas E. Patterson observes in his 2013 book, *Informing the News*. "Journalists' sense of their audience is wrong side up," Patterson argues. "What's happening at the top as it affects the fortunes of those at the top is not what interests most people" (121).

Those of us who worked in newsrooms during this era trained ourselves to be disengaged journalists. Objectivity was the prevailing mind-set—

young reporters were cautioned against joining community groups, and some editors even refused to vote, remaining proudly and stubbornly neutral as a matter of principle. Of course there were some justifiable reasons for this approach. But it went too far, breeding a paternalistic attitude succinctly expressed in a form e-mail that the *Chicago Sun-Times* columnist Neil Steinberg sent to readers he considered snide or insulting: "The fact that you disagree with or were insulted by my opinion really is not important, at least not to me. This is not a dialogue, this is a lecture, and you are supposed to sit in your seat and listen, or leave, not stand up and heckle" (Romenesko 2004). Even Tom Gorman, now executive editor of the digitally innovative *Las Vegas Sun*, acknowledges that for many of his thirty-two years at the *Los Angeles Times*, "I didn't think a whole lot about readers. I just thought about all the other reporters in town and how I wanted to kick their asses" (pers. comm.).

This traditional insular newsroom culture typifies what Joy Mayer, director of community outreach at the *Columbia Missourian*, calls Wizard of Oz journalism: "Pay no attention to that man behind the curtain . . . don't worry, audience. We know what we're doing. We know what's important, and we're putting it out into the universe for you to consume and enjoy" (2010). Mayer rejects that attitude, arguing that today's journalists must proactively build trust "by meeting people where they are, and participating in conversations they didn't start." In other words, by engaging the audience.

"It's not a fad—you know you have to do it," said Meredith Artley, managing editor of *CNN Digital*. "The days of news organizations' doing a story on whatever format and just pushing it out there, those days are over. They're done. The organizations that get that are the ones that are going to win" (pers. comm.). And why should the public care who wins? Because with every new round of newsroom layoffs and buyouts, communities are losing watchdogs who bring accountability to the powerful, like the local officials in Bell, California, who paid themselves enormous salaries from the city budget until exposed by the *Los Angeles Times*, or like the local leaders of the Catholic Church who concealed decades of sexual abuse until the *Boston Globe* revealed their actions. This style of courageous accountability journalism is extremely labor intensive and has never been profitable by itself. In fact watchdog journalism can end up costing a news organization a great deal of money: Michael Hiltzik, business columnist at the *Los Angeles Times*, recalled that he and a colleague were sued seven times during the newspaper's three-year investigation of patient deaths that occurred after lap-band surgery—and although all seven suits were dismissed, the legal wrangling still left the *Times* with a six-figure bill (2014:B7).

For decades advertisers seeking to reach a mass audience through double-truck ads, Sunday inserts, or network television commercials subsidized this system of accountability journalism. But as consumers turn their attention away from mass media in favor of more personalized web and mobile platforms, the news industry is beginning to rely less on advertising and more on subscribers as a primary source of revenue, creating profound implications both for the practice of journalism and its underlying business model (Coscarelli 2012; Doctor 2012).

Until recently journalists could afford to disengage from their audiences because it was economically practical to do so. But today's news consumers have boundless digital options. Modern news organizations constantly must demonstrate commercial relevance by *actively filling a need* for their audiences. If engagement is to be effective and meaningful, journalists must earn their audiences' attention, build loyalty, and deepen trust while finding new revenue streams to subsidize the public-interest journalism that market forces have never supported anyway.

"Engagement is everything," said John Yemma, who as editor of the *Christian Science Monitor* from 2008 to 2014 led a transformation during which the century-old newspaper stopped printing daily editions and adopted a web-first model. "The media environment that we've been living in, and we're going to be living in, is going to be one of constant change, in terms of reader preferences for how they get information" (pers. comm.).[2] Indeed the half-century or so during which journalists disengaged from the audience may well have been a historical aberration—during earlier eras journalists were more closely tied to the readers they served (see Rosen 2013b). Perhaps in today's era of engaged journalism we are returning to a norm in the relationship between the professionals who produce news content and the public that consumes it.

DEFINING ENGAGEMENT

Definitions of engagement are notoriously ambiguous and fluid.[3] Even journalists who prioritize and practice engagement define it in different ways. For Mark Luckie, manager of news and journalism for Twitter in New York, engagement means "not just talking *to* people but listening to them" (pers. comm.). For Tracy Record, cofounder of the nationally well-regarded *West Seattle Blog*, engagement boils down to a mix of collaboration and conversation, "something that shows you're on the minds of people" (pers. comm.). Steve Buttry, formerly an executive with Digital First Media, defines engagement as when news organizations make it a "top priority to listen, to join, lead and enable conversation to elevate journalism" (2011). Frank Blethen, publisher of the *Seattle Times*, said engagement suggests that news consumers are "putting their time in, and they value that. And they're getting some reward out of it" (pers. comm.). Meghann Farnsworth, senior manager of distribution and engagement at the Center for Investigative Reporting, said engagement means that "people are doing something meaningful with our content after reading it, or seeing it, or hearing it" (pers. comm.). And Mayer, an associate professor at the University of Missouri School of Journalism who spent a year studying news engagement as part of a Reynolds Journalism Institute Fellowship, ultimately arrived at a definition that combines "a focus on, respect for and enthusiasm about the role of the audience" (2011).

The academic world also has yet to reach consensus in defining engagement. Perhaps the most comprehensive book to date on the subject, *Medill on Media Engagement*, defines it as "the collection of experiences that readers, viewers, or visitors have with a media brand," further explaining that engagement "causes people to 'use' the media brand by reading, viewing, or interacting with it" (Malthouse and Peck 2011:4). Philip Napoli's *Audience Evolution* offers a model that distinguishes between passive exposure to content and active audience behaviors that indicate deeper levels of engagement (2011:91).[4] For Dan Kennedy, whose book *The Wired City* (2013a) extensively profiles the online-only *New Haven (CT) Independent*, engagement is a form of creating community through a mixture of events and online interaction that together form "the hub of a civic ecosystem" (2013b).

All these explanations ring true, but there's still one idea missing: What does all this mean for the bottom line? I try to incorporate the economic aspect by defining engaged journalism as *the degree to which a news organization actively considers and interacts with its audience in furtherance of its journalistic and financial mission.*

A CROSSOVER FROM ADS TO SUBSCRIBERS

The newspaper business is going through what the industry analyst and consultant Ken Doctor (2012) calls a crossover. Digital subscriptions are starting to at least partially replace declining ad revenues at some companies, including the Telegraph Media Group (London), Star Tribune Media, and the New York Times Company. In mid-2012, for the first time in decades, the *New York Times*'s News Media Group began to earn more revenue from paid circulation than from advertising (Coscarelli 2012).[5] This was a fundamental shift. For years most journalism executives assumed that digital platforms would follow the same advertising-driven business model that long supported newspapers, magazines, and television. But as digital ad rates continue to fall and the connection between page views and revenue proves ever more tenuous, the relationship with loyal, paying, *engaged* customers becomes increasingly important. And online consumers, with myriad choices at their disposal, will pull out their credit cards to subscribe only if they feel truly engaged.

Web traffic tripled at *Seattletimes.com* during David Boardman's first six years (2006–12) as executive editor of the *Seattle Times* (pers. comm.). But as digital ad rates fell during that same period, web revenue fell by half. To help bridge this gulf between online traffic and revenue, the newspaper installed a digital subscription plan in early 2013. Two years earlier Boardman had reorganized his newsroom around the concept of audience engagement—in large part, he said, because a subscriber-driven future demands finding more ways to serve the *Times*'s most loyal, engaged, and *paying* readers.[6]

"It's the Holy Grail, both journalistically and financially," Boardman said. And the stakes couldn't be higher. For the news business, engagement equals survival. Engaging people to the point where they feel compelled to pay for a digital subscription, though, requires an audience-centric mind-set that regards journalism as not just a public service but also customer service.

Still, paywalls alone aren't enough to solve the engagement riddle. The free content model capably sustains readership magnets like *NBC-News.com* and *Yahoo! News*, in addition to a number of engagement-driven hyperlocals, niche sites, and nonprofits, as I also will explore. The point is, whether news outlets require subscriptions or provide content for free, they must constantly interact with—and demonstrate relevance to—their audiences. "It's time to stare down the high priests of the news industry who say nothing short of unmanaged, unaccountable journalism that never takes into consideration whether people are reading it is the modus operandi," declared Earl Wilkinson, CEO of the International News Media Association. "Let's take this moment of change and find ways to connect unique and valued journalism with unique and valued audiences" (2012). Whether a news organization's business model is based on click-driven reach, premium content, nonprofit sponsorships, or some other hybrid, ensuring the attachment of an engaged loyal audience is paramount. And it is imperative for today's journalists to understand that their work must be viable commercially in a much more direct way than ever before, particularly at a time when employment in U.S. newspaper newsrooms has dipped below forty thousand for the first time since 1978 (Pew Research Center 2013).

But while engagement certainly means convincing readers to pay for indispensable journalism, it also means convening the audience in person through events, festivals, and meetups. It means leveraging social media to create conversation, crowdsourcing, and community. It means relentlessly targeting journalism to the specific audience being served, especially if the common denominator for members of that audience is geography or a topical niche. It means empowering the audience with interactive news products such as databases, quizzes, games, and even coloring books. And it means finding a reliable way to track and measure whether all these efforts are making a difference.

These are some common practices I encountered while examining reader engagement strategies at more than two dozen newsrooms in the United States and the United Kingdom. I conducted more than one hundred interviews, from Seattle to London to Austin to New York to Kalamazoo, Michigan. I observed newsroom meetings, combed through internal documents, and talked to readers, viewers, and online users. The result is this book, aimed at media professionals, academics, teachers, students, and anyone else interested in the future of journalism. My intention is to highlight a modern set of best practices, while noting a few false starts and wrong turns, to provide a road map that can lead to effective sustainable journalistic engagement. I will closely analyze both the journalistic and business imperatives of audience engagement. But more than anything, I argue that for journalism to survive and thrive, news providers must listen to, interact with, and *fill a specific need for* their audience, whose attention can no longer be taken for granted.

FIVE GUIDING PRINCIPLES OF ENGAGED JOURNALISM

While visiting newsrooms on both U.S. coasts, in the Midwest, the Southwest, England, North Wales, and my home state of Texas, I found that news organizations' engagement strategies were driven by five guiding principles:

- *They convene audiences in person.* Face-to-face events that deliver a memorable worthwhile experience can deepen loyalty to a news organization while also generating cash to pay for more journalism. The latest breed of news event goes beyond traditional notions of "civic journalism" that once prompted media outlets to convene their audiences out of some sort of solemn obligation to serve as a town square. This new strategic approach to in-person engagement regards live events not merely as a civic obligation but as an entrepreneurial opportunity.

News organizations are in a unique position to convene the types of educated and influential audiences that corporate sponsors want to reach. By hosting face-to-face events that combine networking with education and/or entertainment, news outlets can build a sense of community while boosting the bottom line.

- *They interact with audiences at every step.* Perhaps the most fundamental element of engaged journalism is seizing the most effective digital tools of the day to foster an ongoing conversation with the audience. By now it has become second nature for most newspapers, television stations, and news websites to engage their audience through such techniques as social media, real-time coverage, crowdsourcing, beat blogging, user-generated content, and comment threads. Still, there is a clear difference between halfhearted robotic use of these forums and well-thought-out strategies that forge an authentic relationship with the audience, solidifying a news outlet as a trusted hub for information.

- *They serve the "passionate vertical."* Topical niches (verticals) and geographic areas offer news organizations separate but related opportunities to reach motivated audiences that are willing to pay for specialized and localized content. The most successful ventures in niche and hyperlocal journalism manage to fill a distinct—and previously unmet—information need for the communities they serve. In some cases that means providing minutely detailed coverage of specialized topics ranging from politics to high school football; in other instances it means providing residents of communities like West Seattle or New Haven with a degree of localized coverage they can't get from traditional news outlets.

The growing adoption of smartphones, tablets, and other mobile devices, coupled with the web's "long tail," as the author Chris Anderson (2006) calls it, presents an unprecedented opportunity to engage audiences that are invested in a particular niche or neighborhood. Reaching these audiences on their own terms is crucial, whether through the latest mobile platforms, low-tech e-mail newsletters, or creating forums where niche and hyperlocal audiences can communicate with each other. But mustering a profitable business from these smaller-scale audiences can be challenging.

• *They empower audiences to satisfy their own curiosity.* Data-driven news applications personalize the news by allowing users to easily search for the information that matters most to them or even to contribute to the project itself. In a similar vein, newsy quizzes, games, and contests challenge participants by tapping into their curiosity and competitive instincts. At their best, both styles of participatory journalism provide interactive news platforms that transcend the one-way dispatches of years past. And digital audiences, which vote with their clicks, often prefer interactive apps to traditional stories.

• *They measure effectiveness and capture value.* Today's news organizations have myriad digital metrics at their disposal to track the effectiveness of their engagement initiatives—and to ascertain whether those efforts are helping the bottom line. However, it is incumbent on news organizations to identify and track the measures of success that best reflect their journalistic and financial mission. Re-tweets and Facebook "likes" are nice to have, but the most conclusive metric for any engagement strategy is whether it helps a news organization stay in business.

In this book I will highlight numerous examples of how engagement can boost journalism, but I also will explore how engagement strategies can go awry and trigger frustrations, mistakes, and regrets. Still, lessons learned from failed experiments can better inform the next try. And while other authors have chronicled the evolution of news into a two-way conversation, my goal here is to add to the dialogue by explicitly connecting journalistic engagement with financial sustainability, which the leading scholar Jay Rosen has labeled "the number one problem in journalism at the moment" (2013a).[7]

At its core engaged journalism is the latest incarnation of the age-old journalistic dilemma between covering what the public needs versus what the audience wants. In their sweeping report *Post-Industrial Journalism*, C. W. Anderson, Emily Bell, and Clay Shirky make an important distinction between *public* ("that group of consumers or citizens who care about the forces that shape their lives and want someone to monitor and report on those forces") and *audience* (consumers "newly endowed with an unprecedented degree of communicative agency") (2012:14–16).

In this book I argue that *audience*-focused engagement is essential to help sustain the watchdog journalism that benefits the *public*. Boiled down to a single tweet, it might read something like this:

> Engagement is crucial to journalism's survival. But to be effective it must fill a specific audience need. And it comes with perks & costs.

Raju Narisetti, a lead digital executive for News Corporation and, previously, the *Wall Street Journal*, champions the idea that today's news organizations must provide not only superior journalistic content but also habit-inducing user experiences that keep people coming back for more. "You need great content and to be managing technology to create an amazing experience for users who can go anywhere they want," Narisetti said. "The experience is what will make them stay and come back" (Silverman 2012). Good journalism always will be the lifeblood of the news industry, but engaged journalists also must deliver a news *experience* that meets the needs of digitally empowered audiences.

HOW THE BOOK IS ORGANIZED

The challenge of writing a book about connecting with digitally empowered news audiences lies in the danger that its findings will be dated by the time the book appears in print. After decades of stagnation the news industry is transforming at a breakneck pace as more news organizations adopt a nimble iterative mind-set more typical of a Silicon Valley start-up than a staid media conglomerate.[8] Admittedly many of the audience-engagement initiatives I describe here have evolved since I conducted my fieldwork during the latter half of 2012 and the early summer of 2013. However, I have organized the chapters around the previously described five guiding principles of engaged journalism, which together underpin news providers' ongoing efforts to fill a need for their audience in the twenty-first century. Tools and tactics are always changing, but the chapters that follow reflect the larger conceptual themes that will shape engaged journalism for years to come.

In chapter 1, "Face-to-Face Engagement," I consider how news start-ups and traditional media outlets are connecting with their audience in person through live events and other forms of face-to-face engagement. Such initiatives can attract revenue while also building a sense of community and loyalty, but not all journalists are comfortable taking on a more extroverted and chummy role in which they serve as public ambassadors for their employers.

In the second chapter, "News as Conversation," I explore how newspapers, broadcast stations, and digital news outlets are using digital tools and social media to move beyond the one-way lecture model of journalism. In this chapter I sketch a portrait of the engaged user and delve into some of the more prominent methods of digital news engagement, such as real-time coverage, crowdsourcing, social media curating, beat blogging, comment forums, and user-generated content, as well as a renewed emphasis on old-school professional etiquette. I also explore some pitfalls of maintaining an audience conversation that never ends.

In chapter 3, "Mining Niche Communities," I consider how legacy media and news start-ups are serving niche audiences with digital coverage of subjects from business to politics to mixed martial arts. Digital and mobile technology offers new ways to reach demographically attractive niche audiences, but finding the sweet spot that supports a sustainable niche is tricky business, as a number of failed nonprofits, start-ups, and mobile initiatives can attest. I also examine how both traditional news operations and start-ups are engaging so-called hyperlocal audiences, combining journalistic skills with community interaction to build loyalty that transforms news sites into indispensable hubs for neighborhoods.

In "Search, Explore, Play" (chapter 4), I examine how newsrooms are drawing readers into journalism through participatory experiences. Many metropolitan newsrooms have long had at least one reporter who collected, analyzed, and interpreted large sets of data, then presented the findings to readers in static one-way form. Today's journalists are using online tools to publish rich volumes of data that readers can dig through themselves, although reporters and editors should scrutinize the numbers with the same degree of rigor as any fact that they choose to include in a story. In this chapter I also examine efforts to "gamify" the news through fun, and often competitive, features that challenge readers' curiosity—quizzes, contests, scavenger hunts, news games, and even coloring books. Games can build loyalty and keep the audience coming back for more, but they take extra work that can be difficult to sustain, and journalists sometimes wonder whether gamifying the news is cheapening the core product.

In "Sustaining Engaged Journalism" (chapter 5), I tie together my argument that for journalism to survive and thrive, news providers must constantly prove their relevance by listening to, interacting with, and filling a specific need for their audience, whose attention and financial support news providers can no longer take for granted. I also scrutinize how news organizations measure the effectiveness of their engagement efforts—and how they convert engagement into revenue. Whether news outlets offer their content for free, hide it behind paywalls, or devise some sort of hybrid model, financial success increasingly depends on attracting, retaining, and, yes, finding ways to monetize the loyal news consumer, that is, converting engagement into revenue. The stakes are immensely high for society, because the Fourth Estate can fulfill its watchdog role only if journalism remains financially viable.

THE SEARCH FOR AUTHENTIC ENGAGEMENT

While visiting newsrooms for this book, I repeatedly encountered a deep-seated conviction: To have any hope of success, engagement has to be—above all—authentic. Suki Dardarian, the former director of audience development for the *Seattle Times*, says too many media outlets approach engagement the same halfhearted way grocery cashiers do when they scan your loyalty card, print out your receipt, and butcher your name while ostensibly thanking you for your business (pers. comm.).

"There's nothing worse than feigned, shallow engagement," Dardarian said. "If it's going to be phony, don't do it." Helen Bennett, city editor of the *New Haven Register*, has a similar disdain for lip-service engagement: "If you get 50 or 60 or 70 likes, who cares? It helps your algorithm on Facebook, but is it really engagement?" (pers. comm.). And Joy Mayer, the *Missourian* engagement director and professor who came to be nicknamed the "minister of engagement" during her yearlong fellowship, argues that audience interaction simply "needs to be baked into everything a newsroom does—not just added on at the end" (Mayer 2012).

In mid-2012 *Wired* magazine published a chilling article headlined "Rise of the Robot Reporter," describing how a company called Narrative Science has created a computerized formula that turns box scores and financial reports into coherently written articles. The company's algorithms "produce ultracheap, totally readable accounts of events, trends and developments that no journalist is currently covering" (Levy 2012:134). The article is humbling to any journalist who reads it; its message is that if you're just going through the motions, if a robot can replicate your journalism, you might as well start looking for another line of work.

The same can be said for engagement. If your halfhearted efforts to engage your audience amount to robotically re-tweeting story links, or slapping a generic "Tell Us Your Thoughts" box at the end of every story, or pleading with your viewers to simply blabber on about whatever they reckon, you might as well start looking for another line of work. Authentic engaged journalism requires a human touch.

1

Face-to-Face Engagement

How News Organizations Build Digital Loyalty and Generate Revenue Through the "Original Platform"

On a clear cool summer evening in June 2012, hundreds of Seattle techies gathered at a concert venue in the city's SoDo warehouse district, cheerfully drifting between an eight-table Ping-Pong tournament, two bars, catered spreads, and a photo booth equipped with costume gear. The slick Summer Bash party—hosted by *GeekWire*, an upstart tech news site—drew more than five hundred people from the Seattle tech scene, most of whom had paid at least $50 for the chance to mingle with their peers over drinks and maybe win some table-tennis bragging rights (figure 1.1). Rebecca Lovell, *GeekWire*'s chief business officer, grabbed a microphone and welcomed the crowd with a greeting appropriate for Seattle's start-up culture and grunge music roots: "We're just so delighted to get you out of the garage tonight!"

The event also drew fourteen corporate sponsors, generating thousands of dollars for *GeekWire*, a privately held news site started in 2011 by two former *Seattle Post-Intelligencer* reporters. Summer Bash was

FIGURE 1.1   *GeekWire* Summer Bash, Seattle, June 2012. Photo: Jake Batsell

one of nine 2012 events that collectively represented about 40 percent of the site's annual revenue, Lovell said (pers. comm.). Perhaps equally important, these events brought *GeekWire* more credibility as not only an essential source for news but as a physical hub for the Seattle tech community. "People in Seattle, they have a personal connection to this thing," said Haresh Sangani, a local tech executive at Summer Bash who shook hands and networked with colleagues and competitors when he wasn't playing Ping-Pong. "I see [*GeekWire*] as a community gathering place resource, where we kind of feed them and they feed us back" (pers. comm.).

News organizations have long assembled their readers in person through various forms of high-minded civic journalism (see Denton and Thorson 1995; Perry 2004). But more recently traditional newsrooms, and especially online news start-ups, have begun to embrace live events—not out of some sort of solemn civic obligation nor as a half-hearted corporate marketing exercise but as a strategic opportunity to meaningfully engage readers by raising visibility, building community, creating newsworthy editorial content, and, perhaps most important, helping pay for journalism. Across the United States journalists are snapping out of deadline mode and hosting audiences at events that range from news quiz nights in San Francisco to chef battles in Chicago to wonky political forums in Austin.[1]

"You cannot wait for people to come to you; you have to go to them," said Evan Smith, CEO and editor-in-chief of the *Texas Tribune*. "You've got to create the highest possible likelihood that people will embrace what you're doing, will listen, will think, will talk back" (pers. comm.). Indeed, events have become a lucrative revenue source for the *Tribune*, an Austin-based nonprofit political news site. In 2013 events generated more than $1.1 million, accounting for roughly one-fifth of annual revenue (Smith 2014). The *Tribune*'s events strategy reflects a trend among nonprofit news outlets to become less reliant on charitable donations and seek greater financial sustainability by operating as "mission-driven businesses" (Davis 2013).

Face-to-face engagement is emerging as an increasingly vital complement to newsrooms' digital engagement strategies. I visited many of the news organizations I mention in this book because they have been particularly aggressive in embracing in-person events as part of their wider engagement efforts. These outlets' success with events, while not necessarily typical, merits a closer look as the U.S. news industry searches for sources of supplemental revenue to support and sustain the journalism once subsidized by a now-disappearing advertising model. On top of generating revenue that can help support more journalism, events and other forms of face-to-face engagement can establish news providers as trusted conveners of community—building goodwill, raising brand awareness, and reinforcing the idea that a news site's editorial content is essential for readers to stay in the know. In this sense old-fashioned, real-life, face-to-face engagement is more important than ever for news organizations seeking to establish and deepen digital loyalty while remaining financially viable. As Smith puts it: "Before there was audio and video, before there was blogging, before there was tweeting and Facebooking and G-chatting and iChatting, people got in a room and talked to each other. Real time was the original platform. Real time was the thing that we first accepted as a way to deal with one another" (pers. comm.).

EVENTS: AN OPPORTUNITY, NOT AN OBLIGATION

The notion that journalists had a duty to convene and enlighten members of their communities flourished during the civic journalism movement of the 1990s. An undated summary from the website of the now-defunct Pew Center for Civic Journalism defines the practice as "both a philosophy and a set of values" based on "a belief that journalism has an obligation to public life—an obligation that goes beyond just telling the news or unloading lots of facts." Newspapers, academics, and radio and television stations combined forces to craft experimental town hall–style projects designed to boost voter participation and "draw people into the public sphere" (Denton and Thorson 1995).

A bibliography published by the Poynter Institute (Shedden 2002) lists dozens of books and special reports on the topic, most from the 1990s and early to mid-2000s. During this era the terms *civic journalism* and *public journalism* often were used interchangeably, as reflected in the titles of two influential titles from the genre, *Doing Public Journalism* (Charity 1995) and *The Idea of Public Journalism* (Glasser 1999). Whatever moniker it assumed, the movement's underlying premise was controversial at the time—that news media not only should dispassionately report the facts but also should seek ways to improve the quality of their communities.

During and after the economic recession of 2001, many of these altruistic experiments began to disappear as newsrooms had fewer resources available to devote to their "obligation to public life." In some ways the civic journalism movement was an important precursor to the modern era of constant audience interaction. But the movement never seriously explored the financial opportunities created by face-to-face engagement.

By the end of the decade the news industry was still grappling with economic struggles while simultaneously searching for ways to build audience loyalty in an increasingly digital media landscape (Peck and Malthouse 2011; Napoli 2011). Against this ubiquitous backdrop of dwindling advertising and subscriptions, more news organizations began to see face-to-face events as a potential source of revenue. "People who won't pay $15 for a digital subscription, the theory goes, may pay $20 instead for wine, cheese and a panel of journalists," instructor Jeremy Caplan (2012) wrote at the start of a live web chat on the subject hosted by the Poynter Institute. Magazines had organized such events for decades, but during the 2000s a handful of tech-focused start-ups—including *Gigaom, paidContent, Mashable,* and *Techcrunch*—embraced events as a key component of their revenue strategy (Briggs 2011:78). This new wave of events clearly owed some degree of inspiration to the civic journalism tradition, but there was a key distinction: news start-ups regarded events as an entrepreneurial opportunity, not obligations, as the Pew Center once called them.

In 2009, the year after the stock market crash of 2008 triggered a global financial crisis, American City Business Journals still managed to draw more than 100,000 registrants to events put on by the national chain's sixty-plus publications. And by 2013 annual event attendance had more than doubled to 225,907, according to the chain's corporate website, ACBJ.com. "Part of our readers' loyalty to the paper is because of the events," said Michele Matassa Flores, then–managing editor of Seattle's *Puget Sound Business Journal,* which regularly hosts sponsored interview panels as well as ticketed gatherings celebrating special publications like the *Journal*'s "40 Under Forty" issue (pers. comm.).[2]

CREATING VALUE THROUGH MEANINGFUL EXPERIENCES

At around the time the 2008 economic crisis hit, WBEZ-FM in Chicago started its Off-Air Series of events, giving the public radio station a boost in terms of both community buzz and the bottom line. By its fifth year the series had drawn about thirty thousand station supporters to a lineup of events that included chef battles, drive-in double features for zombie movies, and children's storytelling performances (Hall 2012). The events often carry a fee of $10 or $15, with discounts for members, while sponsors provide the rest of the funding.

"For our brand to grow, we needed to create experiences that had meaning and value," said Daniel Ash, WBEZ's vice president of strategic communications. Ash said the station realized that raising money while also fostering community required a creative approach that went beyond black-tie fund-raisers. And, he said, WBEZ's parent company, Chicago Public Media, averaged 4 percent growth in individual giving in each of the five years after the Off-Air Series began, an increase fueled in part by a rise in regular monthly donations. With more money coming in, he added, WBEZ was able to reduce its number of on-air pledge days by 30 percent during that same period (pers. comm.).

Events certainly don't deserve *all* the credit for improving the station's financial fortunes, but Ash said the Off-Air Series is an important extension of a bedrock idea: "Build a relationship, and the money will take care of itself . . . with our core audience, those that know us, there's a sense of deeper connection." Since launching the Off-Air Series in 2008, the station has seen an overall increase in fund-raising despite a decline in total audience, he said. So while the station's programming is reaching fewer people, avid supporters are giving more money—and Ash credits events for accelerating that trend. "It took me many, many moons to sell the theory that if we have meaningful experiences, the ultimate return would be membership dollars," he acknowledged (pers. comm.).

Across the turbulent U.S. media landscape, newsrooms large and small are staging similar events in search of supplementary income. The *New York Times*, for example, offered an array of ticketed events in 2012 that ranged from a cooking lecture by Paula Deen in Manhattan ($35) to a panel discussion at the Newseum in Washington, D.C., about the impact of gay issues on the presidential election ($25)—both brought to you by Citi, an official TimesTalks sponsor. About twenty-five hundred miles west, the nonprofit *San Francisco Public Press* invited members to "show off your big brain and support local public-interest journalism" at News Quiz Night, a $30-per-ticket fund-raiser that gave guests the chance to enjoy wine, beer, appetizers, and dessert while flexing their mental trivia muscles.

ATTRACTING SPONSORSHIPS
FOR INFLUENTIAL AUDIENCES

In the Pacific Northwest, events helped propel *GeekWire* to profitability within a year of launching the tech news site (Roush 2012). Lovell, the chief business officer, declined to reveal specific revenue figures, but she said that in 2012 *GeekWire*'s nine events—quarterly casual meetups and five signature events—represented about 40 percent of total revenue, with a profit margin of about 20 percent. "We're proud to be creating community, and events have been an effective means for our constituents to make connections, stay informed, get inspired, and accelerate their careers," Lovell said (pers. comm.). In a live chat with Jeremy Caplan for the Poynter Institute, Lovell added that *GeekWire* generally relies on ticket sales to help cover event costs, while sponsorship revenues provide the windfall (Caplan 2012).

Sponsors consider these events to be a worthwhile investment because they provide an opportunity to reach *GeekWire*'s professional niche audience in person, according to Todd Bishop, *GeekWire* cofounder. "It ends up being a galvanizing force for those companies, because they can come out and connect with the community but also present their own products through the venue we provided," he said (pers. comm.). Events aren't a foolproof route to profitability, however: Bishop later told me that a fall 2012 event—which *GeekWire* took over from another site—presented a number of "logistical quirks that we had a hard time overcoming." That event, combined with planned expenses related to staffing and strategic development, left *GeekWire* "just short of profitability" for the full year, Bishop said. However, by mid-2013 *GeekWire* reported that it was profitable once again (Wolf 2013).

In Austin, where the local alternative weekly, the *Austin Chronicle*, started the now-massive South by Southwest conference in 1987, the

Texas Tribune is likewise attracting dozens of event sponsors. "Live events are a really great way to get companies in front of people," said Tanya Erlach, the *Tribune's* founding director of events. She joined the *Tribune* before it began publishing in 2009, after she had spent eight years producing events for the *New Yorker*. The *Tribune's* audience demographics represent an appealing crowd for event sponsors—91 percent are college graduates, 98 percent are registered to vote, and 52 percent have household incomes of more than $100,000, according to internal research. "We can say, 'You will have your logo in front of these prime people,'" Erlach said. And while it's tricky for the nonprofit *Tribune* to precisely measure how events translate into paid memberships, Erlach said both categories have been growing since the *Tribune* started. "As people come to more events," she said, "more of them become members" (pers. comm.).

The revenues from *Tribune* events themselves are more clear-cut. According to Smith, the CEO, events generated more than $627,000 in 2011 and just under $850,000 in 2012 before topping $1 million in 2013 (pers. comm.; Smith 2014). Sponsors provide about 90 percent of event revenues by underwriting policy-minded gatherings, including an Austin-based interview series, on-the-road symposiums across the state, and the three-day Texas Tribune Festival at the University of Texas at Austin. Nearly all events are free; only the annual three-day public policy festival requires a badge that costs between $150 and $300, depending on when you buy it. "You're trafficking in ideas," Smith said. "You're talking about things that matter to everyone in that room, to one degree or another, if you're a Republican or a Democrat or an independent or a Wiccan" (pers. comm.).

The perception of events as revenue sources for news organizations took a hit in 2009 when *Politico* revealed that the *Washington Post* was courting lobbyists to pay up to $250,000 for a series of off-the-record "salons" with journalists and public officials at the home of its publisher, Katharine Weymouth (Alexander 2009). The *Post* later recovered from that debacle by launching Washington Post Live, a series of newsy conferences and panels that became a successful revenue source (Farhi 2012). The *Texas Tribune* likewise has faced scrutiny from critics on social media and local blogs suggesting that the site's lucrative event sponsorships create the appearance of a conflict of interest for its reporters when covering event sponsors in the news.[3]

Smith, however, has maintained from day one that "events are journalism" at the *Texas Tribune* (Phelps 2011). All interviews at *Tribune* events are on the record, captured on video, and frequently covered by reporters from the *Tribune* and other news outlets. At the 2012 Texas Tribune Festival, during a standing-room-only debate pitting Julian Castro, the Democratic San Antonio mayor, against incoming U.S. senator Ted Cruz, a Republican, Castro declared: "I don't believe taxes are inherently evil." Smith quickly turned to the crowd and quipped, "That will be tweeted. Give them a second."

Smith previously served as editor-in-chief of *Texas Monthly*, where he said he grew frustrated because the magazine's events were mostly marketing affairs aimed at advertisers. He envisioned a livelier, more inclusive, series of events that carried an editorial emphasis. "I always believed that there was a place for that type of an ongoing conversation about the world," Smith said. "And I had a notion that there was revenue associated with it that would ultimately come back into the journalism bucket, which has happened" (pers. comm.).

To skeptics who question whether event sponsorships might influence *Tribune* coverage—or, more pointedly, whether such sponsorships breach the news industry's deeply ingrained church-state separation between journalism and advertising—Smith maintains that aside from brand exposure attached to the event, the only rewards for sponsors are "a handshake and a tax letter" (Phelps 2011). The *Tribune* always has listed financial contributors on its site, but after a series of blog posts criticizing its business model in February 2014, editors announced they would begin disclosing specific amounts paid by event sponsors and would add language to event descriptions "stating what has always been true: that sponsors do not have any role in selecting topics, panels or panelists" (Ramshaw 2014).

"I SPENT TOO MUCH MONEY
COVERING THE NEWS"

In contrast to the aggressive events strategy at the *Texas Tribune*, the now-dormant *Chicago News Cooperative*'s events "never reached the level of audience engagement that I would have liked," said founder and editor James O'Shea. The nonprofit *CNC*—which, like the *Texas Tribune*, produced twice-weekly sections for local editions of the *New York Times*—halted operations in February 2012, citing funding problems (Banchero and Belkin 2012). The *CNC* did host a few events during its twenty-eight-month run, including a forum on public school choice for parents and a live interview with the political consultant David Axelrod. But, O'Shea said, "we couldn't convert that into support. People said, 'You've got the *New York Times*, you've got the MacArthur Foundation, you don't need our help.' We never could get out from under the shadow of the *New York Times*" (pers. comm.).

If he could do it over again, O'Shea said, he would hire an events specialist from the beginning to generate more revenue, visibility, and goodwill.[4] "I didn't put enough attention or devote enough of the assets that I had on audience development and engagement," he told me, adding with an ironic laugh: "I spent too much money covering the news."

As O'Shea belatedly realized, events are producing revenue that sustains watchdog journalism in Seattle, Chicago, Austin, and beyond. In 2010 events produced more than 20 percent of revenues at a number of online news start-ups; among them were NewWest.net, a site focusing on news in the Rocky Mountain region, and the *Terminal*, a local news site in Birmingham, Alabama (Briggs 2011:100). "An event brings in new revenue and raises the site's profile at the same time," Mark Briggs writes in his book *Entrepreneurial Journalism* (2011:99).

The financial windfall that events have produced for the *Texas Tribune*, *GeekWire*, WBEZ, and others may not be typical for all news outlets, but media outlets that fail to prioritize such events may be missing a prime opportunity. A *Nieman Reports* article coauthored by legendary Harvard business professor Clayton M. Christensen, author of *The*

Innovator's Dilemma, identifies events as one of three potential revenue streams upon which news organizations should pounce. Christensen and his coauthors (2012) draw a comparison to the music industry, which was stricken by falling record sales in the 2000s, thanks to digital disruptors like Napster and iTunes. Music labels recouped some of those lost revenues through a renewed emphasis on musicians' concert tours. "Live performance ticket sales and merchandise were once viewed more as a marketing exercise to increase sales of albums; they are now considered a key source of revenue" (Christensen, Skok, and Allworth 2012:12). Why shouldn't the U.S. news industry explore a similar path, leveraging its considerable brand equity to create more revenue that can help fund solid journalism?

CREATING THE "YOU-HAVE-TO-BE-THERE VIBE"

Two days before the second annual Texas Tribune Festival in September 2012, Tanya Erlach, events director, sipped iced coffee in her second-floor office while monitoring a frenzy of updates coming in to her laptop, office phone, and the occasional knock on her door. Suddenly her iPhone started buzzing with mobile photos: "My assistant's at the printer, and she's sending me pictures of the lanyards," she explained (pers. comm.). On the opposite wall a huge grid on a silver corkboard mapped out the weekend's forty-five sessions and 150 speakers booked to discuss a range of topics that included health, race, and criminal justice. Over Erlach's right shoulder was a whiteboard showing tallies for the latest registration numbers and social media followers.

All the planning somehow came together forty-eight hours later, when a packed ballroom swelled with applause as Smith welcomed Texas governor Rick Perry to the interview chair for the festival's opening session. By the time the final session wrapped up two days later with a surprise appearance by the University of Texas marching band, the festival clearly had achieved buzzworthy status among Austin political insiders. Jason Stanford, a prominent Democratic political consultant, referred to the approaching Austin City Limits (ACL) music festival when he tweeted: "Is #TribuneFest the ACL for politicos? It's now a fixture on my calendar . . . Kudos, @TexasTribune."

"It's just a real you-have-to-be-there vibe that we've been able to create," Erlach said. Consider Romeo Arrieta. The government affairs director for a Dallas real-estate association drove two hundred miles to Austin on a Friday afternoon to attend Perry's opening session, during which the governor revealed that he would propose a four-year college tuition freeze and also delivered a memorable zinger, calling left-leaning Austin "a blueberry in the tomato soup" of Texas (Root 2012). Arrieta, an avid Twitter user, noted that while he could follow the festival from afar through social media, attending in person *and* tweeting live "allows you to be more efficient" in taking advantage of perhaps the festival's biggest draw: networking. As Arrieta walked to a members-only reception following Perry's talk, he said the festival—which drew more than fifteen hundred participants in 2012 and more than two thousand attendees in 2013—has become one of the Texas political scene's premier networking opportunities. "This event, in general, has people that work policy in every respect—they promote it, they pass it, they write it," he said (pers. comm.).

Networking was the primary appeal of the 2012 festival for Kristen Carrillo, a recent college graduate who shook hands with Mayor Castro and spoke briefly with him after his festival appearance. "Prior to this event, I'll be honest, I didn't follow the *Texas Tribune*," Carrillo said. "When I saw some of the speakers they were bringing, that's what motivated me to come. . . . It can certainly be a resource for me that I didn't know [about] until they had this festival." Carrillo said her experience at the festival was nudging her toward becoming a *Tribune* member, especially to gain access to members-only events like the festival's opening-night reception (pers. comm.).

Before the *Tribune* started its festival, Smith aggressively pursued an events strategy designed to elevate the site's visibility among the state's political power brokers. At one of the first early-morning TribLive interview events in March 2010, more than 250 people gathered at the downtown Austin Club to watch Smith interview the Democratic gubernatorial nominee, Bill White. "It's becoming Texas's version of *Meet the Press*," said the political consultant Rudy England (Batsell 2010:41).

The *Tribune*'s reporters and editors are encouraged to embrace the events as an extension of the site's mission to "promote civic engagement and discourse on public policy, politics, government and other matters of statewide concern." Aman Batheja, a staff writer, moderated a Twitter chat with a state senator about transportation issues to promote the 2012 festival, and Batheja later hosted two panels at the event. For Batheja this was a more public and extroverted role than he ever had taken on during his eight years of reporting for the *Fort Worth Star-Telegram*. Batheja sees his responsibility at these events as a mix of promoting the *Tribune*, interacting with readers and sources, and using his journalism skills to steer the conversation. "It's engagement, but it's also publicity," Batheja said. "It actually feels like journalism, while you're publicizing the site, the event, and everything" (pers. comm.). Other journalists I interviewed weren't as comfortable switching gears from skeptical watchdog to sociable host. During a trivia night at a barbecue restaurant in Washington, D.C., for subscribers to *Politico Pro*, *Politico*'s niche service, I asked Patrick Reis, a *Politico* reporter, if he enjoyed cohosting the Google-sponsored event. He politely declined to answer yes or no. "My sense is, it's more geared toward the business side than the journalism side," Reis said. "But I've gotten a source or two" (pers. comm.). Reis's hesitance to embrace the role of promotional emcee is understandable, given the traditional arm's-length relationship between journalists and their sources. But the business model for news has been permanently disrupted, so it's up to managers to convince their employees that tactfully sponsored events can help sustain newsroom jobs and fund more journalism, a notion any reporter should be able to embrace.

BUILDING LOYALTY THROUGH EVENTS

In Seattle, events contribute to a sense of loyalty for readers like Sangani, the tech executive who attended *GeekWire*'s Summer Bash. Sangani said *GeekWire*'s gatherings are an efficient way for him to reconnect with business contacts and make new ones. "Networking is a big component for me," he said. "It's hard to make time one on one. I kind of know that [contacts] are going to be here, so I just show up and shake hands." Events keep Sangani in the habit of visiting *GeekWire* and deepen his loyalty to the site's journalists, to whom he sends story tips. "I go to *GeekWire* and get my fill," he said. "Because I like *GeekWire*, and because I respect the guys and the team, I'll throw them a scoop" (pers. comm.).

The *Oakland Press* in Pontiac, Michigan, has found another way to build loyalty with influential readers: by hosting free community blogger workshops. On a Wednesday afternoon in mid-August 2012 the newspaper hosted an hourlong training session for about a dozen local bloggers who write about everything from pets to the local golf scene. Karen Workman, the paper's community engagement editor at the time, led a presentation full of basic blogging tips, including search engine optimization, customizing blog designs, and how to post photos.

"You have a feeling like you're really part of the community," said Rebecca Kohler, who regularly attends the blogger workshops. "I may not be a journalist, but I have a legitimate voice and point of view." The workshops deepen the newspaper's relationships with local influencers like Kohler, a freelance designer from a nearby suburb who started a blog called *Bye Buy Clothes* to document her experimental year of not buying new clothes, shoes, and accessories. Kohler, a longtime *Press* print subscriber with no background in journalism, said the workshops taught her headline-writing tricks and how to use Google Analytics to track her blog's growth. Attending the workshops at the *Press* newsroom, she said, has helped instill in her a sense of kinship with the newspaper (pers. comm.).

ENGAGING THROUGH GARAGE SALES, BOOK CLUBS, AND PHOTO BOOTHS

Newsrooms' face-to-face engagement efforts take many forms, but they are guided by a firm belief that connecting with the community goes beyond simply reporting the news. For example, the nationally respected *West Seattle Blog* organizes an annual neighborhood-wide garage sale, charging residents a small fee to be listed on an interactive map. The garage sale, which drew nearly 250 registrants in May 2012, is "very much a connecting thing," Tracy Record, a cofounder, said. "It really fits the mission of something people can be excited about and benefit from" (pers. comm.). Meanwhile at Chicago's WBEZ-FM local nonprofits can reserve a community room and third-floor deck overlooking Navy Pier and Lake Michigan that also has an impressive view of the Chicago skyline. "By opening this space, you're opening this flow of people who are in your building," said Ash, the WBEZ vice president (pers. comm.).

Other newsrooms are taking more extreme steps to facilitate face time. In early 2012, after a wave of layoffs, the *Kalamazoo (Michigan) Gazette* vacated the historic but imposing downtown newsroom it had occupied since 1925 and moved to a street-level space a block away. The move was part of a statewide strategy by its parent company, MLive Media Group, to relocate to smaller newsroom "hubs" designed to be more open, collaborative, and inviting to the public, said John Hiner, MLive's vice president of content (pers. comm.). MLive is owned by Advance Publications, which later applied the same controversial hub strategy to newspapers in Alabama and New Orleans (Myers 2012).

The Kalamazoo hub, outfitted with sleek minimalist furniture and surrounded by windows at the busy corner of South and Burdick streets, has the feel of a small Ikea showroom, with touches of Starbucks, OfficeMax, and NBC's *Today Show*. "We're right in the thick of things," said Mickey Ciokajlo, the *Gazette*'s editor (pers. comm.). "You can wave people in," added Linda Mah, the paper's community engagement specialist. "I think people like that sense of transparency, that this is a place they can just walk into" (pers. comm.).

The mayor of Kalamazoo, Bobby Hopewell, did just that on a Tuesday in mid-July, walking one block over to report an error in a story about the city's charging fees when Korean War veterans wanted to reserve a local park (Klug 2012). "He walked down here, he came in, and he wanted to talk to me," Ciokajlo told me. "Maybe in the past he would have called, or he would have stewed over it. This space is encouraging [interactive] behavior, both on the reporters' part and the community's part."

The hub's most visible space is the corner interview room, where passers-by can get a glimpse of journalists at work. *Gazette* staffers do not have assigned desks; they have laptops and backpacks and are encouraged to move around. On special occasions—such as monthly Art Hop events or a downtown scavenger hunt for first-year students at Western Michigan University—the *Gazette* sets up a photo booth in the interview room and invites the public to pose for silly shots.

THE "OPEN NEWSROOM": A RADICAL EXPERIMENT IN ENGAGEMENT

One of the most closely watched experiments in face-to-face engagement began in late 2010 at the *Register Citizen* in Torrington, Connecticut, when the paper moved its newsroom into a converted factory space that now includes the Newsroom Cafe, which is open to the public. Taking a page from a similar news cafe pilot project in the Czech Republic (Pecoskie 2010), the *Register Citizen* transformed a historic factory where local workers once made sewing needles and ball bearings into a reader-friendly newsroom where community members can enjoy coffee, muffins, and free wi-fi and, if so inclined, offer story suggestions or sit in on the daily 4 P.M. news meeting (figure 1.2). "Anybody can literally walk up to us at our desks and ask a question," Emily Olson, the managing editor, wrote in *Nieman Reports*. "No hiding. No turning away from any man, woman or teenager who walks in" (2011).

Not long after the paper started the cafe, a man walked in and asked to speak with a reporter about a neighboring city's efforts to shut down his farm stand, leading to a story that drew more than fifty comments (Agogliati 2011). Olson noted in her *Nieman Reports* piece that while the man's story may have drawn similar interest and coverage when the newspaper was at its former location, "our open doors, wide spaces for people to walk through, and the availability of a reporter gave this man the confidence he needed to stop by and ask us to talk with him." More

FIGURE 1.2 The *Register Citizen*'s Open Newsroom. Torrington, Connecticut, November 2012. Photo: Jake Batsell

than a year later Olson said the accessible atmosphere had endured. "The news gets in here in a way that it would not if we did not have this open-door policy from seven to seven," she said. "I really believe that. Ivory-tower journalism doesn't work. It used to, because people used to have more of a reverence for journalism" (pers. comm.).

The *New York Times* characterized the news cafe as "Starbucks meets Lou Grant," but nine months after it opened, Matt DeRienzo, the *Register Citizen*'s editor, said it had become clear that the experiment was less about selling coffee than an ethic of accessibility (Applebome 2010; DeRienzo 2011). When I visited Torrington in November 2012, the *Register Citizen*'s newsroom had settled into the familiar feel of a public institution, much like a library. Tutors met with pupils in the cafe; local artists displayed their work on commission, groups gathered in a community meeting space to explore genealogy or study the Bible. Self-serve coffee cost 75 cents from a coin-operated Keurig machine, with pastries and muffins offered alongside an honor-system cash box. The newspaper broke even on the snacks, DeRienzo said, but "it's really about the engagement, not so much making money on it. . . . We try to provide this continuum of ways to engage with us" (pers. comm.).

The paper also opened up its daily newsroom story meetings, inviting the public to attend in person or view a live webcast. Several months before I visited the *Torrington Register Citizen*, I asked Tom Gorman, executive editor of the *Las Vegas Sun*, for his thoughts on Torrington's Open Newsroom. "My concern is, you'd get the same twelve gadflies, and it wouldn't be as democratic as I see it through my rose-colored editor's eyes," Gorman told me. DeRienzo conceded Gorman's point, that attending a news meeting appeals mainly to a small universe of particularly motivated readers, but he added: "You hear from those people anyway, right? So by broadening it [offering amenities such as the cafe] you get beyond those people" (pers. comm.).

In fact public participation in *Register Citizen* news meetings tapered off after the initial fanfare. Instead, staffers told me, people were more likely to visit the newsroom for a group meeting in the community classroom, research local subjects tucked away in more than a century's worth of microfilm archives, or take advantage of free wi-fi from the comfort of a leather chair or couch. During the first month she lived in Torrington in the fall of 2012, twenty-year-old Jaycee Taylor visited the newsroom nearly every weekday to access the web on one of several public computer stations. "I don't have Internet at my house," Taylor said. "It's a nice, safe place to hang out." She said she used the public computer to search for work and eventually found a listing that led her to a job selling women's clothes at JCPenney (pers. comm.).

It's all part of a reader-friendly environment that DeRienzo calls "a fundamental shift in the relationship with our audience" (pers. comm.) What's harder to gauge is how it contributes to the bottom line. Two years into the Open Newsroom experiment, digital revenue was increasing at the *Register Citizen*, DeRienzo said, but not more than at other papers within the same chain. He shared anecdotal examples of business owners' buying ads after coming to the Open Newsroom for a social media training session. But regardless of the financial impact,

DeRienzo told me, the *Register Citizen* unquestionably has become more relevant to its community—even if that relevance isn't always related purely to journalism:

It's a mind-set. It has improved our reputation in the community, for sure. We kind of set ourselves up as a resource to help in so many ways. It kind of redefines the mission of the newspaper. . . . Our print audience loves this place, way more than the people who might be doing more with us on social media. You cannot substitute good reporting and good editing with anything. Our quality rises and falls with that. But the fact that people feel open to come in and tell us we're wrong, and the fact that we embrace that, makes us better.

Still, *Register Citizen* reporters and editors have wondered at times how much their readers really care about participating in the news process. On the eve of the 2012 presidential election, two editors and two reporters gathered for the *Register Citizen*'s 4 P.M. news meeting. No readers attended, and nobody bothered to tune in for the live webcast. Emily Olson, the managing editor, looked up at the monitor hovering over the meeting table and noticed that the UStream viewer counter showed zero.

"Why isn't anybody watching us?" she asked half-plaintively. Olson acknowledged that public attendance at the 4 P.M. news meetings has dwindled since the initial heady days of the Newsroom Cafe experiment, when the paper had roughly a dozen visitors per meeting, including students from local high schools. But the Open Newsroom still sees plenty of other types of activity, whether it's amateur historians scrolling through the microfilm archives or an exercise group practicing *qigong*. "What hasn't died down is that our newsroom is the public's as much as it is ours," Olson said. "That, I think, makes us a success. . . . I think just the fact that people get in here and get in our faces, that keeps us mindful of the reason that we have a newspaper at all" (pers. comm.).

The *Register Citizen*, like Michigan's *Oakland Press*, is run by Digital First Media, which under John Paton, its CEO, has dramatically transformed the former Journal Register newspaper chain (Kirchner 2011). The company has drawn national attention—and scrutiny—for a series of bold experiments, including a centralized digital news desk in Manhattan called Operation Thunderdome (Benzing 2011) that was shut down after three years, the open newsroom in Torrington, and mobile "pop-up" newsrooms at community events in California, Minnesota, Pennsylvania, and Connecticut (McAthy 2012). The financial success of the company's digital initiatives has been difficult to decipher—the chain filed for bankruptcy twice in three years, yet by the end of that three-year period Paton reported that Digital First had realized an operating profit of 41 percent (Haughney 2012; Beaujon 2013). Finances aside, it would be hard to argue with Olson's assessment of how the Newsroom Cafe has bolstered her paper's efforts to engage readers: "As journalists, we are now more a part of the community that we report about" (Olson 2011).

CAREER COUNSELING, BOOK CLUBS,
AND TRIVIA PARTIES

The *Seattle Times*, a prominent practitioner of civic journalism during the 1990s, updated its face-to-face engagement efforts in June 2012 when it hosted a career-counseling event in connection with its front-page "Recession Generation" series. The event, free to twentysomethings who were in the job market, included résumé critiques, presentations about how to network and craft your "elevator pitch," and one-on-one career counseling. Some of the thirty-five millennials who showed up were sources profiled in the series, said Sona Patel, a social media producer at the *Times*. "Engagement is not just commenting or talking to people online," Patel said. "I think it's just as important, if not more important, to meet the people you're talking to" (pers. comm.).

Face-to-face engagement need not always entail hosting events. At public meetings reporters for the *Columbia Missourian* (who also happen to be students at the Missouri School of Journalism) distribute informational handouts with summaries of the key facts framing that night's discussion, according to Joy Mayer, the *Missourian*'s director of community outreach. Before the tenth anniversary of the September 11, 2001, terrorist attacks, the *Missourian* prepared a handout with tips on how to discuss 9/11 with children and delivered the fliers to day-care centers (Mayer 2012).

Other examples are manifold. *GeekWire* hosts game nights at Seattle area restaurants, with local techies competing at board games like Risk and Settlers of Catan. The *Dallas Morning News*'s Sunday editorial section, Points, sponsors a free summer book club, convening readers first on a blog and then meeting to discuss the book in person. The *Washington Post*'s Chris Cillizza, author of the popular political blog *The Fix*, holds regular Politics and Pints trivia parties at a local bar. And *Politico Pro*, a Beltway rival of the *Post*'s, also routinely hosts trivia nights for subscribers, serving up free brisket sliders and pitchers of Shiner Bock beer at a Texas-themed restaurant while peppering four-person teams with Beltway-themed questions. David Barmore, a lobbyist who subscribes to *Pro*'s technology coverage, said events like Trivia Night deepen the bond between *Politico* and its subscribers. "It's already an awesome resource that I use professionally—the fact that it has this for fun is also great," Barmore said after his team won an election-themed trivia night (pers. comm.).

As the news industry obsessively focuses on how to digitally engage readers, it's easy to forget the importance of face-to-face connection. Linda Mah, the *Kalamazoo Gazette*'s community engagement specialist, said that with all the time she spends behind her laptop, she often finds herself wondering: "Is online really engagement? Are you really forming relationships? Is this really a conversation? To get to that point, you need to have face-to-face interaction" (pers. comm.).

MEASURING SUCCESS

When it comes to events, measuring success can be as simple as tallying RSVPs, ticket sales, and corporate sponsorships. But other forms of face-to-face engagement are harder to quantify.[5] In August 2012 the

Morning Sun in Mount Pleasant, Michigan, set up a makeshift satellite newsroom—a portable table stacked with a few freebies—in the lobby of a downtown art gallery as part of a community event called Art Walk Central. As visitors wandered into the gallery on a Tuesday morning, Lisa Yanick-Jonaitis, a photographer who doubles as the paper's community engagement editor, offered them a free copy of the *Morning Sun*'s Art Walk Central tabloid, which included a map and "passport" that readers could get stamped to enter a drawing for prizes. The tabloid brought in $2,100 in advertising revenue, Yanick-Jonaitis said. But beyond that, clear metrics for the newspaper's monthlong engagement project were elusive. "To me, the fact that we made money is a success," she said. "I think the fact that we went to businesses and got them excited about what we were doing is a success. I don't know how you measure that" (pers. comm.).

During lulls at the gallery Yanick-Jonaitis ran a trivia contest from her laptop, quizzing the *Morning Sun*'s 4,458 Facebook fans about Mount Pleasant history. Some readers responded within seconds in the hope of claiming the prize: a vintage softball t-shirt from the parks and rec department. "I feel like it's such a new thing, we're not really sure what we're doing yet," Yanick-Jonaitis said. "You have to accept that not everything's going to be a success, because it's not" (pers. comm.). Meanwhile her boss, Rick Mills, editor of the *Morning Sun*, said he was convinced that the Art Walk Central project was a worthwhile investment of time and newsroom resources. "There's got to be a multiplier there in terms of goodwill and knowing we're accessible . . . that we're not just sitting in a corner covering our community, but we're part of the community," Mills said (pers. comm.).

While supervising the Art Walk project, Yanick-Jonaitis also was brainstorming ideas for another community engagement project aimed at highlighting the spiritual traditions of local Native Americans. She had plenty of ideas for journalistic content but was having a harder time coming up with ways to make the project pay. "I feel like there are a lot of people in my industry who are struggling with this," she said (pers. comm.). Indeed, she is not alone. Many of the engagement specialists with whom I spoke at newsrooms across the country talked about feeling pressure to justify their efforts with metrics showing a clear return on investment.

Yanick-Jonaitis's *Morning Sun* colleague Holly Mahaffey, a community engagement producer, said she considers her job a hybrid of customer service and journalism (pers. comm.). When measuring the return of journalistic engagement efforts, then, it may be useful to consider a customer-service example from the retail world. The famous no-questions-asked returns policy at Nordstrom department stores subtracts revenue every time a customer takes advantage of it, but it has helped the company build an iconic customer-friendly reputation that keeps people coming back (Martinez 2011). Similarly, newsrooms must accept that some of their face-to-face engagement efforts may produce intangible results but are still necessary to build loyalty and goodwill with their audience.

The pitfalls of face-to-face engagement extend beyond fuzzy metrics. Michele Matassa Flores, managing editor of the *Puget Sound Business Journal*, acknowledges that hosting events "blurs the lines a little bit between the newsroom and your marketing side. You're a little more cozy with your sources when you're putting on events" (pers. comm.). And Todd Bishop, the *GeekWire* cofounder, notes that successfully pulling off an event requires the ability to juggle a myriad of logistical details. "It's a different skill," he said. "We've learned so much about events and how hard they are. There are so many moving pieces" (pers. comm.).

COMMON ELEMENTS OF EFFECTIVE FACE-TO-FACE ENGAGEMENT

As the U.S. news industry scrambles to unearth new revenue sources, more online news start-ups and traditional media companies are turning to live events and other face-to-face opportunities to engage and monetize their audiences—that is, use them as a source of profit—while also building community. This new paradigm of face-to-face engagement differs from the civic journalism that once inspired news outlets to convene their audience out of an obligatory duty to serve as a town square, and it goes beyond the advertising-driven events put on by magazines for decades. Instead the newer, more entrepreneurial, approach views in-person engagement not merely as an obligation but as an opportunity to attract revenue while building a mutual sense of loyalty between journalists and their core audience.

Through trial and error, news organizations that prioritize this style of face-to-face engagement have learned some common but important lessons:

• *Designate an event planner.* Ideally a full-time specialist can assume the role. But depending on the scope, event planning also can be handled part time by a staffer on the business side or by a community engagement manager in the newsroom. Regardless, successfully executing an events strategy demands a singular sense of focus and accountability—without which, as O'Shea learned with the *Chicago News Cooperative*, events are unlikely to take off.

• *To make money, seek out sponsors.* Ticket sales mainly cover overhead costs. The real money in events—90 percent in the case of the *Texas Tribune*—comes from corporate sponsorships. And the main way to attract sponsors is to convince them that the event's audience will be demographically desirable and therefore worth the sponsorship dollars.

• *Recognize that networking is a prime draw.* Events with a "you-have-to-be-there vibe" carry a higher probability of success, particularly among professional niche crowds—think *GeekWire*'s legions of Seattle techies or the scores of lobbyists and government staffers who follow *Politico Pro* and the *Texas Tribune*. And events that are consistently perceived to be worthwhile can have a spillover effect, bringing a news site more readers, subscribers, members, and/or donors.

• *Make sure the newsroom buys-in.* When hosting events, giving newsroom staffers a prominent role boosts their visibility and motivates them to act as positive ambassadors for the news organization. Certain events also help feed the news flow by providing fresh content and can build buzz by conveying the sense that attendees are witnessing news in action. However, newsroom leaders must convince the staff that directly engaging the public through face-to-face events is an important part of twenty-first-century journalism and does not violate the hallowed church-state separation of news and advertising.

• *Provide memorable experiences.* Not every event needs to be a brainy, newsy, networking extravaganza. Watching a zombie double feature at the drive-in, talking food with a celebrity chef, or competing in a local trivia contest can deepen the affinity between attendees and the news outlet hosting the event.

• *Be aware that returns are not always quantifiable.* Children's story-telling performances in Chicago, book clubs in Dallas, and art walks in mid-Michigan may not rake in tens of thousands of dollars, but one would hope they have the multiplier effect described by Rick Mills, the *Morning Sun* editor, generating a sense of goodwill and loyalty among readers in Mount Pleasant, Michigan. This style of face-to-face engagement contributes to the sense that a news organization not only covers the community but actually is part of that community.

The *Texas Tribune*'s Smith acknowledges that not every newsroom can generate roughly $1 million a year through live events, as his staff has managed to do. "I don't know that the scale of what we do is replicable elsewhere," he said. But Smith said he's convinced that any news organization can find ways to bring together its community through face-to-face engagement and can find a way to make those efforts help pay for journalism. "You know what? It's there, it's there, it's there," he said. "You've got to know where to go, you've got to figure out who it is, you've got to be creative about it, but it's there" (pers. comm.).

Beyond the bottom line, people who attended events put on by news organizations from Washington State to Texas to Michigan in 2012 told me that the gatherings made them more likely to make a habit of returning to that organization's content as a source for news. Kohler, the freelance designer in Michigan, said the *Oakland Press*'s blogger training workshops symbolize the newspaper's faith in the community. "They acknowledge us, and we acknowledge them," Kohler said. "That's engagement" (pers. comm.).

2

News as Conversation

Not Just Informing but Involving the Audience

Where was God in Aurora?

It was a frank, arresting, and painful question to ask in the days following the macabre shooting spree that left twelve people dead and dozens of others injured at a screening of a Batman movie in Colorado on July 20, 2012. Still, the question struck a nerve for hundreds of thousands of readers of CNN's *Belief Blog*.

The blog aims to intertwine religion with news. But in the shocking aftermath of Aurora, Dan Gilgoff, religion editor of *CNN.com*, and his colleagues in Washington, D.C., were struggling with how to bring perspective to such a senseless tragedy. "It was actually a little bit desperate," Gilgoff said. "The thought occurred to me, 'Where is God in this tragedy?'—which is this age-old question in religion. So I just put it out there" (pers. comm.). He first posed the question on Twitter, then summarized the emotional array of responses a few hours later in a blog post that itself attracted more than ten thousand comments (Gilgoff 2012a).

Gilgoff's question triggered a week's worth of impassioned, generally thoughtful, debate as readers argued about the notion of divine
sovereignty versus human free will. The episode showed how journalists can create community by actively involving the audience in the stories they cover. As I will explore in this chapter, an engaged journalist's
role in the twenty-first century is not only to inform but to bring readers directly into the conversation through digitally powered techniques
such as real-time coverage, alternative story forms, crowdsourcing,
beat blogging, user-generated content, and comment forums.

AURORA'S AFTERMATH:
AN AUDIENCE-DRIVEN CONVERSATION

In the days following the Aurora tragedy, Meredith Artley, managing
editor of the Atlanta-based *CNN Digital*, watched in amazement as the
post featuring Gilgoff's question attracted two thousand comments
during the first six hours after it was published. The comments quickly
grew to five thousand. Then ten thousand. Over the next week "Where
was God in Aurora?" became a fervent but largely civil conversation,
driven by the audience. "It's not our job to say, 'OK, everyone, we're
done,'" Artley said. "We just kept it going. People kept on wanting to
talk about it" (pers. comm.).

As Gilgoff's original post gained traction, "it was not only a conversation, it was a unique conversation that CNN provoked and was starting to own," Gilgoff said (figure 2.1). To keep the momentum going, he
said, "we wanted to do something that was educationally meaningful
that would showcase the conversation, and do it in a way that would
show more depth." So the next natural step, Gilgoff said, was to bring
in other voices. He invited a religion scholar, Stephen Prothero (2012),
and a Colorado pastor, Rob Brendle (2012), to write columns explaining
their take on the where-was-God question. That's another opportunity
in convening a community like this, Gilgoff said: connecting experts
and the masses. "It allows you to kind of give the keys to someone else,
as opposed to calling them to get a quote," he said.

FIGURE 2.1   Dan Gilgoff, religion editor at CNN.com, is interviewed about the CNN *Belief Blog*'s "Where Was God in Aurora?" project. Washington, D.C., July 2012. Copyright © CNN. Image: CNN

Days later, as the conversation began to wane, Gilgoff wrote a recap post noting the strong presence of atheists during CNN's where-was-God conversation, demonstrating how the Internet can serve as a "de facto global church" for nonbelievers during times of crisis (2012b). In all, *Belief Blog*'s Aurora-related posts drew about two million page views during a single week. Earlier in his career, when Gilgoff worked for *U.S. News and World Report*, "we had no window into who was consuming our content, other than newsstand sales," he said. Had he been assigned a reflective piece like the where-was-God story during his days at the magazine, Gilgoff told me, he might have interviewed ten or twelve sources for a seven-hundred-word story that left 90 percent of his reporting on the cutting-room floor. He also probably would have moved along after writing that single story. "Before, you would think a story has come and gone," he said. "What the Internet allows you to do is see that people are still talking about it. We didn't know that a few years ago."

However, tapping into the power of a digital community requires shedding some of the work habits of a traditional reporter. Today's journalists can't just gather facts and quotes and dispense them to the public; they must actively seek out their audience and create opportunities for interaction. "If you don't hear from your readers, the tendency is to have a very insular notion of your beat," Gilgoff said. "If you open it up, there are a zillion angles that wouldn't have otherwise" come to light (pers. comm.).

Plenty of journalists remain wary of the onslaught of social media and audience interaction—even CNN's president, Jeff Zucker, has called Twitter a "frenemy" (Thornton 2013). But by asking questions that respect readers' intelligence, journalists can raise the quality of the dialogue surrounding their stories, as evidenced by the *Belief Blog*'s where-was-God discussion. "When you start a conversation like this, the comments tend to be a lot more thoughtful and constructive," Gilgoff said. "If the comments were lame or less than meaningful on that post, we wouldn't have done it." With each new Aurora post, Gilgoff said, the goal was not to generate easy clicks but rather to listen and react to the *Belief Blog* community, moving the conversation forward: "It had a lot of integrity and substance. It wasn't advancing the conversation in an attempt to ride the wave. We were harnessing what our readers were saying to teach them something, too. . . . It's not as cynically done as, 'Can we get 250,000 more clicks on this?' That's the effect, but it's not the cause." [1]

For Gilgoff, the provocative reader-driven conversation that followed the Aurora tragedy demonstrated the value of interactive journalism. "Our whole mission is meeting the audience," he said. "For the moment they are caring about that, we want to meet them. We can shed light on what everybody's thinking about today. I think that's the primary goal of journalism" (pers. comm.).

AN "IMPROVED FORM OF JOURNALISM"

It's one thing to channel audience reactions during a hot-button news event like the Aurora or Newtown shootings. On a more typical news day, identifying pathways to conversation can take a bit more effort. However, it's becoming easier through the use of analytical tools that identify trending topics on news sites, search engines, and social media. "The tools allow us to know what's on people's minds," said David Clark

Scott, online director of the *Christian Science Monitor*. "The question, I think, has to become: How do we want to enter that conversation?" Scott, a former foreign correspondent, once thrived during journalism's era of one-way dispatches. But he says he prefers working in today's interactive news environment. "To me, it's an improved form of journalism," he said. "Too often we say, 'I wrote about it three days ago.' Do you want to enter the conversation and be more relevant or do you want to take the position, 'Oh, there's nothing to add here'?" (pers. comm.).

Entering that conversation, though, requires a commitment to proactively seek out audiences, wherever they might be talking. "A lot of the conversation is never going to come to the newspaper or the newspaper's website," said Steve Buttry, former director of digital transformation for Digital First Media. "So we need to join the conversation where it is" (pers. comm.). And effectively joining those conversations requires a more sincere effort from journalists than the usual robotic self-promotion of news stories on social media platforms. Andy Carvin, whose exhaustive crowdsourcing for NPR during the Arab Spring uprisings of 2011 demonstrated Twitter's power as a journalistic medium, says too many newsrooms approach social media with superficial strategies. Instead Carvin asks:

> Why aren't we engaging the public more directly? I don't mean engagement like encouraging them to "like" us on Facebook or click the retweet button. That is not engagement. By engagement I mean, why don't we use these incredibly powerful tools to *talk* with them, *listen* to them, and help us all understand the world a little better? Perhaps we can even use social media to do the exact opposite of its reputation—to slow down the news cycle, help us catch our collective breaths and scrutinize what's happening with greater mindfulness. (Carvin 2013)

Regardless of the tactics, news as conversation at its essence amounts to simply caring about the audience. When I visited the *Oakland Press* in Pontiac, Michigan, during the summer of 2012, the newspaper's outgoing community engagement editor, Karen Workman, was in the process

FIGURE 2.2 Karen Workman (at laptop), outgoing *Oakland Press* community engagement editor, trains her successor, Monica Drake. Pontiac, Michigan, August 2012. Photo: Jake Batsell

of training her successor, Monica Drake (figure 2.2). I sat in as Workman presented Drake with a seven-page single-spaced overview of her new job responsibilities, with this warning on the first page: "Don't cheapen it. This is not all about pushing links out on social media or adding new blogs for the sake of adding them." Workman glanced up from the list, looked at Drake, and paraphrased: "Really, it boils down to caring about our audience. You are our point person for caring about our audience." Workman—who was promoted to Digital First Media's internal wire service, Project Thunderdome, and later joined the *New York Times*—said her duties as community engagement editor in Pontiac entailed a mix of customer service, training other journalists and community bloggers, mastering tech tools, and finding ways to integrate social media into the paper's journalism (pers. comm.).

DIFFERING PORTRAITS
OF AN ENGAGED USER

Who is an engaged user, exactly? Not surprisingly, it depends on whom you ask. Eric Ulken, an assistant managing editor at the *Seattle Times*, said his idea of an engaged user is someone who deliberately chooses a news site and spends "significant time" there. Ulken's engaged user frequently comments on stories, shares news links by using social media, and, perhaps most important, returns to the site frequently (pers. comm.). For niche news sites focused on a particular subject, the degree of engagement is likely to be more intensive. Emily Ramshaw, editor of the *Texas Tribune*, thinks of an engaged user as someone who is interested politically, shows up at events, connects with reporters electronically and in person, and tweets about the *Tribune*. "They're people who really care—before work, after work, and on their lunch hour," Ramshaw said. "And I'm proud of that" (pers. comm.).

For Mark Luckie, Twitter's manager of journalism and news, an engaged user is simply "someone who recognizes you by name and will recommend you to a friend" (pers. comm.).[2] Paul Bass, editor of the *New Haven (CT) Independent*, has a mental picture of an engaged user who is much more active: she comments on stories, e-mails reporters, and submits photos. "The big thing is reading and talking and doing something about it," Bass said (pers. comm.). Practiced to its fullest extent, engaged journalism can bring a community together around an issue. For example, Bass said, the *Independent*'s persistent coverage of traffic safety issues in New Haven helped connect residents who later successfully pressured the city to slow traffic in their neighborhoods (MacMillan 2012). "They really kind of found each other through the stories in the *Independent*," Bass said (pers. comm.).

Journalists may conjure up different mental pictures of their audience, but they agree on a fundamental point: engaged users stay loyal to a news site because its content is relevant to their lives. Colleen Stone, director of digital operations for the MLive Media Group chain of newspapers in Michigan, acknowledges that she utters the word

engagement so much that "I'm sick of hearing it come out of my mouth."
But Stone said an engaged proactive attitude toward the audience helps
reporters get to know their community better, infusing their work with
more relevance. "I really do believe that engagement, whether it's just
watching your numbers or actively interacting, really helps improve the
reporting," she said (pers. comm.). John Hiner, MLive Media Group's
vice president of content, believes engagement leads to well-informed,
better-directed reporters—which, in turn, drives commercial success
because "we're more in tune with what the community's actually interested in. It removes that hierarchical view that editors used to have. The
readers are often right" (pers. comm.).

"Without engagement, we're not relevant," said David Beard, director of digital content for the *Washington Post*. Beard, whose journalism career spans more than three decades, said print journalists for too
long have been consumed with the art of their profession while hardly
ever thinking of—or interacting with—their readers. Today, Beard said,
"the world is communicating with us every second. We'd be silly to mute
those voices and claim to be representing our readers" (pers. comm.).
Matt Hufman, editorial page editor of the *Las Vegas Sun*, said his job has
expanded beyond proclaiming the paper's stances on the issues of the
day and now includes the equally important role of facilitating reader
discussion of those issues. When Hufman began his journalism career,
timely messages from readers arrived not through e-mail but by way of
phone message slips. "And in some ways, I miss it," he jokes. But he has
come to appreciate the value of interacting with readers. "The editorial
voice of a newspaper that came down from on high, my two-cent theory
is, that voice irritates people," Hufman said (pers. comm.).

In fact, at a time when anyone with a Twitter or Facebook account can
spread news instantaneously, some might question the need for journalists at all. But Christensen, Skok, and Allworth (2012:14) convinc-
ingly argue in *Nieman Reports* that "the value for news organizations
now increasingly lies in providing context and verification—reporting
the 'how, why and what it means'—and *facilitating communities around
that news and information*" (emphasis added). Context and verification
always have been hallmarks of professional journalism. But to excel in

the era of engagement, news outlets now must devote the same degree of effort to interacting with their communities.

ENGAGING IN REAL TIME, AS A DAILY HABIT

On the day before the November 2012 general election, a handful of editors and reporters gathered for the regular 10:30 A.M. news meeting at the *New Haven Register* in Connecticut. The meeting took place not around a mahogany table or inside an editor's office but on the live-chat platform ScribbleLive, where *Register* editors logged on and discussed the day's news outlook, both in person and virtually, with other staffers from Digital First Media newspapers around the state.

Also invited: you, the public. Reader Kevin G. checked in to the chat at 10:32 A.M., prompting a greeting from Ed Stannard, the *Register*'s community engagement editor: "Did you do OK in the storm, Kevin?" Superstorm Sandy had struck the area a week earlier, and many residents remained without power. For Kevin the weekend had been fortuitous: "Got it back Sat morning .. Lights .. Power .. Shower!! Yee Ha." Later in the chat Kevin suggested a story angle related to authorities' handling of the outages.

"The idea," Helen Bennett, the city editor, said, "is to let everybody know what we're doing. The hope is getting the public to participate in the process as it's going along. . . . We try a lot, and if we fall flat on our face, we keep going" (pers. comm.). Kevin G. turned out to be the only reader who participated in that morning's meeting, but *Register* staffers were unfazed. "To be really honest, we get very little public participation," Stannard said. So, with minimal interest among readers, why invite them at all? "I think it goes to our credibility as a public institution that we be open to the public in as many ways we can be," Stannard said. "In the long term it's better to have a window than a brick wall" (pers. comm.).

Daily news meetings may not draw much participation from the public, but newsrooms are finding other ways to meet readers' real-time needs. During the breakfast hour, a time when you could hear crickets chirp in many American newsrooms, the *Daily Post* in North Wales, United Kingdom, already buzzes with the sounds of clacking keyboards, animated phone interviews, and editors chatting with each other about the day's news agenda. David Powell, a breaking news reporter for the *Post*, begins work at 6:30 A.M., feeding the *North Wales Live Blog* with what editors call "snackable" nuggets of practical information—weather, traffic, overnight headlines—for readers to scan over coffee before they set out for the day. "It's really important that we keep [the live blog] going, not with trivia but with useful information," Alison Gow, the paper's editor, said. "It may be a slow news day, but you can still tell people things that are important to their day, like road closures, events coming up on the weekend." Since the live blog made its debut in fall 2012, Gow said, it has become the site's most engaging feature, averaging more than three minutes per visit: "It's the only place locally where you've got that rolling news update if you want it" (pers. comm.).[3] The live blog was among a series of changes the *Daily Post* introduced as part of a "Newsroom 3.0" campaign designed to create a more digitally focused workflow.

Beyond the newsroom, journalists are using real-time platforms to cover live events ranging from political debates to red-carpet strolls to sports matchups. Danny O'Neil, who for seven years covered professional football for the *Seattle Times*, said in-game *CoverItLive* chats not only help him connect with Seattle Seahawks fans but also identify what his readers perceive to be pivotal moments in the game. That feedback, O'Neil said, shapes the questions he'll ask the head coach in the postgame press conference: "It'll point out, 'This is something I need to get an explanation for'" (pers. comm.).

O'Neil was among many newspaper reporters with whom I spoke who described ways they'd found to integrate real-time reporting into their workflow for the daily print product. With the news industry devoting more attention to online engagement, veteran print journalists and more than a few readers have worried aloud that an increasingly digital focus would erode the quality of the print newspaper. For example, MLive Media Group, owned by Advance Publications, combined its eight Michigan newspapers into a digitally centered news operation, reduced home delivery to three days a week, laid off hundreds of employees, and refocused newsgathering efforts around its flagship website, *MLive* (Hoogland 2011; Jones 2011). The changes wrought by the parent company would later draw criticism from, among others, a *Kalamazoo Gazette* reader who posted a comment questioning why, when Kalamazoo-based Western Michigan University beat state rival University of Michigan for a conference hockey championship, the *Gazette*'s story did not appear on the sports cover of the newspaper (Keep 2012).

When I asked the *Gazette*'s editor, Mickey Ciokajlo, about that reader's complaint, he said: "If you had gone on our site or our Facebook page during that game, we were blowing it up. We were doing real-time reporting on *MLive* and social media" (pers. comm.). That may be true, but even the most digitally savvy Western Michigan hockey fans can still appreciate prominent coverage of a conference championship in the next day's newspaper. The *Gazette*'s retooled newsroom structure failed to deliver that experience, and its readers noticed. That's not to bemoan *MLive*'s digital strategy, but it does highlight the perceived trade-offs that can come along with web-focused newsroom overhauls.[4]

Across the pond in Wales, the *Daily Post* also has reduced newsroom staff, but the paper continues to emphasize its print editions and sister publications. When the newspaper reorganized its editorial workflow in late 2012 under the banner "Newsroom 3.0," editors were careful to present the new strategy as "digitally *enhanced*"—not digital *first*. In fact, nine months into the Newsroom 3.0 era, a telling poster still hung on a newsroom wall near the editor's office: "Before undertaking any activity, ask this simple question: Does it sell newspapers? If the answer is no, it isn't worth doing." The *Daily Post* routinely repurposes web content, including weekly "Ask the Expert" chats and daily stories that began as nuggets of breaking news on the live blog, for the next day's paper. The paper's journalists have come to understand that digital content helps fuel the overall news operation—which still very much includes print, said Dan Owen, executive editor for digital. "We're asking people to do ultimately what is the same job in terms of telling stories, but we're getting people now to do it in a very different way," Owen said (pers. comm.).[5]

ALTERNATE STORY FORMS: "EVERYTHING'S ABOUT THE READER"

The Internet is blissfully exempt from the format constraints that long required cramming a news story into fifteen column inches or a ninety-second broadcast segment. When executed well, digital storytelling can help the audience experience a news story so intuitively and naturally that it is almost effortless.

For example, in the destructive aftermath of Superstorm Sandy in late October 2012, the *New Haven Independent* published an unusual story. The storm had upended a large tree on the New Haven Green, unearthing a centuries-old human skeleton that was tangled among the tree's gnarled roots (MacMillan and Bailey 2012). But instead of filing a traditional inverted-pyramid text story, the *Independent*'s reporters, Thomas MacMillan and Melissa Bailey, filed continuous updates from the scene, posting sixteen photos and a slew of updates throughout the night in the form of a running blog entry that drew more than eleven thousand likes on Facebook. National outlets, including the *Huffington Post* and the *Drudge Report*, picked up the story, triggering a crush of traffic that temporarily shut down the *Independent*'s site. The story was translated into Arabic and Russian, and, days later, the mysterious old skeleton even spurred a joke on *Saturday Night Live*'s "Weekend Update" segment.

Meanwhile the *New Haven Register*—no stranger to digital engagement—was considerably less imaginative than its local online competitor. The *Register* posted a print-style, two-hundred-word story about the skeletons, with only one photo (Kaempffer 2012). The *Independent*'s scrollable, blog-style, picture-heavy presentation was more accessible and intuitive to navigate—which, of course, helped it attract more attention. "We don't do things to pick up hits; we want to make it easy to read," said Paul Bass, editor of the *Independent*. Bass noted that the *Independent* could have presented the skeleton story as a photo slide show with each image on a separate web page, a tactic many news sites use to generate more page views. But that approach, Bass said, probably would have annoyed readers: "Everything's about the reader. We never want to snooker them. We'll click you right to the story" (pers. comm.).

The quirky but compelling skeleton story shows how online journalism, practiced effectively, empowers readers with options to experience news on their own terms. That same user-first attitude prevailed a week later throughout *Yahoo! News*'s twelfth-floor newsroom in midtown Manhattan on election night 2012. As the first results began to trickle across Times Square news tickers three blocks away, *Yahoo!*'s political bloggers, editors, programmers, and developers locked their focus on the night's mission: putting users in charge of their own experience, in real time, on the most anticipated political news night of the year.

The night's centerpiece was the Election Control Room, a new immersive portal with elements that included a video stream of *ABC News*'s on-air coverage, a live blog with *Yahoo!* editors and pundits, real-time interactive electoral maps, and an algorithmic feature called "The Signal" that combined tweets, Facebook statuses, and blog posts from across the web (figure 2.3). *Yahoo!* users could switch back and forth between each feature as they saw fit or step back for the bird's-eye view to see them all at once.

E. J. Liao, a senior product manager, said the goal in designing the Control Room was to give readers the same range of options that a television producer has when overseeing a live broadcast: "We took that as a concept and said, 'What if we made them the producer, with a wall of different options?'" (pers. comm.). Throughout the night Liao moved around the newsroom with his laptop in one hand and cell phone in the other, orchestrating the Control Room in collaboration with *Yahoo!* staffers from Taiwan to Texas to California.

The portal's live blog was peppered with constant updates from *Yahoo!* reporters, editors, and political commentators, including the political pundits Virginia Heffernan and Jeff Greenfield. Scores of readers sent

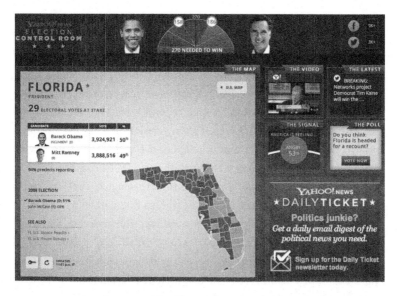

FIGURE 2.3 On Election Night 2012, *Yahoo! News*'s Election Control Room empowered users to click and choose however they wanted to experience the story. Copyright © *Yahoo! News*. Image: *Yahoo! News*

comments to the live blog, which had drawn nearly 300,000 clicks by midnight, but producers published only a small fraction of them. In the midst of a real-time national news event, what type of comment makes the cut? "It kind of depends on the flow of the conversation, the narrative at the time," said *Yahoo!*'s Jason Sickles, who co-moderated the live blog. Sickles scanned the sea of comments in search of quick on-point responses and interactions. For example, when Heffernan mentioned that she had taken her children to the polls, Sickles quickly published several comments from readers who replied that they had done the same. "You want to keep the conversation moving," Sickles said (pers. comm.).

The night had its dicey moments, particularly when the *ABC News* video stream kept crashing, producing the dreaded error message. But a team of engineers, including three who had been flown in from Taiwan, fixed the problem several hours before the night's climactic announcement that President Barack Obama had been reelected.

The staff gave the Taiwanese engineers a standing ovation when they left for the night.

It all added up to a record-setting performance. The Election Control Room delivered more than 768 million page views, including 4.2 million live streams, setting an all-time *Yahoo!* record, according to Carolyn Clark, a company spokeswoman (pers. comm.). For Liao the milestone demonstrated the simple power of giving readers choices. "It all comes back to handing the control of the experience to the user, and having them decide what's important to them," he said (pers. comm.).

Earlier in the 2012 election cycle the *Washington Post* created a video analysis tool that readers could scan to find and watch the most talked-about video clips from political convention speeches and presidential debates (Haik 2012). The feature, called "Say What," synced the most-tweeted moments of a speech or debate with its corresponding video clip, enabling readers to watch the highlights in context. A reader who may have missed the previous night's broadcast could quickly scan through the most-talked-about video highlights over coffee and breakfast.

"Say What" was guided by the same principles that a savvy retailer brings to customer service, said Ryan Kellett, the *Post*'s national digital editor. "[Newsroom staffers] get a little nervous when we talk about customer service," Kellett said. "I don't think anyone should shy away from that. We have customers. That's a real thing. How can we serve them with an incredibly high-quality experience?" (pers. comm.).

The following summer another combination of politics and video enabled viewers to control their own news experience—this time as news unfolded in the middle of the night. On the final day of a special thirty-day legislative session in June 2013, Texas state senator Wendy Davis, a Democrat, stood in the senate chamber and spoke continuously for eleven hours during a filibuster aimed at blocking a bill that would create stringent abortion restrictions. As the midnight deadline to pass the bill approached, nearly 200,000 people from around the nation and world tuned in to the *Texas Tribune*'s live stream of the proceedings, watching every moment of the drama unfold. Cable news networks remained strangely oblivious to the story, but as the story spread on Twitter, newspaper websites from the *Washington Post* to the home-state *Dallas Morning News* embedded in their websites the YouTube live stream set up by the nonprofit *Tribune*, which instantly raked in more than $25,000 in donations from grateful viewers around the world (Smith 2013). "We hadn't considered the possibility that by the transmission of this live stream it would become the national and international story that it did," said Evan Smith, the *Tribune*'s CEO and editor-in-chief. The raw live stream and its accompanying coverage shattered daily web traffic records at the not-quite-four-year-old *Tribune*. The live stream's success, Smith said, validated the site's mission to bring greater transparency to state government by making it easier for people to participate on whatever platform they choose. "You've got to give people multiple ways in, talk to them on devices they rely on, and on platforms they embrace," he said (Friedman 2013). The *Tribune* later parlayed the momentum from the filibuster by using the crowdsourcing platform Kickstarter to raise more than $60,000 for remote video equipment that would enable the site to provide live video coverage of the 2014 Texas governor's race.[6]

The most mesmerizing interactive news projects follow this same principle of easy-to-navigate digital storytelling. For example, the *New York Times*'s "Snow Fall: The Avalanche at Tunnel Creek" (Branch 2012) and the *Guardian*'s "Firestorm: The Story of the Brushfire at Dunalley" (Henley 2013) both were widely acclaimed for seamlessly integrating multimedia content at precisely the right moment in each story's written narrative. But sometimes the user's prerogative is choosing what *not* to read, as the *Guardian* cleverly recognized during its royal baby coverage in July 2013. As the Duchess of Cambridge went into labor, prompting a predictable flood of oversaturated news coverage, the *Guardian* enabled readers to hide royal baby coverage by clicking a button—an option that drew 700,000 clicks (Marshall 2013). Whether it's experimenting with alternate story forms or helping readers steer clear of coverage they don't want to see, today's news outlets must empower users with the ability to dictate their own news experience.

COLLABORATING WITH THE CROWD

Half a generation ago television still reigned as the dominant medium for live news events. Whenever major news broke, networks would switch away from scheduled programming and turn things over to anchors and correspondents, who dispensed nuggets of real-time information to an audience that had limited news options.

Today's breaking news routine follows a much different trajectory. Television networks still spring into action, but their on-air coverage often runs behind the frenzy of activity that unfolds on social media. Ordinary citizens break news on Twitter, bypassing news outlets completely. Meanwhile journalists scramble to gather facts, confirm them, and, if need be, debunk unfounded rumors. At its best this ecosystem of real-time news produces citizen journalists like Janis Krums, the ferry passenger in New York who in 2009 famously tweeted the first photo of passengers safely evacuating from the US Airways jet that had landed in the Hudson River (Beaumont 2009). At its worst the hyperconnected system rapidly spreads misinformation, as when users of the online forum Reddit amplified erroneous speculation—re-tweeted by a handful of journalists—that a missing Brown University student was a suspect in the Boston Marathon bombings (Bidgood 2013).[7]

For better or worse, collaborating with the crowd is the reality of today's news landscape, and journalists ignore it at their peril. In a *New York Times Magazine* piece deconstructing the Boston transgressions fueled by Reddit and Twitter, the writer and editor Jay Caspian Kang argued:

> This is what media is now, a constantly evolving interaction between reporters working for mainstream companies; journalists and writers compiling and interpreting news for online outlets; and thousands of individuals participating on their own in the gathering and assembling and disseminating of information. It's a tremendously messy process, at times thrilling and deeply useful, and at times damaging in ways that can't be anticipated.

How it all gets straightened out, how some rules might become codified, is going to take awhile.   (Kang 2013:51)

In November 2009, when social media's role in the breaking news cycle was still in its infancy, the *Seattle Times* used Twitter, Facebook, and the now-defunct Google Wave to team up with readers to track the progress of a forty-hour manhunt that followed the execution-style slayings of four police officers in Lakewood, Washington. The newspaper's "swift use of available tools to tell a breaking story" was a key factor in awarding the *Times* the 2010 Pulitzer Prize for breaking news reporting. It also set the standard for future entries, according to Sig Gissler, the Pulitzer administrator (Moos 2011). "That was the moment when the *Seattle Times* staff, beyond the digital staff, realized how important it was to make journalism a two-way conversation," said Kathy Best, the *Times*'s digital managing editor during the Lakewood coverage. "It woke up the newsroom to the fact that we can't just keep doing things the way we used to" (pers. comm.).

David Boardman, then the executive editor, ran the *Times*'s Twitter feed for fifteen hours during the manhunt. Still, Boardman said he came away from the pioneering prize-winning experience even more convinced that crowdsourcing, for all its benefits, can play only a supplementary role in the newsgathering process. "I believe violently that professional trained journalists who are paid to spend their days collecting, vetting, and analyzing information are essential for a community," Boardman said. "I don't think the crowd is enough. But the crowd is a valuable tool" (pers. comm.).

Channeling the crowd to supplement shoe-leather reporting has become second nature for Brian M. Rosenthal, a *Times* staff writer. Through Twitter he found the lede for his story questioning how Seattle school officials handled a rare snowstorm in January 2012 (Rosenthal 2012). Using the Twitter hashtag #seasnow, Rosenthal connected with a medical librarian who had dropped her son off for a late-starting school day and was at work for fifteen minutes when she was forced to immediately return to pick her son up because the school district had called for early dismissal. "It was just a great story, and I wouldn't have found it without Twitter," said Rosenthal, who previously interned with the *Washington Post*'s interactive team. "The story is not coming from Twitter. Twitter is being used to supplement what you know and broaden your understanding of what's going on" (pers. comm.).

For feature stories that are less time sensitive, calling out to the crowd on social media can be significantly more effective than simply knocking on doors. Allison Linn, a senior economics reporter with *NBC News Digital*, wanted to humanize a 2011 Census report placing the national household median income at just under $50,000 a year. Linn, who writes about how the economy affects regular Americans, began to report on the median income project with a four-paragraph blog post on *MSNBC.com* headlined "Hey Middle Class, Tell Us About Yourselves" (Linn 2011a). More than seven hundred responses later Linn had more than enough material to compile readers stories' from around the country for a project entitled "We Are the Median: Living on $50,000 a Year" (Linn 2011b). Earlier in her career, when Linn worked for the Associated Press, her stories were widely disseminated but produced scant feedback from her audience. Today Linn gets twenty to thirty daily e-mails from readers, some of which can be quite critical. But overall, Linn said, "I feel like I do have an intimate sense of engagement. For the most part it makes me feel like I'm not pushing stuff into the void" (pers. comm.). That same sentiment holds true for Omar Gallaga, technology columnist for the *Austin American-Statesman* who often uses Twitter to crowdsource ideas for his *Digital Savant* blog about new technology. "When I'm wading into the water of something I'm not too familiar with, I get such good responses to that," Gallaga said (pers. comm.).

In Chicago WBEZ-FM created an entire series, "Curious City," around the idea of crowd-powered collaboration. A question bubble at the top of Curious City's web page asks: "What do you wonder about Chicago, the region or its people that you want WBEZ to investigate?" Listeners submit questions, the crowd votes, and once a query is selected, WBEZ invites the listener who asked the question to tag along during the reporting process. For example, in August 2012 a listener's question about the progress of so-called green roofs atop Chicago buildings led to a story reporting that developers were continuing to plant native landscapes on top of the city's skyscrapers, although even Chicago, which officially encourages green roofs, does not yet have enough of them to demonstrate their environmental effects (Martinez 2012).

Creating targeted groups on Facebook can be another effective crowdsourcing tool. When the *Seattle Times* began reporting its "Recession Generation" series in 2012 about how local millennials were faring in the job market, the newspaper set up Facebook groups for recent alumni of three area high schools. The *Times* used the groups to distribute a survey that drew 160 responses and also helped reporters identify sources. Jim Simon, a *Times* assistant managing editor, said that before the era of social media, the newspaper probably would have relied on high school counselors to find sources for a project like this. "It would have been very time consuming to find enough people to even do the story," Simon said. "This is incredibly efficient compared to the type of reporting we would have had to do five years ago" (pers. comm.). Likewise, *ProPublica*'s Patient Harm Community on Facebook, which documents the human cost of medical mistakes, had grown to more than two thousand members by March 2014 and spurred a Tumblr blog on the same subject (Allen and Victor 2012).

At the *Oakland Press* in Pontiac, Michigan, reporters and editors frequently pull comments from the newspaper's social media channels and insert them in news stories. "We try to quote readers in whatever stories are possible—if it's a knowledgeable quote," said Julie Jacobson-Hines, the paper's local news editor. Jacobson-Hines said plucking story quotes from social media fits with the *Press*'s philosophy of "reaching out to our audience in whatever way possible, online and in print." She added, "In the old days it was just quoting experts. You can't just forget the experts, but a lot of times [with social media] you get commenters who are more straightforward with their answers than the experts are" (pers. comm.). Facebook comments sometimes appear verbatim in *Press* stories with the commenter's real name; in other cases reporters follow up on points raised in the comments. When covering a story about a summer car crash involving five teenagers, Monica Drake reported Facebook comments in her story, but the comments also spurred her to look up the state law governing the maximum number of passengers allowed in a car driven by a teenager (Drake 2012).[8]

It's all part of a wider campaign by the *Press* to "turn our paper over to the people," Glenn Gilbert said. The newspaper, now part of the Digital First Media chain, got serious about reader engagement in late 2008, opening a citizen journalism institute to train the public on journalism basics like the inverted pyramid and how to frame photos (Gilbert 2008). The paper also hosts community bloggers for abbreviated newsroom internships. "We still own the platform," said Gilbert, who recently as retired executive editor. "But we're turning it over to the people" (pers. comm.).

When it's time for anniversary and holiday stories, the *Press* uses social media to crowdsource in search of new angles. For Valentine's Day 2012 the paper asked readers to share the sweetest thing their significant other had ever done for them. A man responded with a touching tribute to his wife for helping him recover from a double knee replacement while she continued to work her job for Chrysler (Workman 2012). Karen Workman, the community engagement editor, led her front-page Valentine's Day story with the husband's testimonial. "It may not be watchdog journalism, but it's still a story worth sharing," she said. "All of General Motors was sharing the story that day." Workman said crowdsourced stories like the Valentine's Day tribute may not win awards, but they help connect a newspaper with its community. "Telling stories in a way that people enjoy is as much a part of what we do as the watchdog element," she said. "I think it's really important you have both" (pers. comm.).

One of Workman's colleagues, Steve Buttry, the digital transformation editor, said that while crowdsourcing doesn't replace basic newsgathering by any means, it can make finding sources more efficient. "The fact that the community is having this conversation makes it easier to find the sources and do better journalism," Buttry said. "The promotional and feel-good aspects of community engagement—which I don't dismiss at all—to me, they're secondary to the journalism" (pers. comm.).

Even in the wake of crowdsourced blunders like the misidentified Boston bombings suspect, asking how to curtail public participation in the news process "is the wrong question," the Seattle journalist Monica Guzman writes in *Quill* magazine. "The right question is, how do we help?" Guzman continues:

> It's easier for journalists to pay lip service to the idea of collaborating with the public than it is to actually do it. There are good reasons it's tough: Control. Values. Trust. But public voices are here, speaking alongside ours, and for the good of the information we share, at least, we've got to see past the barriers between us. That begins with understanding what drives public voices, and seeing how it's not so different from what drives our own.
>
> (Guzman 2013:24)

EMBRACING "ACTS OF JOURNALISM"

Another important element of news as conversation is bringing users' own "acts of journalism" into the flow (Gillmor 2010). Mark Luckie, Twitter's manager of journalism and news, said that when he notices a news site prominently displaying readers' photos and videos, he knows the site "gets it" when it comes to audience engagement. "People see themselves and say, 'Oh, I want to be part of that,'" Luckie said. "Readers like to see themselves as part of the process. A lot of news organizations do it as an add-on" (pers. comm.).

At 3TV News in Phoenix, Lori Santa Maria, the social media manager, began asking local photographers to send their most stunning shots of Arizona landscapes—desert sunsets, lakeside sunrises, and the like. Santa Maria published the best shots as the daily cover photo on the station's Facebook page, encouraging readers to hit the like button if the shot dazzled them. "At first, I was like, 'Am I being cheesy? Am I just trying to boost my engagement numbers?'" Santa Maria said (pers. comm.). But when the station's Facebook fans started asking for more, Santa Maria decided to make it a regular feature. "It's not hard news, but it's taking a break to share an Arizona moment, and it's local—that's huge," she said. At KING-5, the NBC affiliate in Seattle,

Evonne Benedict, its social media manager, similarly used Facebook to encourage local photography enthusiasts to submit shots of a rare supermoon in May 2012. The resulting photo slide show drew ninety thousand page views over five days. "Creating this excitement about a fun event, I think, helps build community," Benedict said. But perhaps more important, she said, soliciting user-generated content on soft topics can serve as an icebreaker, increasing the chances that users will send photos and videos the station's way whenever harder news breaks. "If you do that with something fun," Benedict said, "then when the shit hits the fan, you've already created that safe place" (pers. comm.).

BUILDING MICROAUDIENCES

Journalists used to quantify their audience through newspaper circulation figures or television ratings, without knowing what portion of that aggregate number actually took the time to read or watch their stories. Today beat reporters create and interact with their own microaudiences through beat blogs, e-mailed newsletters, and social media.

Mastering these digital forums is a subtle art. Reporters often write in a more informal and personable style but take care to steer clear of personal opinions that might taint their neutrality. The *New York Times*'s internal standards for blogging (2009) encourage reporters to blog with a "distinctive point of view"—but to make their case with reported facts, not rhetoric. Another key role of a modern beat reporter is to serve as a trusted filter, guiding and directing the audience to relevant coverage or information, even if written by the competition. Linking to other news outlets may go against a journalist's competitive instincts, but it can build loyalty by establishing a reporter's newsletter or Twitter feed as the go-to source for the latest information on a given subject. Jeff Jarvis, a journalism professor and media consultant, coined the mantra for this mind-set: "Cover what you do best. Link to the rest" (2007).

Dave Levinthal first built an audience as a beat blogger when covering city hall for the *Dallas Morning News* in the late 2000s. "That was the first time I realized that engaging a group of highly intelligent readers about a particular topic has very few downsides and boatloads of benefits," Levinthal said. Perhaps the biggest benefit, he said, is using a blog to build sources, a skill he later used when coauthoring *Politico Influence*, a daily newsletter covering lobbying in Washington, D.C. (pers. comm.). Creating a digital community through beat reporting is no halfhearted endeavor. Levinthal said it requires a level of commitment that can be all consuming. "You want to build an audience, and the best way to do that—bottom line—is content," he said. Responsiveness is another essential trait, he told me:

> If you're not willing to respond to e-mails at 11:30 at night, or at 2 A.M. when you get up to get a drink of water, or at 6 A.M. to do a radio hit, then this may not work out so well. But if you're willing to treat this like you're talking to an extended family, the benefits are demonstrable. . . . You're on the train, you get an e-mail, you get a text, you get G-chatted, and you fire right back. When I'm on, I'm all for engaging however people want to engage.
>
> (pers. comm.)

The pace can be invigorating for a news junkie, but it raises one of the chief human drawbacks of engaged journalism: done well, it never ends. Daily journalism always has been hard work, Levinthal said, but with today's beat demands, "you find yourself having to work in several directions at once and be able to maintain your journalism at a high level. I think we all struggle with how to do that without burning yourself out." In January 2013, after producing 438 editions of *Politico Influence*, Levinthal left *Politico* to become a senior political reporter at the Center for Public Integrity. Two months earlier, when I interviewed him at *Politico*, Levinthal was candid about the level of intensity that penning a daily newsletter demands. "It's a juggling act day after day after day," he said. "It takes a hell of a lot of planning to manage the chaos. I've always got to be thinking three, four, five days ahead of time about the column, so I have time to do meaty reporting." Still, he said, "as a reader, it's an absolute net positive." At the Center for Public Integrity,

Levinthal contributes to a political finance blog called *Primary $ource*, but his new position allows more time for enterprise reporting.

CNN's Gilgoff can relate on both counts. Building and serving an audience through a beat blog, he said, is invigorating and profession-ally satisfying—but the pace can be personally taxing. "You don't have as much time to think," Gilgoff said. "The Internet never closes down; you're posting a zillion times a day, so there's not as much time to reflect. It is more chaotic." Gilgoff also stressed that beat blogging should supplement—not supplant—the time-honored traditions of good watchdog reporting. "It should amend what we're already doing, rather than replacing it," Gilgoff said (pers. comm.).

Consuming as they may be, these digital platforms can bring a higher profile to a short-term assignment, as Jordan Fenster learned in 2012 when covering a local congressional race for the *New Haven Register*. Fenster created a blog, a Facebook page, and a Twitter feed to supple-ment his print coverage of a tumultuous campaign that included two federal investigations. Fenster broke plenty of stories during the race, but he also liberally linked to competitors' work, from both his blog and social media. "If you wanted to know about that race, Jordan's Twitter feed was the place to go," said Digital First Media's Steve Buttry. "He was tweeting in a conversational way. If people are re-tweeting him, he's thanking them for it. He's asking questions. He's having a running conversation about the race, without trying to make it all about him" (pers. comm.). In early 2013 Fenster's blog on the race for the congres-sional seat won an EPPY award from *Editor & Publisher* for best political news blog with less than one million unique visitors.[9]

READER COMMENTS: STAYING
IN THE FRAY—AND ABOVE IT

Online comments from often-anonymous readers have persistently frus-trated journalists since news websites began to adopt comment forums in the mid-1990s (Santana 2011). Nearly two decades later, if you browse the comments attached to any typical mainstream news story, you'll quickly see that the tone of discussion remains as polarizing as ever. In early 2013, just before he resigned from the *Seattle Times*, ending a forty-year sportswriting career, the columnist Steve Kelley told the local alternative weekly that reader comments were part of the reason why he quit. "The reader comments section, it's a free-for-all," Kelley said. "The level of discourse has become so inane and nasty. And it's not just at the *Times*, it's ESPN, everywhere—people, anonymous people, take shots at the story, writers, each other. Whatever you've achieved in that story gets drowned out by this chorus of idiots" (R. Anderson 2013).

If you don't believe Kelley, just ask his former boss, the paper's publisher, Frank Blethen. "Look at 90 percent of the morons that send comments to stories," Blethen told me during an interview in mid-2012. "It's not that you don't get some good stuff once in a while, but 90 percent of these guys are idiots. There's a debate raging about whether you even should have comments, because it's such a small group and they're not very valuable customers."

So journalism's future depends on engaging a bunch of idiots? Matt Hufman, opinion editor at the *Las Vegas Sun*, puts it more diplomatically. "Maybe we're looking for unicorns or snipes—the people who are open to new ideas and are civil about it," Hufman said. "Sometimes it feels like a snipe hunt." Hufman frames the challenge this way: "Can we be in the fray, and above it?" (pers. comm.). Tom Gorman, the *Sun*'s executive editor, says journalists in his newsroom have a responsibility to enter—and moderate—the comment streams. "I've seen so many stories get hijacked in the comments," Gorman said. "Sometimes, someone needs to get in the middle of that mess and say, 'Hey, guys, you've missed the point'" (pers. comm.). Indeed a recent University of Texas study found that when reporters take the time to interact with commenters, news sites' online forums become more civil (Stroud 2013).

Engaging readers in comment streams has become a more formal part of reporters' duties in the newsrooms of MLive Media Group throughout Michigan. Reporters receive training in techniques aimed at keeping comments on topic and steering conversations in a more productive, civil direction. "One of the expectations for our reporters is that they are engaged, go into the comments, be active, and look for trends," said Kelly Adrian Frick, *MLive*'s statewide director of community news. "Listening to the reader, watching the numbers to grow audience, that's the ultimate goal." When evaluating reporters' engagement efforts, Frick said she looks for those who respond to comments and take action, as well as for consistently high numbers of comments (pers. comm.). *MLive* editors said they ultimately expect reporters to proactively shape their stories' comment streams into something more like a coffee klatch than an argument. "We're really looking at more than just, 'Thanks for commenting,'" said Colleen Stone, *MLive*'s statewide director of digital operations (pers. comm.).

Those sound like worthy corporate goals, but how is it working on the ground? Has the new system made comment streams more civil? "I think it's getting there," said Linda Mah, community engagement specialist for MLive Media Group's *Kalamazoo Gazette*. Mah said that taking control of a comment stream often can be as simple as reminding hostile commenters "that we're talking about members of the community, people who have families" and insisting that the discussion remain respectful. "Some people say, 'OK, thanks,'" she said. "Others say you're trampling on their rights" (pers. comm.).

The cofounders of *GeekWire*, the Seattle-based tech news start-up, receive an e-mail alert for every comment posted on the site. John Cook, one of the cofounders, said that while *GeekWire* strives to be accurate, the site welcomes comments that point out errors and works to correct mistakes quickly: "Oftentimes, getting something wrong is not the worst thing in the world—it can spur a dialogue," he said. "We're firm believers that the readers are smarter than us" (pers. comm.).

ABANDONING THE "RABBIT HOLE" OF READER COMMENTS

As the MLive Media Group chain prodded its reporters to take a more active role in their stories' comment streams, another newsroom retreated from such participation. In September 2012 the *Christian Science Monitor* disabled comments for most stories. John Yemma, the editor, explained in a column that the paper made its decision after an extensive review of two years' worth of comments: "Some have been thoughtful. Some have added useful information or pointed out our mistakes. Thank you for those. But many comments have been nonproductive. . . . We value our readers and want *CSMonitor.com* to dignify their intelligence, empathy, and civic-spiritedness" (2012b).

In an internal memo to the newsroom Yemma made clear that while disabling comments would be the default option, *Monitor* bloggers and editors were free to turn on comments for any story they wished. Most didn't. "I was kind of relieved—frankly, reading some of them is so demoralizing," said Marjorie Kehe, the books editor (pers. comm.). Added Eoin O'Carroll, the online news editor: "I used to have an anarchist view: 'Just open it up and goodness will emerge.' Instead, it's Somalia. . . . It's kind of personally toxic to read comments all day" (pers. comm.). Amelia Newcomb, the foreign editor, also welcomed the new policy: "Even on sites that have a pretty intelligent readership, the comments can devolve so quickly. There are conversations you want to have, and then there are conversations where you're kidding yourself to call them conversations" (pers. comm.).

But as I talked to more *Monitor* journalists about the policy to disable comments, I began to understand that the new policy wasn't simply a matter of taste. It was a business decision, too. As Dave Scott, the online director, explained:

> I've watched reporters get flustered and sucked into the rabbit hole by getting in a fight with readers. We have to make decisions about, what are the best ways for reporters to spend their time. Frankly, a story is more valuable. . . . We'd rather have a reporter write another story than spend half a day or a day engaging in discussions with a reader. A new story can reach a much larger audience.   (pers. comm.)

In the more than two years I spent working on this book, I encountered the entire spectrum of journalists' attitudes toward reader comments, from Steve Kelley's "chorus of idiots" dig to John Cook's proud assertion that his readers are smarter than he is. Still, Scott's explanation for why the *Monitor* shut down comments struck me as a revelation. With shrinking newsrooms paying ever more attention to scarce resources, it's worth asking: How economically viable is it for reporters to spend their time responding to reader comments? Sure, you can make comments more civil by asking reporters to mediate them, but what, exactly, is the return on investment of policing a troll in the comment threads? And can those precious newsroom resources be better spent elsewhere, as Scott suggests? "The conversation now is, if we're going to do this, what are you *not* going to do?" Scott said (pers. comm.). One of the *Monitor*'s answers, at least for now, is that they're not going to bother with comments.[10] You can agree or disagree with the decision, but at least the *Monitor* made a deliberate choice about which forms of engagement best align with its journalistic and financial mission.

The *New Haven Independent* also shut down comments in February 2012. But the staff later outvoted their editor, Paul Bass, 11–1, to bring comments back. "The stories felt naked without it," Bass said. "Reporters wanted feedback." All comments on the *Independent*'s site are moderated—but unlike editors at *MLive*, the *Las Vegas Sun*, and in other newsrooms, Bass advises reporters not to enter the fray. "The readers should have the last word," he said. "I kind of feel like we need to err on the side of shutting up" (pers. comm.).

Like many journalists, the *Texas Tribune*'s Aman Batheja is not a fan of reader comments, and understandably so. When Batheja worked at the *Fort Worth Star-Telegram*, commenters used racial slurs to insult him. "I glance at the comments, but I tend not to engage," Batheja said (pers. comm.). Instead Batheja prefers to interact with readers through Facebook and Twitter, which he uses as a barometer for reader interest in stories. That mirrors the experience of Omar Gallaga, technology columnist for the *Austin American-Statesman*, who said he has noticed that reader engagement is shifting from comment threads to social media. Gallaga said most feedback he receives from readers is now splintered among Facebook, Twitter, and Pinterest: "Blog comments seem to be dying off for us," he said (pers. comm.).

A ray of hope in the arena of reader comments emerged in June 2013. In anticipation of the U.S. Supreme Court's sure-to-be-controversial rulings about whether same-sex marriages should be recognized by the federal government, the *Washington Post* and *New York Times* created structured comment forums to gather readers' reactions. Instead of offering a forum for the usual free-for-all, the *Post* designed an interactive feature asking readers to first answer a multiple-choice question: "Why do the Supreme Court's decisions on gay marriage matter to you?" After clicking a button indicating whether the decision "impacts someone I know" or "engages my moral or religious beliefs," and so on, readers then were asked to use their own words "to tell us how these decisions resonate with you."

Meanwhile the *Times* selected half a dozen excerpts of Supreme Court justices' written opinions, then asked readers whether they agreed or disagreed with each. Having indicated their approval or discontent, readers could then "respond to the justices." The *Times*'s project drew just under a thousand responses; the *Post*'s attracted 3,598 responses. In both cases the tone was remarkably civil.

Can these structured comment projects be deemed a success? Again, when assessing engagement, newsrooms must weigh the results of a project against the resources expended to produce it. A four-person team produced the *Post*'s interactive feature, while the *Times* assigned five staffers to its project (Benton 2013). Those staffing levels, of course, aren't realistic for smaller newsrooms, but the *Post* and *Times* have created a promising template for a more productive and edifying form of reader comments.

COURTESY AND ETIQUETTE ON WHATEVER PLATFORM

Reader relations have not always been journalists' strong suit. Tom Gorman, executive editor of the *Las Vegas Sun*, spent thirty-two years at the *Los Angeles Times* and acknowledges that "back in the old days, when I was growing up, it was more, 'Oh, don't talk to them—send them to the editor's office or the PR office.'" But at a time when media outlets can no longer afford to take their digitally empowered audiences' attention for granted, and when snark and sarcasm flow so freely across computer screens, it's more crucial than ever for journalists to be courteous, professional, and responsive whenever readers contact them. "In a way," Gorman said, "we're a service utility for people" (pers. comm.).

That may sound overly earnest, but it's a sentiment I encountered repeatedly while visiting newsrooms large and small, legacy and start-up, corporate and nonprofit. "I think you have to be more willing to interact, both digitally and personally," said Jim O'Shea, who edited the nonprofit *Chicago News Cooperative* during its two-year run. Back when O'Shea was managing editor at the *Chicago Tribune*, he said, "people were stunned" whenever he would return readers' telephone calls. "There are a lot of little things you can do," he said. "You've got to give the reader the idea that you're not unapproachable . . . the whole thing is having the attitude that you want to reach out, not hide" (pers. comm.).

Elise Hu, a technology and culture reporter at NPR, said she and her colleagues try to seek feedback from their audience continuously, not just when a story airs or is published. "I think of it as a relationship with your audience that happens sometimes before a story is even conceived," Hu said. "Where we want to do better is [at the] front end, before the story" (pers. comm.). And audience engagement often doesn't relate to a story at all—it's simply a matter of replying to an e-mailed question or acknowledging a mention on social media. "Some of the most meaningful engagement we have doesn't show up on the site," said Tracy Record, editor of the *West Seattle Blog* (pers. comm.).

On social media channels a sense of decorum should prevail regardless of whether a journalist is on or off the clock. "At least two-thirds of my tweets have nothing to do with my job," said Omar Gallaga, technology columnist for the *Austin American-Statesman*. "I don't sound like a robot, I don't sound like a reporter. I sound like a real person. . . . I never wanted to be this faceless reporter behind the byline. I like to share that I'm a real person who has kids" (pers. comm.). Letting one's guard down on social media is harmless in the context Gallaga describes, but it can be damaging when things get confrontational. Andrew Goldman, a freelancer for the *New York Times Magazine*, was suspended for a month in October 2012 after he profanely insulted a female author on Twitter, prompting Margaret Sullivan, the public editor, to publish the newspaper's social media guidelines: "We treat our readers no less fairly in private than in public. Anyone who deals with readers is expected to honor that principle, knowing that ultimately the readers are our employers. Civility applies whether an exchange takes place in person, by telephone, by letter or online" (2012).

Of course, while tools abound for online engagement, the most basic way to cultivate an audience hasn't changed: spending time in the community. The *New Haven Independent*, a hyperlocal news site founded in 2005, has outlasted many of its peers and won national awards for its digital engagement experiments. But Bass, the editor and founder, said the most fundamental aspect of engagement is "going out and reporting stories in person, just being around. I don't think that's so new. What's new is how it moves at hyperspeed" (pers. comm.).

ADOPTING A READER-FOCUSED WORKFLOW

For a glimpse of what may be the new normal in an era of audience engagement, consider a Monday in the life of Fritz Klug, then a reporter for the *Kalamazoo Gazette*. On August 13, 2012, Klug's first digital byline appeared at 7:30 A.M. with a daily blog feature called *Kalamazoo Today*, "your early morning look at what's ahead in Southwest Michigan." As the day went on, Klug would file three reported blog posts, two follow-up stories, and a gallery of photos he shot over the weekend at the scene of a homicide—a story he broke after he got a tip on Twitter. All the while he interacted with readers on Twitter and kept tabs on his stories' comment streams. "It's just a continuous flow of posting stories and posting information as it becomes available," said Klug, who was born and raised in Kalamazoo and graduated from his hometown college campus, Western Michigan University. Engaging with readers, Klug said, is a huge part of his daily routine: "It's just like writing. You have to do it every day to keep your skills up and keep it sharp. . . . You need to find a good work-flow that works for you and just have at it" (pers. comm.).

Six months after I visited Kalamazoo, Klug was promoted to *MLive*'s bureau in Lansing, the state capital. So the reconfigured *MLive* structure, which corporate parent Advance Publications has since expanded to other cities, would seem to reward the same qualities historically emphasized in a newsroom meritocracy—curiosity, tenacity, productivity. "A good reporter's always been engaged in the community—you were plugged in, you knew what was going on," said Ciokajlo, the *Gazette*'s editor and a former staff writer for the *Chicago Tribune*. "A good reporter is someone who's out cooking their beat, interviewing people, and trying to get to the bottom of things, in the community and in real life, but also on Twitter and online" (pers. comm.). I thought of Klug in September 2012 when the media insider blog *JimRomenesko.com* published a memo leaked from the Advance-owned *Portland Oregonian*. The memo described expectations for a beat reporter's typical "digital day" in the future *Oregonian* news-room, and it sounded a lot like what I observed Klug doing in Kalamazoo. "The keys for you are time management, attitude and agility," the memo read. "Your work flow will be your own. Reorient your thinking to what you can deliver for the web today. Cover your beats, push information, don't worry about where or whether a story will play in print. Editors will worry about that for you" (Romenesko 2012).

The *Oregonian* tipster who sent Romenesko the memo was incredu-lous: "It's so wonderfully glib in describing a brave new world that some journalists would find disturbing." And, yes, the memo's condescend-ing tone was upsetting, especially given the context—the new work-flow was part of a corporate overhaul that produced massive layoffs in Advance newsrooms, including *MLive*, the *Oregonian*, *New Orleans Times-Picayune*, and the *Cleveland Plain-Dealer* (Chittum 2013a). Critics decried the ongoing strategies, deployed most prominently by Advance and Digital First Media, to downsize newsrooms and pump up page views. "This is not a cost-free experiment," wrote Dean Starkman of the *Columbia Journalism Review*. "Once the newsrooms are degraded, there is no clear path to redeeming them" (2012).

As a former rank-and-file newsroom staffer myself, I was skeptical about the drastic reorganizations at Advance and Digital First, which is why I made a point to visit their newsrooms for this book. But to my surprise, I didn't observe anything degrading about the new workflow carried out by the surviving journalists at those chains' papers. I met reporters and editors of all ages who seemed sincerely invested in their new audience-focused mission, realizing that their jobs depended on it. And I met dozens of journalists with an awakened sense of respect for their readers, as reflected in this internal memo from Workman, the outgoing *Oakland (Michigan) Press* community engagement editor, to her successor, Drake:

> Be real with people. Recognize when it's appropriate to apologize. Don't take down posts or comments because they're negative toward us. Check messages and interactions on social media. Respond to them. Ask questions that spark good discussions about important things. Remind people not to launch personal attacks on one another. Share content that people like, and understand that content is not limited to the written word. Create content that people like.

Workman's memo reflects a reader-focused mind-set that demonstrates relevance to the audience by transforming news into conversation. "Maybe start with, 'What's the value to somebody in what I'm going to be doing? Why is this going to be meaningful to them? Why is it going to be worth their attention? Why is it going to help me build trust?'" said Digital First Media's Steve Buttry. "Once you start from that audience focus, I think that will guide your execution" (pers. comm.).

COMMON ELEMENTS OF EFFECTIVE
NEWS AS CONVERSATION

Compared to past generations of news consumers, today's digitally empowered audiences demand a more active role. This new reality means that, to do their jobs effectively, journalists must inform readers while also routinely interacting with them through some of the techniques described in this chapter. Specific tactics and strategies differ widely, depending on a news outlet's mission, geography, and business model. But newsrooms that prioritize the goal of news as conversation follow a number of common practices:

- *They empower an "audience czar."* Any relevant twenty-first-century newsroom needs someone whose chief responsibility is to advocate for the audience, whether that person is a community engagement editor, social media manager, or, even better, has a position higher up the chain of command. This newsroom audience czar should have real internal clout, unlike many of the newspaper ombuds or reader representatives of years past, whose presence often was made known only in a weekly op-ed column. "I need somebody who actually is on my command desk, fighting for the audience and what they want at every point in the newsgathering process," said Alison Gow, editor of the *Daily Post* in North Wales. Gow created the new position of head of audience engagement in May 2013, replacing the less powerful role of community editor because she wanted somebody "coming at it from a completely different perspective and quite possibly saying, 'That story that you think is so great is actually repelling people'" (pers. comm.). The imperative to bring more audience perspective into newsroom decisions extends far beyond North Wales and the United Kingdom—it's an emphasis I repeatedly encountered in American newsrooms from Arizona to Michigan to Washington, D.C.

- *They decide what they are not going to do.* These newsrooms align their audience engagement strategies with their business mission and deploy resources accordingly. In the midst of a radical digital transition, the *Christian Science Monitor* shut down reader comments on its website, in part because managers felt staffers could be more productive in other pursuits if spared from the often-hostile "rabbit hole" of reader vitriol. The counterintuitive move risked alienating the very online readers the *Monitor* is trying to court (Groves and Brown 2013). But give the *Monitor's* editors credit for this: instead of trotting out empty exhortations to do more with less, they weighed the pros and cons, carefully considered the opportunity costs, and decided to turn comments off.

When I visited the *Daily Post* in North Wales in July 2013, nonstop media coverage was flowing throughout the United Kingdom about the soon-to-be-born royal baby, later named Prince George of Cambridge. But unlike many British media outlets, the *Daily Post* had no plans to run a live blog chronicling the royal birth. "We wouldn't even try to do that, because it's not what readers are coming to us for," Gow said. She noted that the baby's father, Prince William, a flight lieutenant, was stationed at a base in North Wales, so the *Daily Post* certainly would cover any royal developments that might affect the lives of local readers, such as a parade celebrating the birth. "It's that kind of touchstone information that they're interested in," Gow said. "If somebody wants a royal live blog, go to the *Mirror*—they're doing a royal live blog. We're not" (pers. comm.).[11] A week later, when the duchess gave birth in London, the *Daily Post* stuck to its local plan, topping its home page with a story about a man who got stuck waist deep in mud (Williams 2013). The paper acknowledged the royal birth, of course, but it was clearly secondary to the *Daily Post*'s local mission.

"You need to decide what to do less of, what to stop doing, what to do to a lower standard—which is a tough thing for a journalist to do," said Digital First's Steve Buttry. "But if you're just doing more, you're going to do something to a lower standard, so you should decide which one it's going to be" (pers. comm.).

• *They cultivate a newsroom culture that rewards engagement.* When Kate Day makes presentations on the massive projection wall that looms above Telegraph Media Group's newsroom in central London, she makes a point to highlight successful examples of digital interactivity. Day, the *Telegraph*'s director of digital content, said it's important to bring attention to small victories.[12] "There's nothing like highlighting best practice in front of the editor and have that seen as a very public thing," Day said. Recognizing minor everyday successes in engagement has helped drive change at the *Telegraph*, Day said: "I'll now get journalists really proud of the fact that they made it to the most-shared list, or that their tweet was highlighted as particularly interesting, or they managed to get something to trend. Because it's much more visible, whereas previously that sort of little win wouldn't have been so publicly celebrated" (pers. comm.).

• *They understand it's not all about them.* Blind dates don't go so well when people talk only about themselves. So why do journalists so often use social media as a one-way platform for self-promotion? "We still have this tendency to use social media like a big megaphone," said Meredith Artley, managing editor of *CNN Digital*. "That's one of our biggest challenges and opportunities" (pers. comm.). As Buttry puts it, "Think of social media and put it in other social contexts—at a party, or a circle of friends in high school, or whatever. The person who's always talking about themselves is not a popular person" (pers. comm.).

After three years as CNN's religion editor and coeditor of the *Belief Blog*, Dan Gilgoff left the network at the end of 2012 to become *National Geographic*'s director of digital news. In his farewell column, published on New Year's Eve, Gilgoff linked to the "Where Was God in Aurora?" coverage from six months earlier and ended his column with a plea to readers:

> In the world of digital journalism, your voice matters more than ever. With the proliferation of reader comments, social media and instantaneous metrics on what our audiences are clicking and how they're responding, your choices and opinions are shaping our coverage more than ever. Some of our best content from the last year was more about conversations happening around the news than about the news itself. We choose to do certain stories and skip others partly based on whether you're engaged in those stories or not. Use your power wisely.   (Gilgoff 2012c)

The comments beneath Gilgoff's farewell featured the usual smattering of trolls and religious arguments but also a genuine sense of gratitude from readers. "A big THANKS to you and cnn for letting the discussions flow so freely on your site," one commenter wrote. "I cannot tell you all how interesting and important this blog is to me and i read it every day," added another. Like a good pastor, rabbi, or imam, Gilgoff had convened a vibrant community, and the congregation kept coming back.

3

Mining Niche Communities

Serving Topical and Hyperlocal Audiences
Through Digital and Mobile Platforms

In November 2012, at the close of a record-setting month fueled by nonstop coverage of the presidential election and its aftermath, John Harris and Jim VandeHei, cofounders of *Politico*, sent a congratulatory memo to the newsroom. As they celebrated digital traffic milestones, including fifty-four million page views on election night and twenty-five million unique visitors in November, Harris and VandeHei also heralded the success of the premium service *Politico Pro*, describing it as a "very exciting experiment in subscription journalism" and "an unambiguous success" since its launch in February 2011.

Politico Pro charges about $9,000 per institutional subscription for up-to-the-minute customized coverage of niche policy topics ranging from defense to health care to transportation. *Pro* subscribers receive instant mobile alerts, daily e-mail newsletters, and access to exclusive events, among other features. Allbritton Communications, which owns *Politico* and is privately held, does not disclose financial results, but the

Harris-VandeHei memo crowed that *Pro* "has exceeded the high business and editorial expectations we have set" and validated the site's strategy to place niche subscriptions "at the heart of the hybrid newsroom that we are building." The momentum continued into the new year, as *Politico* announced in March 2013 that *Pro* had a thousand subscribers and was reaching roughly seven thousand policy professionals at a whopping 96 percent renewal rate (Owen 2013).

Politico Pro's founding editor-in-chief, Tim Grieve, said the subscription service covers the nitty-gritty details of federal policy "at a level of specificity that you can't get anywhere else." Busy subscribers don't comment much on stories, Grieve said, but "are engaged in the most basic, fundamental way—they're paying for the product" (pers. comm.).

Politico is hardly alone in its quest to deliver journalistic expertise to niche audiences through the latest in digital technology. With online and mobile tools allowing consumers to bring a more personalized focus to their news diet, "giant ocean liners like AOL and Yahoo are being outmaneuvered by the speedboats zipping around them, relatively small sites that have passionate audiences and sharply focused information" (D. Carr 2011). As the news industry searches for ways to remain financially viable, online start-ups and traditional newsrooms alike are engaging—and monetizing—niche audiences through digital and mobile coverage of subjects ranging from politics to technology to high school football. Digital news delivery aimed at niche audiences—one newspaper executive I interviewed calls them "passionate verticals"—can build competitive advantage and attract loyal readers who are willing to pay for information that keeps them in the loop (Batsell 2012:41).[1] And, yes, paying for news is itself a form of engagement. Researchers at the Lear Center Media Impact Project at the University of Southern California—a project supported by grants from the Bill and Melinda Gates Foundation and the John S. and James L. Knight Foundation—have identified five fundamental "verbs of engagement": *consuming, amplifying, contributing, subscribing,* and, finally, *transacting.*[2] Indeed, paying for news absolutely is an act of engagement, because it represents a news consumer's deliberate vote of confidence during an era of infinite choices.

I chose to visit many of the news organizations I discuss in this chapter because they have identified niche coverage as an essential part of their strategy to build an engaged and loyal digital audience. As I previously mentioned, while these outlets' experiences with niches are not necessarily typical, their successes and failures warrant a closer look by anyone concerned with how journalism can be supported and sustained during an age of digital disruption.

NICHE JOURNALISM
IN A DIGITAL AGE

Niche journalism is nothing new. The push to reach targeted audiences through digital and mobile platforms builds upon the troves of newsletters, trade publications, and hobby magazines that have long served professionals and enthusiasts on a wide range of subjects. But on the Internet, no limits exist—news outlets can provide as much content as niche audiences are willing to consume: "In such an environment the content provider can make all available content accessible, and not have to make editorial judgments about which content to carry and which content not to carry based on [often wrong] predictions regarding consumer tastes" (Napoli 2011:61).

Niche audiences tend to be more motivated about their subject than the typical general-interest news consumer, and news outlets can earn a higher degree of customer loyalty by capably serving the needs of the niches. "Nothing is worse than being a lonely nerd, and niches bring nerds together," said Ross Ramsey, former editor of *Texas Weekly*, an online political newsletter founded in 1984. When a news consumer signs up for a niche subscription, "part of what they're buying is expertise, trust," said Ramsey, who sold *Texas Weekly* to the *Texas Tribune*, where he is now executive editor, in 2009. "The passionate niche has nothing to do with technology and everything to do with, 'I'm talking to this audience.' If you're a beat reporter, you're already working a passionate niche. Everything else is just presentation" (pers. comm.).

However, the expectations of niche audiences are high—not only with respect to the content itself but also in the way a journalist approaches the subject. "True loyalty only develops when there is a shared narrative, emotional connection, and respect for the cultural mores of the audience," writes Steven Merahn, vice president of modernmedicine.com, a business-to-business web portal focused on the health-care industry (Malthouse and Peck 2011:8). For example, Merahn explains that in the case of health-care professionals, industry mores include responsiveness, respect, simplicity, ease, and value.

Niche audiences always have required more careful tending than the general public, but today's news providers have more digital tools than ever to meet these audiences' elevated needs through such features as push notifications for mobile devices, real-time updates, social forums, geolocation, and other functions. One global news outlet that has flourished in this environment is *Bloomberg News*, whose editorial staff of twenty-three hundred employees relentlessly focuses on "fast delivery of core information" to a business-focused audience of more than 250,000 users worldwide (Machin and Niblock 2010:786).

Subject-focused niche audiences, which may be dispersed around the country or world, have different information needs than so-called hyperlocal audiences, which have geography in common. Indeed hyperlocal journalism is its own peculiar niche, as I will explore later in this chapter. But the niche and hyperlocal approaches can overlap when news blogs tackle topical niches in a geographic setting—sailing in the Pacific Northwest, for instance, or horse racing in Kentucky. Nicholas Carr, a technology writer, calls this the "great unbundling" of news—instead of searching for personally relevant news in a bundled package like a newspaper or television broadcast, "we're able to indulge our personal tastes as never before, to design and wrap ourselves in our own private cultures. The vast array of choices is exciting, and by providing an alternative to the often bland products of the mass media it seems liberating as well" (N. Carr 2008).

BIGGER IN TEXAS: ENGAGING THE
HIGH SCHOOL FOOTBALL FAN

The niche-meets-hyperlocal model certainly applies to the *Dallas Morning News*'s mobile coverage of high school football. When it became available in August 2011, the SportsDayHS iPhone app (later released for Android devices) was believed to be the most extensive ever created for high school sports, featuring real-time scoring and live play-by-play coverage of about fifty games a week (figure 3.1). "It's taking local to another level," said Mark Francescutti, the *News*'s senior online managing editor of sports (Batsell 2012:39).

During the fall of 2011, I spent several months following the *News*'s app and other outlets' digital coverage of Texas high school football for my *Columbia Journalism Review* article "Friday Night Bytes."[3] Rich Alfano, the *News*'s general manager for sports, repeatedly used the phrase "passionate vertical" to describe the newspaper's strategy to pursue niche markets with highly motivated followings (Batsell 2012:41). Alfano told me the SportsDayHS app was part of that strategy, springing from the realization that avid smartphone-equipped high school football fans are no longer satisfied to wait until Saturday morning to pore over newspaper box scores:

> How long will the newspaper be valuable on that Saturday morning after the games are over? Isn't somebody else going to come in and figure this out? Isn't there going to be a better technology solution where you can follow your team and follow the other teams in your conference, or your player or your school, in a mobile environment? So I'm just glad we were the first ones to do it. Because I think it makes the whole franchise more valuable.

High school sports and professional sports attract different breeds of fans, because school teams involve so many personal connections between the players, their families, their classmates, and the

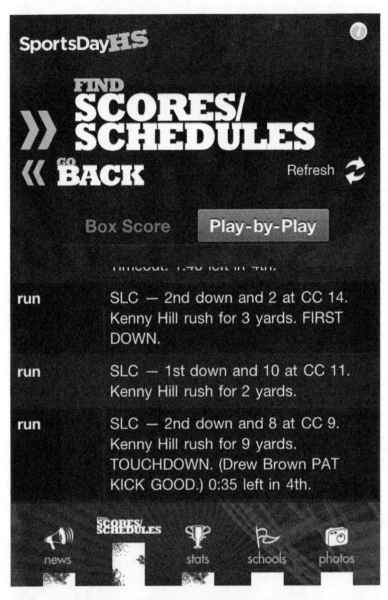

FIGURE 3.1 Real-time, play-by-play scoring delivered by the *Dallas Morning News*'s SportsDayHS football app, August 2011. Copyright © *Dallas Morning News*. Image: *Dallas Morning News*

community. "You have parents, you have grandparents, you have the students themselves," Francescutti said. "It really rallies communities of people, and that can be very intense. And obviously in Texas, it's one of the most intense experiences in the nation" (pers. comm.). As news consumers, fans of high school sports tend to be more loyal—in 2010 the typical visitor to the SportsDayHS pages of the paper's website clicked on fourteen pages per month, nearly twice the rate of clicks on the paper's main online sports section (Batsell 2012:41). The trick, though, is figuring out how to serve this highly motivated niche during the relatively short period of their lives that people care about the subject: "You just need to be there for that group when they want it," said Eric Zarate, who edits high school sports for the *Fort Worth Star-Telegram* (pers. comm.).

From day one, the *News*'s real-time scoring app was wonderfully comprehensive and, for the modest download fee of $1.99, less expensive than a grande Americano at Starbucks. But it faced free competition from mainstream media rivals like the *Star-Telegram* and ESPN Dallas, as well as from local citizen-journalists who created Facebook fan groups and even a crowd-powered app called Friday Night Rivals. The week before the 2011 state football finals, the free Friday Night Rivals app had been downloaded to more than twenty-two thousand devices, whereas SportsDayHS had been downloaded fewer than five thousand times (Batsell 2012:40–41).

The *Seattle Times* can relate to football fans' reluctance to pay even a few bucks for enhanced mobile coverage. In 2010 the *Times* unveiled a University of Washington football app with all sorts of enticing features: in addition to the latest stats, news, and analysis, Husky fans could even shake their phone to summon audio of a barking dog (Boardman 2010). But the newspaper would later abandon the app, which cost downloaders $2.99, after fewer than ten thousand users had subscribed to it. "It was a poorly conceived project with very little oversight by me or anybody else," acknowledged Frank Blethen, publisher of the *Times*. As Blethen describes it, the app's content was worthwhile, but news and advertising executives did not fulfill plans to further monetize it through ads. Also, Blethen said, managers did not show enough discipline in controlling costs, particularly for information technology. "[A] really important point about any of this stuff is really having some rigor around it." Blethen said the Husky football app "cost us a ton of dough . . . to me, the most important thing about these things is what we learned from them. We learned from this thing that you've really got to be careful with your rigor around these things, or you will lose money" (pers. comm.).

The *News*'s SportsDayHS app also initially failed to engage a critical mass of users, at least to the point that they would pay. Still, Alfano called the rollout of the app a success. He pointed out that the newspaper already was paying to send freelancers to approximately fifty high school games every Friday night, so the app was simply another platform for publishing that content. He also explained that the app was part of a wider campaign to expand the *News*'s high school presence through digital, television, and radio platforms. "I think that the mistake that companies make is they look at a mobile app as a stand-alone product—they look at it as success or failure," Alfano said. "The reality is, it's an extension of your strategy. It's an extension of you reaching an audience through print, online, and mobile" (pers. comm.).

In subsequent seasons the *News* continued to offer the SportsDayHS app—but this time for free. And the newspaper promoted the app with an advertising campaign at local high school stadiums that included program ads, announcements over the public address system, video commercials, and field signs. By the end of year 3, app downloads had surpassed forty thousand (iOS and Android combined), and the real-time scoring initiative as a whole was generating revenue through targeted banner ads for relevant products, such as single-game tickets for Dallas Cowboys games, as well as through bundled multimedia sponsorships and an annual awards banquet.[4] "This is one of TDMN's most successful and popular apps," Kyle Whitfield, an assistant sports editor, told me in an e-mail in late August 2013, just before SportsDayHS began its third season of real-time coverage. "I think users can expect it to stick around for a long, long time."

KNOWING YOUR NICHE

To effectively engage a sophisticated niche, journalists must be in tune with the nuances and sensibilities of their audience. *GeekWire*, the tech news site started in 2011 by two former Seattle newspaper reporters, relentlessly covers technology and innovation in the Pacific Northwest, with a particular emphasis on the area's start-up culture. "We're acting as a megaphone for what's happening here," said *GeekWire*'s Todd Bishop (pers. comm.). Its cofounders, Bishop and John Cook, said *GeekWire* aims to connect the Seattle tech community in the same way that *TechCrunch* serves as an information hub for Silicon Valley. And while *GeekWire* extensively covers corporate giants like Microsoft, Apple, Amazon, and Google, the site especially caters to Northwest techies with an entrepreneurial streak. *GeekWire* even distributes a promotional infographic with cartoon caricatures comparing the typical Silicon Valley geek (shaggy hair, aggressive, idolizes Facebook founder Mark Zuckerberg) and the archetypal Seattle geek (faux hawk haircut, passive-aggressive, idolizes Microsoft cofounder Bill Gates). The caricatures are a joke, but the message is clear: *GeekWire* knows its readers, from their sleeve tattoos down to their REI hiking boots. That sense of familiarity has helped build a loyal audience that, by summer 2013, had propelled *GeekWire* to twentieth place on the influential Techmeme Leaderboard, ahead of more established institutions like the BBC, *Fortune* magazine, and *Ad Age*. And by the end of *GeekWire*'s second year, its hybrid business model—which includes advertising, events, corporate sponsorships, premium memberships, and a job board—was producing a quarterly profit (Wolf 2013).

The casual hoodies-and-jeans crowd isn't the only niche audience in Seattle's business universe. Michele Matassa Flores, managing editor of the *Puget Sound Business Journal*, said her newsroom covers technology from the perspective of the paper's core audience: executives, business owners, and chamber of commerce types. "The niche is what it's all about, to know our audience," Flores said. "They want to know about technology in a different way than twenty-year-olds who run start-ups out of their garage" (pers. comm.). The *Business Journal* may not show up on the Techmeme Leaderboard, but its media kit boasts that it reaches an audience of 135,750 monthly readers with an average household income of $259,000. It's a demographically desirable niche, to be sure, although perhaps a bit buttoned-down for the tastes of Cook and Bishop, who left the *Business Journal* in 2011 to start *GeekWire*. Cook said he and Bishop saw an opportunity to continue their aggressive coverage of local technology while expanding their scope "to incorporate more of an entertainment style, a fun style" (Timmerman 2011). The point is, whether they target hipster geeks or the more staid establishment crowd, these niche business news outlets in Seattle can coexist and remain viable because both know their core audience and respond to its needs.

The *Christian Science Monitor* also sees niches as part of its future. In late 2012 the *Monitor* was developing strategies to deliver subject-specific international news to global business leaders. "We need all the focus we can get, and we can't be everything to everybody," said Marshall Ingwerson, the managing editor, who has since succeeded John Yemma as editor. "This whole idea of finding your niche and focusing on the people who will pay for it is really important" (pers. comm.). Amelia Newcomb, the foreign editor, observed that with global news, "your most likely form of engagement is people who are engaged in the topic already. . . . I think our future is in those more dedicated readers, especially in international" (pers. comm.). By early 2014 the *Monitor* had reported that it was enlisting its international correspondents to contribute to niche products called *Frontiers Market Monitor* and *World Business Monitor*, described as "more specialized reporting for business and NGOs and other audiences that really care about international news in a more granular way" (Ellis 2014).

Tactics for engaging a niche audience depend on that group's accepted norms and tastes. For instance, Ross Ramsey, executive editor of the *Texas Tribune*, said reader comment forums aren't a good fit for political insiders. "The funny thing about the lobby in politics is that they don't want to talk to each other," Ramsey said. Instead the *Tribune*'s subscriber-only newsletter, *Texas Weekly*, gathers about 150 responses each week to its poll, which it publishes in a feature called Inside Intelligence. The poll gathers subscribers' responses to hot-button questions, summarizes the overall results with pie charts, and publishes individual answers anonymously. "It's clearly inside the bubble," Ramsey said. "Things like that stitch people together" (pers. comm.).

Other niche sites see engagement strategies as a way to expand their audience beyond the usual insiders and experts. "Reader engagement is particularly important to niche sites, because they have a danger of preaching to the choir all the time," said David Poulson, editor of the *Great Lakes Echo*, an environmental news service based at Michigan State University. To spread awareness of the site and its subject matter, Poulson has used lighthearted quizzes, brackets in the style of March Madness, and other entertaining tools like "carp bombs," in which the *Echo* encourages readers to submit Godzilla-like Photoshopped images depicting invasive Asian carp in human settings (Poulson 2010). "Our niche is important," Poulson said. "I think the general public has a strong need to be informed about environmental issues. I've got to find ways to get them there" (pers. comm.).

The ascendancy of niche news sites was even more evident in 2013 after the six-year-old nonprofit *InsideClimate News* won a Pulitzer Prize for its coverage of an oil spill in Michigan that was largely ignored by other media. "I think it's a very hopeful sign," said Sig Gissler, the administrator of the Pulitzers. "I think it really shows the way the journalism ethos reconfigures itself as times change" (Hajela 2013).

The *Las Vegas Sun*, which won its own Pulitzer Prize in 2009 for investigating construction deaths on the Las Vegas Strip, has built a thriving niche audience around an entirely different subject—the Ultimate Fighting Championship (UFC). The mixed martial arts league has a rabid worldwide following, and its promotion company is headquartered in Las Vegas. Still, the *Sun* hadn't devoted much coverage to UFC until a new interactive editor, Rob Curley, arrived in 2008.[5] "We learned that UFC has an audience that wasn't being served," said Ray Brewer, the sports editor.

Today UFC coverage is one of the more important beats on the *Sun*'s sports desk. Case Keefer, the *Sun*'s mixed martial arts and gambling reporter, approaches his beat as a running conversation with fans, offering prefight predictions, analyzing the odds, and fielding readers' questions on Twitter. On fight nights frugal fans can skip the $50 pay-per-view UFC telecasts and go instead to the *Sun*'s live blog, where Keefer provides real-time updates and scores every round. Keefer even uses the mobile app Shazam to identify the songs that play when fighters enter, then live-blogs about it. During high-profile fights, Brewer said, "our live blog is getting slammed with five hundred views per minute" (pers. comm.).

Much as the *Seattle Times*'s Danny O'Neil used his live Seahawks chats as a barometer for gauging fans' reactions during NFL games (see chapter 2), Keefer monitors social media threads for angles for follow-up stories. When he wrote a story in July 2012 about a fighter's inexplicably running away from public view after winning a match, "the reason I did that story was because I saw what the buzz was about" on social media, Keefer said (pers. comm.).

On his personal blog Curley said the *Sun* pounced on UFC coverage in 2008 because it presented a natural opportunity to build a loyal audience around "Las Vegas' major-league sports franchise" (2009). Before Curley's arrival the *Sun*, perhaps reflecting the institutional hubris of mainstream media, had largely ignored an internationally popular sport that was headquartered in its backyard and worth more than $1 billion (Miller 2008). But to its credit, the *Sun* finally recognized a revenue-generating niche and went after it—even though most of its traditional media peers still do not consider UFC worthy of substantial coverage. "You don't want to say we're a fan site, but we want to give the fans what they want," Brewer said. "You won't find a mainstream news organization that sends a reporter to cover UFC like we do. No 'real media,' for lack of a better word, goes to every card" (pers. comm.). The *Sun*'s coverage of UFC fills a need for a motivated niche, while the newspaper continues to perform watchdog journalism in the public interest.

TAPPING THE POLITICAL NICHE

The most obvious political niches are partisan ones, and plenty of digital ventures aggressively cover that territory. To name just a few examples, right-leaning audiences flock to the *Drudge Report* and Glenn Beck's the *Blaze*, while left-leaning audiences visit *Daily Kos* and MoveOn. org. Here, however, I am most concerned with how audience-focused engagement can help sustain journalism that benefits the wider public, not any particular ideology. In her book *Niche News: The Politics of News Choice*, Natalie Jomini Stroud concludes that partisan media "create and inflate gaps in the citizenry: gaps between those with partisan inclinations and those without, gaps between those who participate in politics and those who do not, gaps between those who affiliate with the political left and those who affiliate with the political right" (2011:183).

In the nonpartisan arena one of the most famous digital experiments in niche journalism is *Politico*, founded in 2006 by the veteran *Washington Post* political correspondents John Harris and Jim Vande-Hei. Harris explains the rationale for starting *Politico*:

> Increasingly, it seemed to us, readers gravitate less to general-interest sites and more to ones that place them in the middle of specific conversations they want to be a part of—whether the conversation is about stocks or stock-car racing. We knew there was a large audience of people, in Washington and around the country, who shared our interest in politics and policy, and—if the journalistic content was good—would read everything we could produce on the subject. (Harris 2008)

With its mantra of "own the morning" and a newsroom full of aggressive, prolific, web-first reporters, *Politico* quickly emerged as an essential news source among Washington insiders. In fact, when the Amazon.com billionaire Jeff Bezos acquired the *Washington Post* in August 2013, the *New York Times* columnist Ross Douthat wrote, "It's *Politico* rather than *The Post* that dominates the D.C. conversation, *Politico* rather than *The Post* that's the must-read for Beltway professionals and politics junkies everywhere, and *Politico* rather than *The Post* that matches the metabolism of the Internet" (2013).

Five years after it began, *Politico* deepened the scope of its niche coverage with *Politico Pro*, the subscription service that covers specific policy topics with a "rapid, granular, and mobile" approach (Ellis 2013a). Accounts can be customized with as many as twenty-five keywords that trigger e-mail and smartphone alerts, allowing congressional staffers and lobbyists to track specific bills and news updates as they scurry about Capitol Hill. "We'll spare you the boring, jargon-laden stories," Martin Kady II, the editor, promises potential subscribers in a welcome note. "Instead, we'll deliver right to your inbox the most up-to-date, actionable intelligence. Our readers receive alerts literally seconds after our reporters learn the news."

Tim Grieve, its founding editor-in-chief, said *Politico Pro* was built to inform policy specialists "at a level of specificity that you can't get anywhere else. . . . These people are professionals. These people are friggin' busy: 'Just tell me what I need to know.'" In this sense *Politico Pro* primarily engages its niche audience not through news as conversation but by empowering subscribers to customize their own high-velocity news experience. *Politico Pro* subscribers "are superengaged," Grieve said, "but maybe in a somewhat more traditional, 'we're talking, they're listening' sort of way." Meeting subscribers' needs requires what Grieve calls a "faster metabolism"—reporters churn out plain-text e-mail blasts every morning, then update them throughout the day with follow-up e-mails, texts, social media posts, and, of course, stories (pers. comm.). It's a content strategy focused on one-way dispatches rather than two-way conversation, but that's the approach that best suits the professional needs of *Politico Pro*'s niche. This customer-focused ethos corresponds with my definition of engaged journalism as actively considering the needs of the audience even when not directly interacting with it.

At the end of 2013 *Politico Pro* was covering Beltway niches that included defense, energy, financial services, health care, taxes, technology, transportation, agriculture, education, and trade. By building and monetizing niche audiences for those ten subjects, *Politico*'s business model appeared to be an exemplar of what Chris Anderson, former editor of *Wired* magazine, calls the "long tail" theory of media consumption (2006). This influential theory argues that technology is pulling consumers away from mass markets as they gravitate toward millions of niches, as evidenced by the success of digital content aggregators such as iTunes, Netflix, and Amazon, which offer a "long tail" of specialized products that bricks-and-mortar stores are unable to offer. *Politico*'s owner, Allbritton, doubled down on the niche strategy in 2014 after acquiring the media and politics site *Capital New York*, announcing that it would introduce another subscription service that would charge nearly $6,000 a year for coverage of such verticals as New York City Hall, New York State government, and the media (Moses 2014).

At the end of *Politico Pro*'s first year, Grieve said, 95 percent of subscribers renewed, most at a higher level. Still, Grieve cautions that it would be difficult to achieve those results anywhere other than Washington, D.C., the epicenter of federal policy. "We have a unique confluence of circumstances here that I don't know are replicable in a lot of other places around the world," Grieve said. The nation's capital, he said, has that "magical combination" of a reader base whose livelihood depends on timely information and can pay for it, and a subject area that can be capably covered with a finite number of reporters, keeping expenses down (pers. comm.).

Still, Grieve believes that niches will figure prominently in the future of news. "Figuring out how you can engage the people who are passionate enough to be engaged—and to pay—in the passionate niche markets, to me, is what's going to work," he said. "I don't know, if you're in El Paso, how you put out a newspaper that is specific enough to be of high enough value to 200,000 people. . . . To be a broad generalist anymore is hard" (pers. comm.).

And that's part of the riddle when serving niche audiences: When is a story too broad, too mainstream, to merit coverage? The *Texas Tribune* wrestled with that dilemma during the very week it made its debut in November 2009, when an army psychiatrist shot and killed thirteen people at nearby Fort Hood. It was instantly a national story, but the *Tribune*, a nonprofit news site that focuses on statewide politics and public policy, opted not to send any of its reporters to the scene just seventy miles away. Instead the *Tribune* led its home page the next day with a story about the top fifty state employee salaries, spotlighting the database that soon would become its signature—and most popular—

interactive feature (D. Carr 2009; Batsell 2010:41). Four months later, when a suicidal pilot crashed his plane into an Austin IRS office, the *Tribune* likewise did not flinch, leading its site with a story about a new school district policy to fire teachers based on students' test scores. "We have stayed true to what we are," said the *Tribune*'s CEO, Evan Smith. "We have never wavered. Not one time. From the very first day we were about [state] politics and public policy and government. We don't cover things that are not in our wheelhouse" (pers. comm.).

Niche ventures into political news are not always as fruitful as *Politico Pro* or the *Texas Tribune*. In 2012 two niche sites of similar scope, the *Arizona Guardian* and *Chicago News Cooperative*, folded within three months of each other. The *Arizona Guardian*, based in Phoenix, began covering the statehouse in 2009 and did so ably for more than three years but ultimately failed to attract and retain enough subscribers willing to pay steep fees (Stern 2012). In addition, it failed to fill a must-have need for its audience—it had no counterpart for the lucrative legislation-tracking services or public notices offered by more established competitors, and it made little effort to convene its community at sponsored events similar to those organized by *GeekWire* or the *Texas Tribune*. The *Chicago News Cooperative* likewise overlooked audience-focused revenue-generating activities in favor of more traditional newsgathering efforts—an approach that ultimately didn't pay the bills, its editor, Jim O'Shea, conceded. "I'm a firm believer that journalists have to start taking responsibility for the business of the journalism," he said (pers. comm.).[6]

THE HYPERLOCAL RIDDLE

Politico Pro's model of niche journalism appeared to be succeeding three years after it launched in February 2011, but the results weren't as heady when its parent company, Allbritton Communications, experimented with hyperlocal news.[7] To much fanfare Allbritton unveiled *TBD.com* during the summer of 2010, blanketing Washington, D.C., and its suburbs with news that could be specifically tailored to readers' ZIP codes. However, by early 2011 Allbritton had laid off half of *TBD.com*'s staff, and the site continued to lose heft before eventually vanishing two years after it started (Wemple 2012). While some media observers—not to mention TBD employees—were surprised to see Allbritton essentially pull the plug after only six months, it was hardly the first high-visibility hyperlocal failure. In 2013, after AOL announced that it would lay off lay off five hundred of more than eleven hundred employees from *Patch*, its local news arm, Rem Reider, former editor of the *American Journalism Review*, called hyperlocal journalism "a seductive pursuit that has broken many hearts." Reider continued:

> The idea behind hyperlocal sounds entirely sensible. People like neighborhood news. Small merchants need a place in which to advertise where they can target their home audience and not pay the freight for an ad in a major metro daily. And as those dailies cut back, there's an underserved market. Problem is, as is so often the case on the Internet, there just aren't enough digital ad dollars to make the numbers work.(2013)

Reider's grim prognosis may aptly describe some attempts to scale the hyperlocal model to mass audiences. But a number of truly local hyperlocals have thrived for years. Consider the *West Seattle Blog*, founded in 2005 by the television news veteran Tracy Record and her husband, Patrick Sand. With dozens of local ads placed by community organizations and merchants from the YMCA to real estate agents to a Montessori school, the blog pulls in enough revenue for Record and Sand to make a living in West Seattle, a peninsula of about 100,000 residents connected to the rest of Seattle by a bridge and water taxi. Record said the site draws roughly one million page views a month because it fulfills its readers' needs for unglamorous everyday neighborhood news—weather, traffic, crime, community events, and even a pets page. "The stuff we do does not win Pulitzer Prizes," Record said. "But it makes a difference in people's lives" (pers. comm.). Record and Sand may not have any Pulitzers on their mantle, but *West Seattle Blog* did win the Online News Association's national Community Collaboration

Award in 2010. The Society of Professional Journalists also gave Record an award for distinguished service, describing her as "a rare force in modern journalism" with "unshakeable respect for the enduring values of journalism, a demonstrated ability to innovate where few have, and a deep respect for her readers—whom she considers partners" (Guzman 2012).

Another enduring experiment in hyperlocal journalism is the *New Haven Independent*, which also got its start in 2005. I interviewed its founder and editor, Paul Bass, at his Connecticut home two days before the 2012 general election. Bass had spent much of the day out in the field covering last-minute campaign news, and his laptop glowed on the kitchen table as he chopped vegetables and cooked soup for dinner while keeping an eye on the site's traffic and reader comments. "It begins with just writing local stories, being there in person," Bass said. "That's 95 percent of it. It's the stories. There's no magic potion." Dan Kennedy, whose book *The Wired City* (2013) profiles the *Independent*, gives Bass considerably more credit. Kennedy notes that the *Independent* has succeeded where many other hyperlocal efforts have failed by building its own distinct community of readers—"an online community that parallels the offline community, a place where people come together to discuss their interests, talk about local news and events, and sometimes bring expertise or new information to the table that enriches the site's coverage and leads to follow-up stories" (Kennedy 2013:38).

Another chain of hyperlocal sites, *DNAinfo.com*, sought to create a similar sense of community in the neighborhoods of New York City when it began in late 2009. The hyperlocal venture, which later expanded to Chicago, is funded by the billionaire Joe Ricketts, who vows to readers in a YouTube video that his sites will deliver "the information that brings it down to your street, down to your pothole, to let you know what's happening in your neighborhood" (Spivak 2013:16). The *American Journalism Review* reported in 2013 that while *DNAinfo.com* had yet to turn a profit, readership was increasing and Ricketts had signaled he had ample patience to allow the venture time to succeed. "They've built an audience, and now must become a must-use for a large enough group to build a business," said Ken Doctor, an industry analyst (Spivak 2013:14). If *DNAinfo.com* endures, it could provide clues about how to be successful in scaling the hyperlocal model beyond a single community.

MAINSTREAM MEDIA AND HYPERLOCALS: COMPETITORS OR PARTNERS?

The proliferation of hyperlocal news outlets presents hometown mainstream media with a choice: compete with them, ignore them, or join forces with them. The *Seattle Times* has embraced the collaborative route, forging content-sharing agreements with more than fifty local blogs as part of its News Partner Network. Launched in 2009 as part of a pilot program sponsored by the Knight Foundation and J-Lab: The Institute for Interactive Journalism, the *Times*'s partner network includes local news sites like *West Seattle Blog*, ethnic media sites like *Northwest Asian Weekly*, and topical blogs covering subjects ranging from cycling to craft beer. On its home page the *Times* prominently showcases recent links from news partners alongside its own journalists' content.

What do the *Times* and its partners get out of this alliance? The local sites get a traffic boost (roughly 150,000 combined monthly referrals from the paper's website, *Seattletimes.com*, as of mid-2012) and free use of some *Times* staff photos. And the partnership appears to be popular with the *Times*'s audience: In an internal follow-up survey of nearly one thousand readers, 84 percent said they found value in the partner network (Seattle Times Company 2011). "There is no way you could provide this level of neighborhood detail using your own resources," one survey respondent wrote. "So it is a smart use of reliable, existing media—benefits you, the other sites & the readers." *Seattletimes.com* gets considerably fewer referrals (about 9,000 per month) from the local blogs, but the partner network was a major factor in the *Times*'s winning the 2010 Associated Press Managing Editors' Innovator of the Year Award (Lail 2010).[8] Boardman said the network broadens the *Times*'s reach and helps to "reestablish and solidify our role as the Town Square. . . . It helps break down the sense of us as some sort of fortress, and [makes us] more of a place for ideas to come together" (pers. comm.).

Despite the industry accolades and the newsroom's enthusiasm for the partnerships, the *Times*'s publisher, Blethen, wasn't ready to call the partner network an overall success. He said the partnerships, while phenomenal journalistically, have been an "absolute bust from a circulation and advertising standpoint. In fact, there's even some concern that we're undermining our own product and our own advertising and that we're helping these people create a platform to compete against us. . . . I have some serious questions about the neighborhood blogs and what they really get for us" (pers. comm.). Adding to the sense of commercial frustration was the collapse of talks between the *Times*, KING-TV, local sites, and a digital advertising firm to create a hyperlocal ad network after they determined that the potential pool of web advertising money wasn't large enough to split four ways.

Bob Payne, the *Times*'s editor for partnerships and audience engagement, said the failed effort to establish a local ad network "was a case of too many hands in the pie." Still, Payne insisted that the partner network has been a worthwhile experiment, pointing to the reader survey results and an overall sense that the *Times*'s website now serves as a more comprehensive hub for hyperlocal news from around the area. "There's no reason to be competitive," Payne said. "I have no fear of putting links to *West Seattle Blog* on our home page and people not coming back to the *Seattle Times*." As for the partner network's return on investment, Payne pointed out that newspapers routinely spend money to bring their readers external content of uncertain direct value—news wire services, for instance. "In our hearts," Payne said, "we know this [partnering] is the right thing to do" (pers. comm.).

MOBILE ENGAGEMENT

In the late 2000s, just as news organizations were starting to get the hang of engaging audiences through social media on quaint old desktops and laptops, another disruptive force forever changed the expectations of news consumers. The arrival of smartphones, perpetually connected to the Internet through wireless networks, suddenly permitted users to receive an endless cornucopia of personalized news while on the go. David Carr, media columnist for the *New York Times*, soon declared himself hooked on his smartphone's Twitter app: "I'm in narrative on more things in a given moment than I ever thought possible, and instead of spending a half-hour surfing in search of illumination, I get a sense of the day's news and how people are reacting to it in the time that it takes to wait for coffee at Starbucks" (2010).

Twitter's cofounder, Biz Stone, summed up the changing patterns of news consumption when he spoke at a conference of newspaper executives in Dallas in March 2011: "Healthy engagement isn't being hunkered over keyboards for nine or ten hours," Stone said. "It's glancing at a mobile device to stay connected and then living your life." And because smartphone users tend to consume their news in short bursts while on the go, news outlets' mobile offerings must be even more targeted, helpful, and relevant for those users.

"This is a battle for people's time," said David Ho, the *Wall Street Journal's* editor for mobile, tablets, and emerging technology. "We need to make it worth their time." I had the chance to hear Ho's thoughts about mobile engagement at a pair of journalism conferences in 2012 and 2013. On both occasions he stressed how important it is to avoid annoying mobile users with layouts and features designed primarily for the desktop. Even adding the words *click here* to a link blithely assumes the increasingly unlikely scenario that the user is sitting at a desk, surfing the web with a mouse. Ho also emphasized the importance of listening to feedback from mobile users about their experience. He said he reads every comment posted about the *Journal's* products at the iTunes app store. "I read them all, and I pay attention to them," Ho said. "If you read enough of them, you can see trends emerge" (pers. comm.).

News consumers' routines are inexorably shifting toward smartphones and tablets. In 2012 a Pew Research Center survey found that 64 percent of tablet owners said they used their devices to access news every week, while 37 percent did so daily. Smartphone owners reported almost identical patterns of news consumption, with 62 percent using their phone to retrieve news each week and 36 percent doing so each day (Sasseen, Olmstead, and Mitchell 2013). And for the first time ever, smartphones outsold basic mobile phones during the second quarter of 2013, accounting for nearly 52 percent of mobile phone sales worldwide (Rooney 2013). Meanwhile U.S. spending on mobile ads—which initially was expected to nearly double to $8.5 billion in 2013 from one year earlier—actually exceeded that lofty projection, instead totaling nearly $9.6 billion and accounting for nearly 23 percent of all digital advertising investments (Macleod 2013; eMarketer 2013). Jonah Peretti, *BuzzFeed* founder and CEO, said his company has found that mobile ads outperform their desktop counterparts when it comes to engaged consumer behaviors, including clickthroughs and sharing. "People are more focused on mobile," Peretti said. "On the desktop there are all those distractions" (Shields 2014).

The market shift toward smartphones and tablets makes it even more urgent for news organizations to find ways to engage mobile users on their own terms. "The reason that audience and loyalty are important is that we need to have an engaged audience so that wherever they go with mobile, we can be with them—or, put another way, our journalism will reach them where they are," said John Yemma of the *Christian Science Monitor* (pers. comm.). And journalists shouldn't assume that mobile users are interested only in distractions while waiting in line— surveys have found that smartphone users actually prefer watching full versions of video content, not snippets. "The second screen, in other words, is quickly gaining primacy in our lives—and for immersive content as well as quick-hit stuff" (Garber 2014).

In the United Kingdom spending on mobile advertising was expected to double in 2013 to nearly £1 billion ($1.68 billion) (Goldhill 2013). "I've read probably every year since 2010 that this is the year of mobile," said Joe Jenkins, mobile editor at the *Telegraph* in London. "Really, it's been the year of mobile in every year, in my opinion, because it's always been growing and growing and growing." Jenkins said U.K. mobile news consumption got a big boost in 2012 when the London Underground added free wireless access for the Olympics: "You've always seen people playing games on their mobile phone on the Tube. But I think now you see a lot more people actually consuming apps." When I met with Jenkins in mid-2013, he reeled off example after example of how Telegraph Media Group was scrambling to generate more revenue from mobile devices—subscriptions, interstitial ads between swipes on an iPad, even sponsored features within apps, such as a special rugby section backed by Land Rover. "Not everything's perfect, but you've got to be out there," Jenkins told me. "Otherwise you're just missing out."

Kate Day, the *Telegraph*'s director of digital content, said mobile users prefer to interact in brief focused ways, such as voting in a poll. "I think it's a fairly light level of engagement," Day said. "A lot of [mobile users] like to have a view on stories, but they don't necessarily want to log on and leave a comment." However, she said that is likely to change over time, as news organizations refine and improve their mobile offerings:

> I think there is appetite for quite lengthy engagement; you've just got to get around those user experience and technical challenges to make that happen. The types of story you'd leave a comment on from your phone would probably be live, fast, and moving, whereas if you sat down and read a very lengthy analysis and then left quite a thoughtful comment, you'd be more likely to do that when you got to your desktop. But it's quite hard to measure that or prove that.(pers. comm.)

Mobile users are busy and on the go, which makes earning their loyalty even more of a challenge. "It's thinking not just that, 'Oh, it's digital, yeah, we've done that already—we've got a website,'" said Kevin Anderson, an American who spent nine years working in the United Kingdom as a journalist and digital media consultant before joining the Gannett chain in Wisconsin in 2014. To effectively engage mobile users, Anderson said, newsrooms need to think through some fundamental questions: "How is mobile different? How do people interact differently with the content? How do they interact differently with the devices? What new opportunities do we have to make sure that we have more revenues for our journalism?" (pers. comm.).

COMMON ELEMENTS OF ENGAGING THE "PASSIONATE VERTICAL"

Online platforms and mobile devices empower today's journalists with more tools than ever to inform and connect a community defined by geography, a common interest, or some combination of the two. Effectively engaging these "passionate vertical" audiences depends first and foremost upon providing a news experience tailored to the particular tastes and customs of each group. That said, the ventures in niche and hyperlocal news that ultimately survive tend to follow a number of common practices:

- *They identify an underserved audience large enough to sustain a business.* What do UFC fans, federal policy wonks, and West Seattle neighbors have in common? They are like-minded groups of tens of thousands of people whose information needs weren't fully served by existing media outlets. The *Las Vegas Sun*, *Politico Pro*, and the *West Seattle Blog* each delivered a more comprehensive news experience than was previously available to these audiences, each of which was large enough to be commercially viable. "If there is a niche fishing group in New England, even if you were wildly successful, it's only a couple thousand people," said the *Dallas Morning News*'s Rich Alfano. "But if you can reach 10 percent of 500,000 people, that's 50,000 people. That's an audience that you've created" (pers. comm.).
- *They help readers customize their mobile experience.* This is especially important with professional niches, as *Politico Pro* has shown with the popularity of its keyword-activated e-mail alerts and push notifications that deliver "actionable intelligence" to the smartphones of busy staffers and lobbyists bustling about Capitol Hill. Niche users want to be in charge of their mobile experience.
- *They stitch their audience together—on its own terms.* The insiders who read the subscriber-only *Texas Weekly* generally don't post public comments about news stories, but their collective answers to a weekly survey are the backbone of Inside Intelligence, a polling report that

taps into the latest political intrigue. The *Las Vegas Sun* saves UFC fans money by live-blogging pay-per-view fights they would otherwise have to pay more than $50 to watch; reporters pepper the live with real-time tidbits like the entrance songs selected by each fighter. Such attention to detail shows that a news outlet truly understands the sensibilities of its audience.

- *They proceed carefully with mobile apps.* Even when device-specific apps are crafted for the most passionate niche audience, their economic considerations are tricky—front-end developer fees, determining whether the app is paid or free, pricing out premium features and advertising, the list goes on. Lackluster downloads eventually prompted the *Dallas Morning News* to stop charging $1.99 for its groundbreaking real-time SportsDayHS app, which the paper now markets aggressively for free as part of its cross-platform suite of high school football coverage. The *Seattle Times*, on the other hand, abandoned its disappointing Husky football app, a project the *Times*'s publisher later said lacked budgetary discipline. "Defining and attracting a desirable [niche] audience is necessary, of course, but not by itself sufficient," write Grueskin, Seave, and Graves. "Acquiring that audience on a tight budget is what sets successful grass-roots ventures apart from the also-rans" (2011:52).

- *They match their audience's passion.* The most successful niche and hyperlocal sites often are led by a veteran business-savvy journalist who is personally committed to covering that community inside and out. However, constantly meeting the insatiable expectations of a motivated niche audience is no small feat. As Ross Ramsey, former editor of *Texas Weekly*, puts it, "You're in a universe where you basically have to keep swimming or die" (pers. comm.). Still, treading those brisk waters can be invigorating, fun, and—with the right mix of journalistic and entrepreneurial drive—sustainable.

4

Search, Explore, Play

Drawing Readers into Journalism
Through Interactive Experiences

The *Texas Tribune* launched in late 2009 with a newsroom of veteran journalists and rising stars. And while that respected crew of reporters, editors, and columnists would go on to unearth their share of political scoops, it wasn't traditional reporting and writing that propelled the *Tribune* to early prominence. Instead, the *Tribune* quickly made its name as an interactive resource for readers to do their own exploring.

During its first year the *Tribune*'s biggest traffic magnet—by far—was a series of more than three dozen interactive databases that enabled readers to scour their neighborhood's school rankings, look up an inmate in the state prison system, or snoop on their office mate's salary. The databases connected readers to more than one million public records they otherwise might not have known how to find. Collectively these databases were an unexpected hit, drawing three times as many page views as the site's stories (Batsell 2010:40–41).

"Publishing data *is* news," the *Tribune*'s Matt Stiles and Niran Baba-lola told readers in a blog post outlining their philosophy. "It aligns with our strategy of adding knowledge and context to traditional reporting, and it helps you and us hold public officials accountable" (Stiles and Baba-lola 2010). Embracing that mentality, the *Tribune* created what almost instantly became its most popular calling card, a database listing the salaries of nearly 700,000 public employees. Emily Ramshaw, one of the *Tribune*'s original reporters who later was promoted to editor, told me the newsroom conversation about the salary database went something like this: "'Why don't we just put the whole thing up there for people to peruse at will? Why not draw them in with that and feed them their vegetables in the meantime?' It sort of miraculously became our shtick."

The salary database drew a flurry of complaints from state employees who considered it an invasion of privacy and from readers who called it the digital equivalent of "water-cooler gossip" (Batsell 2010:41). But ultimately it was an easy-to-use tool that connected readers with pub-licly available information. That ethic of accessibility informs all the *Tribune*'s interactive news or apps. "The first goal is to make the data accessible to real people," Ramshaw said. "In a traditional newsroom, priority one is to break news" (pers. comm.).The databases also help bring in revenue—for example, each salary listing has its own digital page with several ads placed by corporate sponsors.

The *Tribune* is part of a growing tide of newsrooms that are creat-ing interactive platforms for readers to use in whatever ways matter most to them. Major U.S. newsrooms have long employed a handful of computer-assisted reporting specialists who acquired data through public records requests, sorted and analyzed the databases, and summa-rized the most attention-grabbing figures in their stories (or highlighted them in accompanying sidebars and graphics). The approach certainly produced a lot of worthwhile journalism, but a key element was missing: enabling readers to explore the data themselves. In the digital era that basic expectation of interactivity has become one of the most essential components of effective journalistic engagement. "It's not just, 'Hey, here's what I found,'" said Ryan Murphy, who leads the *Texas Tribune*'s news apps team. "It's, 'Here's what I found, and here's all of it for you to look through, and let me know what you find'" (pers. comm.).

AN ETHIC OF TRANSPARENCY—
AND USABILITY

Aron Pilhofer, executive editor of digital for the *Guardian* in London, remembers precisely when his mind-set in regard to data journalism changed. In May 2005 the pioneering journalist–developer Adrian Holovaty launched chicagocrime.org, a website that combined Google Maps with data from the Chicago Police Department to create interactive block-by-block crime maps. The site gave Chicago residents the ability to easily track crimes in their neighborhood, regardless of whether the incidents made television news or the metro briefs column in the *Tribune* or *Sun-Times*. "It totally changed the way I thought about journalism . . . the idea that data itself, presented to readers in a format that they, then, could investigate, could itself be an act of journalism," Pilhofer said during a 2012 training webinar sponsored by the Knight Center for Journalism in the Americas.

At a certain level this new era of interactive data journalism defies newsroom traditions of journalistic competition. "We came from this mentality of not sharing your notes," said Jennifer LaFleur, now senior editor for data journalism at the Center for Investigative Reporting (she previously held computer-assisted reporting positions at *ProPublica*, the *Dallas Morning News, San Jose Mercury News*, and *St. Louis Post-Dispatch*). "Now, we're sharing everything with everybody." LaFleur said creating interactive databases to share with the public in full—not just selected highlights—creates an ethic of transparency that makes stories more relevant and useful to readers. "We try not to just do stuff for the sake of doing it but really put energy into things that are going to help people," she said. "I don't want to put anything up that doesn't serve a purpose and help people" (pers. comm.).

For journalists who do embrace data, the opportunities are proliferating. Emily Bell, director of the Columbia Journalism School's Tow

Center for Digital Journalism, points out that journalists who handle data range "from being a statistics number cruncher or creative interaction designer to being a reporter who uses data skills—extracting the story and/or explaining the bias in it—as part of his or her beat" (Bell 2012:48). Philanthropists have shown a willingness to open their wallets for data projects—several foundations funded a $1.5 million data-driven collaboration called the State Integrity Investigation, which from 2010 to 2012 analyzed corruption and transparency in U.S. state capitols.[1]

Numbers are the foundation for most databases, but any type of data can fuel interactive projects. *CNN.com*'s powerful "Home and Away" project, which documents the casualties of U.S. and coalition troops in the Afghanistan and Iraq wars, uses side-by-side interactive maps to juxtapose the hometown of each fallen soldier and the location where he or she died (Cox 2010). The *Texas Tribune*'s database of state executions during Governor Rick Perry's tenure includes the full text of each inmate's last statement (Murphy, Grissom, and Seger 2011). At their essence interactive data projects engage readers simply by connecting them with "something that's interesting; something you didn't know," said the *Tribune*'s Murphy.

Consider the *Texas Tribune*'s Public Schools Explorer database, created primarily by the developer Noah Seger. The project compiled academic, enrollment, and financial records from eighty-five hundred schools in thirteen hundred districts across Texas. The Texas Education Agency already publishes such data on the web, but the government site forces parents who look for information to navigate a bewildering sea of acronyms, links, and PDFs (figure 4.1). "It's not anything that's feasible for a normal person who wants to find things out," Murphy said. "We thought it was something we could tackle and make more enjoyable to use" (pers. comm.).

In contrast the *Tribune*'s Schools Explorer presents the state's data on easy-to-follow charts, empowers users to create their own side-by-side comparisons, and uses an algorithm to generate summary sentences that give a coherent overview of the numbers (figure 4.2) (Bernier 2012). The app is much easier to use than the state agency's clunky bureaucratic website.

And that's the hallmark of effective data journalism. No matter how artfully an interactive project is designed, the ultimate test is whether the public can use it. "If something's useful, it'll live in the wild," said Matt Stiles, who left the *Texas Tribune* to join NPR's news apps team in Washington, D.C. With every app the NPR team creates, Stiles and his colleagues strive to solve a problem for readers— "not just dump it [data] but to let them explore it with a good experience. . . . What story are we trying to tell? What is someone going to bookmark and use again? What is someone really going to want?" (pers. comm.). For example, NPR's mobile Fire Forecast app synthesizes data from the U.S. Forest Service with interactive mapping technology to give users a personalized current assessment of wildfire danger based on their location (Stiles et al. 2013). "This is a good case for making government data useful," Stiles said. "The new reality is, it has to be responsive, it has to be useful, it has to be durable" (pers. comm.).

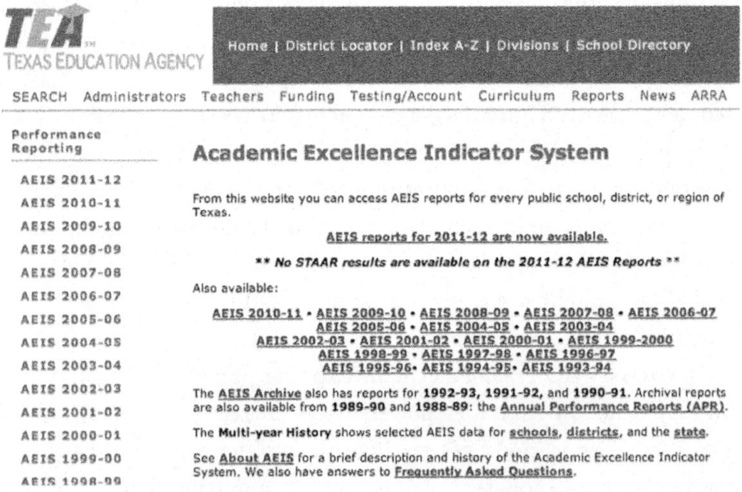

FIGURE 4.1 The Texas Education Agency's data interface, as captured on its website in September 2013. Image: http://www.tea.state.tx.us

ENLISTING THE CROWD

Interactive data projects often are the product of journalists who take unwieldy government data sets and translate them into more accessible formats. But other projects directly enlist the public's help in collecting the data. When the State of Washington opened liquor sales to private businesses in June 2012 for the first time since Prohibition, the *Seattle Times* crowdsourced the impact of the new regulations, asking readers to record and report prices from around the region (*Seattle Times* 2012). Some people directly reported prices using an online form created by the *Times*, while others took pictures of receipts with their smartphones and tweeted from the store using the hashtag #waliquor. The newspaper combined the results with its own reporting and found that

SEARCH DISTRICTS AND SCHOOLS

Find school data by typing your school or district name into the box below.

Start typing to find schools

Not sure which school you're looking for? Use the button below to find schools near you:

◇ VIEW SCHOOLS NEAR ME

Or try a sample campus or district link to find out how the explorer can help you answer the questions below. To dig deeper, follow the "more info" links that appear after the data, or click the "see all" link after the school name.

AUSTIN HIGH SCHOOL ↱ All Data

Demographics ⯈   **What does my school or district enrollment look like?**

Austin High School is an urban school in Austin with 2,350 students. More Info

Academics ⯈   **How is my school or district performing academically?**

Students perform at the state average in passing TAKS scores. More Info

FIGURE 4.2 The *Texas Tribune*'s Public Schools Explorer app repackages data from the website of the Texas Education Agency in a more user-friendly format. Copyright © *Texas Tribune*. Image: *Texas Tribune*

prices had increased for thirteen of the state's twenty most popular brands of whiskey, rum, tequila, and vodka. The results, while informal and unscientific, provided an early indication that privatizing liquor sales would not necessarily reduce prices by introducing competition, as advocates had predicted. "It's better than interviewing ten people and saying what you found," said Cheryl Phillips, the *Times*'s data enterprise editor (pers. comm.).

ProPublica took crowdsourcing to an even deeper level with its "Free the Files" app, which mobilized more than one thousand readers to pore through federal records and log more than $1 billion worth of political ad spending during the 2012 elections. The project's aim was to shine a light on dark money campaign spending by disclosing which political groups actually paid for television ads in key battleground states. The Federal Communications Commission requires television stations to digitally post documents revealing who funded political ad buys. But stations often send the government a hodgepodge of PDF files that are onerous and time consuming to search. The "Free the Files" app demystified the process by creating an app that invited *ProPublica* readers to click a green "Give me a file!" button, review PDFs, and easily enter the data, said Amanda Zamora, *ProPublica*'s senior engagement editor.

ProPublica formed a "Free the Files" Facebook group and used it as a platform to attract readers and motivate them to participate by offering such incentives as free t-shirts and a leaderboard recognizing the most active participants. "You're playing to people's democratic ideals," Zamora said. "It was an inherently altruistic project—people could see how they were helping increase transparency." The Facebook page, Zamora said, essentially became a "superuser group" of about two hundred people who encouraged each other and alerted *ProPublica* staff whenever they encountered glitches using the app. "They were great indicators as to what our larger readership might be struggling with," Zamora said (pers. comm.).

Ultimately more than one thousand people reviewed at least one file. And by the end of election season readers had helped *ProPublica* "free" more than fifteen thousand files, including a record 917 on Election Day (Zamora 2012, 2013). The project also produced some newsworthy scoops, including the revelation of a previously unknown dark money group that had secretly spent more than $1 million on negative ads about Sherrod Brown, the incumbent Democratic senator from Ohio (Elliott 2012). For Zamora, Justin Elliott's story showed how interactive projects can succeed on "concurrent tracks," helping reporters identify individual stories and dig deeper while the crowd assembles the bigger picture. As a reporter, Zamora said, "you're going to home in on what's most newsworthy. [But] there may be other stories hidden in that data." Meanwhile, she said, with every freed file, the crowd contributes to a more comprehensive overview, "giving us a way to open up and tell a more complete story. It doesn't negate the need for reporters to leverage their expertise and figure out what's most valuable and interesting to their audience" (pers. comm.).

GUARDING AGAINST PITFALLS

By doggedly promoting the project on *ProPublica*'s website and social media channels, Zamora kept the momentum going for "Free the Files" for three solid months. Without that degree of continuous and dedicated promotion, data journalists say, even the most dazzling interactive projects can go unnoticed. "Unless it's out there front and center, it gets kind of ghettoized," said Cheryl Phillips, the *Seattle Times*'s data enterprise editor (pers. comm.). NPR's Matt Stiles said it's especially important to promote apps among coworkers in broadcast newsrooms, so colleagues will buy into the project and be more likely to mention the story on air (pers. comm.).

The London-based journalist Kevin Anderson was an early contributor to the much-followed *Datablog* of the *Guardian*, which since 2009 has analyzed data trends in the news while often challenging popular assumptions. Anderson said it's not sufficient to simply publish a database on the web and hope that people will interact with it. "These days, the battle for attention is so acute that you have to reach out, you have to engage," Anderson said. "So adding a social layer to everything you do—even something like data—is really important" (pers. comm.).

For example, posts on the *Datablog* routinely draw scores of comments from curious readers.

Perhaps the biggest pitfall with data journalism is the perception that vast sets of numbers somehow do not require the same level of scrutiny as quotes, documents, and other types of information. LaFleur— who before joining CIR was *ProPublica*'s director of computer-assisted reporting—said that when collecting data for *ProPublica*'s "opportunity gap" series on public schools, she found one high school that claimed to offer twenty-two thousand different AP classes, when only thirty-seven were possible (Coutts and LaFleur 2011). Some schools provided statistics showing that they had more teachers than students. When *ProPublica*'s reporters spotted outliers like those, LaFleur said, she and her colleagues called the school district to verify the data. "It's my job when I interview someone to background-check them," LaFleur said. "Why not background-check my data? It's my job to interview my data just like I interview a person." Posting data online without carefully vetting it first is lazy journalism, LaFleur said: "I don't think a lot of people are aware of how many problems there can be with data that misserves the public. The excuse, 'Well, that's how it is in the government data'— that's unacceptable to me. That's like taking a press release and taping it to a wall" (pers. comm.).

The *Journal News* in suburban New York learned a blunt lesson along these lines in December 2012 when, in the wake of the Newtown shootings, the newspaper published the names of more than thirty thousand handgun permit holders and mapped their addresses online. Readers were irate, and the newspaper's journalists were harassed and received so many threats that the publisher hired armed guards for on-site protection (Haughney 2013). Respected journalists spoke out against the newspaper's decision to publish the names and addresses, saying the *Journal News* did not make a compelling case as to how such a map would benefit the public. "It is one thing to have a public database available that lets me look up whether the neighbor I am feuding with might have a gun permit," wrote David Carr of the *New York Times*. "It is quite another to publish the names and addresses of all my neighbors who own guns. The decision lacked a rationale" (2013).

Adopting a "data as journalism" mentality does not eliminate the
need for human news judgment. To the contrary, as Emily Bell of the
Tow Center puts it:

> Journalism by numbers does not mean ceding human process to
> the bots. Every algorithm, however it is written, contains human,
> and therefore editorial, judgments. The decisions made about
> what data to include and exclude adds a layer of perspective to
> the information provided. There must be transparency and a set
> of editorial standards underpinning the data collection.
>
> (2012:49)

For example, the *Texas Tribune* realized in July 2013 that a state agency
had made errors in assigning federal codes that designate prisoners'
crimes, inaccurately labeling some inmates as having sexually assaulted a
child. The *Tribune* temporarily took its entire Texas Prison Inmates database offline. "We're not comfortable publishing information whose accu-
racy is in question," wrote Brandi Grissom, the *Tribune*'s managing editor
(2013). About a week later the *Tribune* put the database back online after
removing the federal codes—which had been entered manually by state
employees—from individual prisoners' entries (Swicegood 2013).

TESTING READERS' KNOWLEDGE— AND ATTRACTING CLICKS— WITH MULTIPLIERS

Five days before U.S. voters went to the polls in November 2012, the
most popular story on the *Christian Science Monitor*'s website was not an
article about the imminent presidential election but a hundred-question
quiz headlined "Could You Pass a U.S. Citizenship Test?" The quiz, pos-
ing questions from the same naturalization test taken by aspiring U.S.
citizens, tested readers on the basics of U.S. history and the parliamen-
tary mechanics of how a bill becomes a law. The *Monitor* also tempted
quiz takers with a bold, if not somewhat daunting, reminder: fifty-eight

correct answers were required to pass. The message to readers was unspoken but clear: prove your civic expertise—and keep those clicks coming.

The quiz, published by the *Monitor* nearly two years earlier, was often embedded within the text of more recent election stories as part of a wider strategy to boost online traffic with multipliers—evergreen quizzes and lists that entice readers to click on multiple pages. "The great thing is, they keep on giving," said the *Monitor*'s John Yemma. "You do them and keep bringing them back" (pers. comm.). Indeed, multipliers have been a key element of the *Monitor*'s transformation from a century-old newspaper into a web-first newsroom since it stopped daily publication in 2009 (Groves and Brown-Smith 2011, 2013). The *Monitor*'s multipliers are meant to ignite readers' competitive instincts, Yemma said, challenging them to test their knowledge on subjects like geography, science, or politics. "We try to develop multipliers that are consistent with who we are, which is why a lot of our multipliers tend to be a little brainy," Yemma said. "It's a form of journalism. It's not a pure play in journalism, but it's a form of journalism because it is based, usually, on current events. So it at least reinforces the idea of an informed citizenry" (pers. comm.).

Yemma candidly explained that multipliers are designed to draw page views—and accompanying advertising revenue—while also attracting the attention of new readers who might become more deeply engaged with the *Monitor*'s analytical journalism. "Somehow we've got to find a way to make people eat their spinach," he said. In October 2012 seven of the *Monitor*'s multipliers combined for nearly eleven million page views, generating more than one-fifth of overall the site's web traffic during a record-setting month of more than fifty million page views.[2] The record-setting lineup of multipliers included "Could You Pass a U.S. Citizenship Test?," "Are You Scientifically Literate?," "Are You Smarter Than an Atheist?," and a pair of quizzes testing whether readers were more liberal or conservative than Barack Obama or Mitt Romney. Marshall Ingwerson, the managing editor, said quizzes and other multipliers deliver "immediate engagement, and there's the potential to make it more of the distinctive *Monitor* experience that really delivers value." The hope, Ingwerson said, is that "it adds some fun and some 'gamification' to our serious news delivery" (pers. comm.). (See figure 4.3.)

Are you a cat person or a dog person? Take our quiz!

If you suspect that there's a difference between those who prefer the company of cats and those who enjoy spending time with dogs, you just might be on to something. Studies have found measurable differences in the personality traits of so-called 'cat people' and 'dog people.' This quiz should not under any circumstances be mistaken for an actual psychological assessment, but it is based on empirical data that we will share with you at the end.

Answer each question with the description that more closely matches your personality. This quiz is 25 questions.

- Eoin O'Carroll, Staff

⊕ Enlarge

A barn cat spends time with a dog on a farm in Granville Summit, Pa. in 2012. (Melanie Stetson Freeman/The Christian Science Monitor)

Question 1 of 25

1. Any time someone rubs my belly, my first impulse is to...

FIGURE 4.3 News quizzes like the *Christian Science Monitor*'s "Are You a Cat Person or a Dog Person?" are designed to tap into readers' curiosity and boost online traffic. Copyright © *Christian Science Monitor.* Image: *Christian Science Monitor*

Getting the most out of multipliers requires quick opportunistic thinking in response to real-time trends on the web. For example, on February 22, 2012, Google put a new interactive doodle on its home page to mark the 155th anniversary of the birth of Heinrich Rudolf Hertz, the German physicist who proved the existence of electromagnetic waves. Chris Gaylord, the *Monitor*'s innovation editor, wrote a short story explaining the Google tribute, with background information about Hertz and his groundbreaking work (Gaylord 2012). When Google users noticed the doodle and searched for Hertz, Gaylord's story showed up prominently in the results. And once readers called up the Hertz story, they encountered a link to the "Are You Scientifically Literate?" quiz that had been embedded in Gaylord's story. The Hertz story and accompanying quiz tapped into the curiosity of the moment, push-ing the *Monitor* past four million daily page views for the first time in its history.[3] "I wouldn't say it's become the tail wagging the dog in terms of how much time we devote to journalism," Yemma said. "To me they [the multipliers] are part of the whole package of news that you offer people. And if they help to support the core of what we do, then they're a good thing. But they have to be consistent with who we are. We don't do multipliers about the Kardashians" (pers. comm.).

Multipliers at the *Monitor* also can take the form of list stories ("30 Banned Books That May Surprise You") or an alternate form of book review ("'Preschool Gems': 25 Funny Quotes from Preschoolers")—both lists penned by Molly Driscoll, a staff writer who compiles roughly one such multiplier per week for the books and culture sections. Driscoll said she has fun writing multipliers, noting that she laughed while selecting the preschooler quotes from Leslie McCollom's book, *Preschool Gems* (Driscoll 2012). But Driscoll said the more casual format can actually take longer to write than a more straightforward review or blog post. "We definitely try to make it so people will be hooked and say, 'That's something I want to check out,'" Driscoll said (pers. comm.).

Marjorie Kehe, books editor of the *Monitor*, said Driscoll's list of funny quotes from McCollom's book "is something we could have done in a book review. But a multiplier drives traffic like crazy." The click-to-see-what's-next format gets more attention than a traditional book review might, Kehe said. And with review budgets shrinking and audience preferences changing, she added, some books would not be reviewed in any form without the multiplier format. "There's [only] a small pool of readers who want to sit down and read full-length reviews by professional critics," she said. "It's a sad reality." The *Monitor*'s web analytics show that readers have a greater appetite for short snappy reviews, Kehe said, and "we're not in a place anymore where we can tell readers what they want. They're telling us what they want. . . . Even in print, readers are telling us they want more in less space. We're trying to do what readers are telling us they want" (pers. comm.).

In some ways the *Monitor*'s success with list stories mirrors the more far-reaching popularity of what *BuzzFeed* calls "listicles," such as "109

Cats in Sweaters" and "31 Things You Can Make Out of Cereal Boxes" (Shepherd 2010; Armbrester 2013). Many journalists scoff at *BuzzFeed* and consider its content to be vacuous, but the Center for Investigative Reporting's Meghann Farnsworth said newsrooms could learn a thing or two from *BuzzFeed* about how to make news more relevant and accessible to their audiences. "Not everyone's going to be *BuzzFeed*," said Farnsworth, CIR's senior manager for distribution and engagement. "But I think we can take some of those lessons and say, 'How can we improve, so that it fits what our mandate is?'" (pers. comm.).

At the *Monitor* editors sometimes field complaints from readers about having to click through lists and quizzes, Kehe said. But she responds to those complaints by explaining that the digital display ads attached to the multipliers enable the *Monitor* to offer content for free. "I'm grateful for the list stories, which pay the rent to a certain extent," Kehe said, estimating that multipliers make up about one-fourth of her section's content. "They're a huge part of our section traffic. I feel like it's something that we can feel good about. In general they're not junk. They're not things we have to feel ashamed about. They're actually rather respectable." Done well, Kehe said, list stories generate discussion by making people curious (pers. comm.).

Eoin O'Carroll, an online news editor, has crafted some of the *Monitor*'s most popular and enduring multipliers, such as the "Are You Scientifically Literate?" quiz that helped boost the site's daily traffic past four million page views in February 2012. O'Carroll, who was a part-time pub trivia jockey for seven years, has written dozens of quizzes and also has trained dozens of *Monitor* staffers on how to strike the right balance in writing them. "The best quizzes we have are the ones that kind of challenge your identity—"Okay, you may think you know this, but do you really?'" O'Carroll said. "You kind of want to reward the reader by making them feel smart but not make it too easy. Even if you get something wrong, that's a great way to learn."

The quizzes, O'Carroll said, are "fundamentally pedagogical." Collectively they constitute a relatively small—but important—part of his job. "It's probably my main revenue contribution to the *Monitor*, but it's not the biggest part of my time," he said. O'Carroll and his newsroom colleagues are fully aware that the quizzes and multipliers are designed to attract page views and generate more digital revenue, effectively subsidizing deeper forms of journalism. "If you're doing quality journalism that nobody sees, then does it really make any difference that you're doing it?" he said. "We're supporting [deeper journalism] through the lists and quizzes and other things that generate revenue" (pers. comm.).

Yemma said multipliers "aren't the destination engagement that you're looking for, which is the engagement with your deeper journalism, but it's a part of the process of engagement." If readers previously unfamiliar with the *Monitor* have a good experience with a multiplier, Yemma said, the hope is that they'll keep coming back to the website—and perhaps even subscribe to the weekly print magazine (pers. comm.).

GAMIFYING THE NEWS

News outlets can further appeal to readers' competitive instincts by pulling them into digital "gamified" experiences that are even more immersive. The *Telegraph* in London did just that during the summer of 2013 with an interactive feature that was fun, compelling, and wonderfully simple—and took only a few days to build. "How to spot a Stradivarius," published in connection with an Oxford museum exhibit featuring twenty-one of the world-renowned violins, challenged users to listen to three short audio clips and see if they could pick out the fairest fiddle of them all (Palmer, Oliver, and Allen 2013). Users listened to three audio clips, each less than a minute—one played with the Stradivarius, one with an eighteenth-century German violin, and one with a £40 (about $67) violin from the supermarket. Users dragged and dropped each violin into the box that they thought matched the corresponding clip.

Whether you guessed right or not, the Stradivarius challenge provided a brainy five-minute escape and perhaps the impulse to pass the story along to a friend. *Telegraph* readers shared the game repeatedly through Facebook, Twitter, and other social networks, and more than 75 percent of the nearly five thousand users who answered a poll said they got it right. If you nailed it, you might have experienced the same thrill as Cynthia Green, a University of North Texas student who said this in a blog post after taking the challenge during a study-abroad journalism class: "Not only did I have fun taking it, but I felt really fancy and sophisticated when I guessed the answers correctly" (2013).

When I spoke with members of the *Telegraph*'s interactive team in London, they said they considered the Stradivarius project a relative success, especially given the minimal staff time spent creating it. "It's not the best, by far," said Mark Oliver, an online graphics editor who spent roughly half a week creating the feature. "But in terms of the amount of time that we spent building it, it was pretty successful, I think" (pers. comm.). Oliver and Conrad Quilty-Harper, an interactive news editor, said they don't have a fixed formula for gauging the success of interactive games. When a project goes live, they pay close attention to page views, social media shares, and comment activity, as well as more subjective factors like the tone of the comments. The Stradivarius test, which drew roughly five thousand responses from people sharing their results, "was probably a midlevel–high success," Quilty-Harper said. "But then, some graphics we've done have thirty thousand or forty thousand [shares]. If we get something that does fifty shares and we spent three days on it, that's dramatically unsuccessful" (pers. comm.).

On the other hand, a news game that catches on can attract a motivated and loyal subset of users, as the *Texas Tribune* found in 2011–12 with its daily trivia game about Texas politics, Qrank. Rodney Gibbs, cofounder of Ricochet Labs, which developed Qrank, said the game was designed for those "microboredom moments" when you're waiting in line or picking up your kids. "It's a game, but it's not Farmville, just goofing off," Gibbs said. "Ostensibly I'm getting a little smarter here" because of the game (pers. comm.).

Reeve Hamilton, a staff writer, was in charge of updating the daily Qrank quizzes with newsy nuggets and tidbits from the *Tribune*'s stories and interactive features. "There were a lot of inside jokes embedded in it that you would only get if you were paying attention," Hamilton said. "It gave people a reason to come to the site" (pers. comm.). Players accumulated points for correct answers and were ranked on a leaderboard as they competed for monthly prizes worth hundreds of dollars, such as dinner for two at an upscale Austin restaurant. "You basically have to read everything on our site to get a perfect score," said Emily Ramshaw, the *Tribune*'s editor. "The facts we stick in there sometimes are so obscure" (pers. comm.).

The experiment worked in some ways but not others. Players found ways to cheat. And over time the game became a drain on Hamilton's time—he spent roughly an hour every night updating the quiz. "It was quite an undertaking," he said. Gibbs conceded Hamilton's point: "For all its strengths," he said of Qrank, "it took constant feeding." In September 2012 the *Tribune* discontinued the Qrank experiment; Ricochet Labs sold the game's technology to another gaming company, and Gibbs became the *Tribune*'s chief innovation officer (Gibbs 2012).

Still, during its twenty-month run Qrank created a sense of competition and excitement for the roughly eight hundred to nine hundred unique users who participated each month. Even Hamilton called it a worthwhile experiment: "It kept a small segment of our base superamped about waking up and doing that every morning," he said. "If [the new quiz] wasn't up at midnight, I got an e-mail immediately: 'Where's Qrank?'" (pers. comm.). Like NPR's legendary quiz show, *Wait Wait . . . Don't Tell Me!*, Qrank managed to engage a loyal subset of *Tribune* readers by delivering serious news in the form of a fun competitive game. But unlike *Wait Wait*, the momentum ran out.

David Poulson can relate to both the fun of creating news-related games and the ambiguity of their ultimate success. Poulson is editor of the *Great Lakes Echo*, the online news service based at Michigan State University. The *Echo* ran two whimsical contests called the Great Lakes Smackdown, creating March Madness–style brackets and asking readers to vote on which invasive species is most ecologically destructive to the Great Lakes region (Rossignol and Gleason 2011). "It's not scientifically rigorous, but it gets people talking about it," Poulson said (pers. comm.).

The smackdown brackets started as newsroom banter, the product of students' wondering aloud who would win in a fight between an astronaut and a cave dweller. After six weeks of voting readers crowned a tree-killing insect called the emerald ash borer as the 2011 smackdown's ultimate winner. To wrap up the contest student journalists conducted a video interview with a professor who explained the insect's devastating ecological effects.

Poulson said he was disappointed by the Great Lake Smackdown's online traffic and number of comments. However, the contest did generate interest among local scientists and high school students, and a public radio station in Detroit ran a news story about it. "I don't know if journalism happened, but education happened," Poulson said. "There's a heightened awareness of what these critters are capable of" (pers. comm.).

Realized to their maximum potential, news games can spread the impact of journalistic projects far beyond their original publication outlet. Nicholas Kristof, the *New York Times* columnist, and Sheryl WuDunn, a former *Times* reporter, supplemented their best-selling book *Half the Sky: Turning Oppression into Opportunity for Women Worldwide* (2009) with a Facebook adventure game in which players complete quests to unlock actual gifts that support women and girls around the world. Kristof announced on his public Facebook page in August 2013 that the game had reached one million players and raised more than $400,000 for global women's causes. "Games can do good," Kristof told his Facebook followers.

In Brazil, simulation games aimed at young people demystify the news by assigning players enticing roles and missions, such as an undercover cop who poses as a trafficker to infiltrate the mafia. The Brazilian youth magazine *Superinteressante* and its publishing house, Editora Abril, have developed several such games. Fred di Giacomo, the former youth department editor for *Editora Abril*, describes his editorial process in deciding which topics were worthy of a news game:

First you need to think about when it's worth creating a game. Is the story I want to tell best told through a game, a post, or an infographic? If I had wanted to explain how to avoid catching swine flu, for example, I would never do it in a game. Will making a game facilitate understanding of information? That is the starting point. To make a newsgame, you have to ask two questions:

Does the game inform? If it doesn't, it is only a game. Does the game entertain? If not, it is only journalism. (Mazotte 2013)

California Watch, an investigative site founded by the Center for Investigative Reporting, informed and entertained a younger-than-usual audience in 2011 with *Ready to Rumble*, a coloring book released in tandem with an acclaimed series that examined seismic safety in the state's public schools.[4] The nonprofit investigative news outlet published a first run of roughly thirty-six thousand coloring books that educated children on what to do when an earthquake hits. Ashley Alvarado, the public engagement editor, explained that CIR created the book because she and her colleagues wanted to directly reach and inform the children whose safety was the ultimate goal of the series: "While *California Watch* articles are written for adults, we recognize that oftentimes children are those most affected by the stories we report" (2011). Several media partners helped cover printing costs for the coloring books, which were translated into Spanish, Vietnamese, traditional Chinese, and simplified Chinese.

Contests also can help individual bloggers build a bigger following, as Mark Luckie discovered years before he became Twitter's manager of journalism and news. In the late 2000s Luckie started a blog called *10000Words.net* that covered the intersecting worlds of journalism and technology. To promote the blog Luckie began to run contests on Twitter, offering prizes as modest as a $5 or $10 gift card. The contests helped Luckie engage his core audience and attract additional readers to the blog. "That was the point that I realized 10,000 *Words* was a business, and I needed to do something to make it more engaging to take it to the word-of-mouth stage," Luckie said (pers. comm.). Luckie later sold *10000Words.net* for an undisclosed amount to WebMediaBrands Inc. (now Mediabistro Inc.), parent company of *Media Bistro* (Weprin 2010).

The *Texas Tribune* returned to the world of news games in May 2013 with the Session Scramble, a photo scavenger hunt held during the frenetic final two weeks of the state legislative session (Hamilton and Gibbs 2013). "Think of it as Instagram with cut-throat competition instead of sepia tone filters," the *Tribune* proclaimed in announcing the contest, whose assigned hunts ranged from the newsy (taking shots of demonstrations at the capitol) to the silly (legislators high-fiving each other). Funded by corporate sponsors, the Session Scramble drew 1,243 photos from 244 participants vying for prizes that included a spa retreat and three nights at a Caribbean hotel.

Engaging through contests and prizes also is a familiar tactic for *GeekWire*, the tech news site in Seattle that began in 2011. *GeekWire* has a Name That Tech Tune contest on its weekly morning radio show, offering apropos prizes such as a computer mouse commemorating Microsoft's thirtieth anniversary. *GeekWire*'s cofounders, John Cook and Todd Bishop, both former newspaper reporters, said they originally considered gamifying the entire site so their most engaged readers could earn points for comments and re-tweets. But ultimately Cook and Bishop decided against it. "As a start-up, we needed to focus, and we were probably trying to bite off too much," Cook said. "News has a different value than Farmville" (pers. comm.).

Fair enough, but the idea of mixing news with games has proved its enduring pop-culture appeal. Even the venerable Walter Cronkite served as a backup host for the CBS game show *It's News to Me*, which ran on CBS for four years in the early 1950s. Douglas Brinkley, author of an acclaimed Cronkite biography, noted that the legendary anchorman could have "taken a Murrow-esque stance that such mindless drivel was beneath the dignity of a true journalist. But the quiz shows were so wildly popular that he couldn't resist" (2012:158). Whether the medium is a black-and-white television set or a retina-display iPad, gamifying the news has a long track record of engaging the public's imagination.

COMMON ELEMENTS OF CREATING INTERACTIVE NEWS EXPERIENCES

The sheer journalistic effort involved in creating a comprehensive data-driven interactive project is considerably more intense than a light-hearted attempt to engage readers through a newsy quiz or contest.

But from the reader's perspective, the end result is largely the same: journalism becomes more accessible and participatory. News organizations that empower readers to dictate their own experience follow a number of common practices:

- *They regard data as journalism—so they treat it that way.* Most news websites follow the conventional practice of leading their home pages with a lengthy story or an embedded broadcast, not an interactive database. But data-driven projects can anchor home pages and should be presented as journalism in their own right, not extras or add-ons. "It's always a challenge to get an app treated as a story, and not as an accessory to a story," said Matt Stiles, an NPR data editor (pers. comm.). Designing interactive projects to stand on their own also is important because readers are increasingly likely to find them through search or social media, outside their original context on a home page.
- *They keep the data fresh.* To be truly interactive resources, data apps need to be refreshed at least once or twice a year with the most current information available. "We kind of owe it to readers to keep updating it," said the veteran data journalist Jennifer LaFleur (pers. comm.). It's not always possible to refresh every app, but in those cases news organizations should make clear that the apps are not being updated.
- *They err on the side of simplicity.* When building the Stradivarius feature, the *Telegraph*'s Mark Oliver said the goal was to appeal to novices and experts alike: "Is this going to be complicated for a twelve-year-old kid to navigate their way through, or is it going to be easy? At the same time, for a classical music genius, is it going to be too basic for them to enjoy it?" Ultimately the team opted for an approach based on simplicity. "I think you can get a bit carried away with making it into a game," Oliver said. "You can spend, like, six months building a project and people might lose interest after the first level" (pers. comm.).
- *They recognize that games should not be a chore for the staff.* Over time, as momentum for Qrank faded within the *Texas Tribune* newsroom, the game became a burden for Reeve Hamilton. "It was something on top of my daily duties that I didn't get any credit for," he said

(pers. comm.). News games can whip up enthusiasm in, and deepen the loyalty of, core users, but the games take work and can drain energy from other journalistic pursuits. When it's clear that the energy has waned, it's time to move on.

• *They are mindful that interactive features can boost the bottom line.* The *Christian Science Monitor*'s multipliers have been traffic magnets, drawing page views galore and generating enough online ad revenue to help subsidize more serious journalism. The *Texas Tribune*'s public salary database created its own digital ad inventory by giving each salary entry an individual page on the site. However, page views are not the only way to make participatory news features pay. The *Tribune* also seeks out sponsors for contests like Session Scramble and earns several thousand dollars a month from Google by adding sponsored microsurveys to its databases, which earn the *Tribune* a nickel each time a user answers a question. And the *New York Times*, which already sells premium crossword subscriptions, has "some very ambitious ideas around what we can do with games," according to its new CEO, Mark Thompson (McDuling 2013). When newsrooms create interactive platforms that fulfill readers' needs—practical, whimsical, or otherwise—they must somehow find a way to capture that value. Their survival depends upon it.

At its finest, interactive journalism can provide a riveting and memorable experience that you can't wait to share with your friends. That happened in December 2013 when the *New York Times* published an interactive news quiz called How Y'all, Youse, and You Guys Talk (Katz and Andrews 2013). The quiz created a personal dialect map based on participants' answers to which-word-do-you-use questions, such as whether one drinks from a water fountain or a bubbler. The interactive feature was published with only ten days left in 2013, but it still rocketed to the top of the *Times*'s list of most-visited stories for the entire calendar year. "Think about that," Robinson Meyer, the *Atlantic*'s technology editor, writes. "A news app, a piece of software about the news made by in-house developers, generated more clicks than any article" (2014). Astonishing things can happen when a news organization invites its audience to participate.

5

Sustaining Engaged Journalism

Measuring and Monetizing the Audience Relationship

Even when all cameras are turned off at KTVK-3TV in Phoenix, the on-air talent remains under the spotlight. The station's social media manager, Lori Santa Maria, developed an elaborate system to measure the Twitter and Facebook activity of reporters, anchors, meteorologists, and the station's own accounts. Santa Maria's system relies on third-party software to keep tabs on more than four dozen social media accounts, tracking the total number of posts and tweets, and, more important, the acts of engagement they trigger from viewers—replies and re-tweets on Twitter; shares, likes, and comments on Facebook; and several other metrics. She sums up the results in a monthly Social Media Scorecard that is prominently displayed on a monitor in the newsroom, including bar charts that identify leaders and laggards. "Once you get it out in a newsroom, it gets kind of competitive," Santa Maria said. She also sends individual monthly reports to each journalist and a supervisor.

The idea behind the scorecards, Santa Maria said, is to motivate the station's journalists to get in the habit of engaging viewers throughout their entire workday. "Don't spend eight hours a day on three minutes for TV," she said. "Tell us along the way what you're doing" (pers. comm.). The scorecards are just one example of how news outlets are searching for ways to effectively measure digital success.

Page views and unique visitors have long been the default barometers for tracking the reach of an online news story, but those metrics merely document one-way consumption, akin to a newspaper's circulation figures or a television station's Nielsen ratings. Measuring the degree to which digital news engages readers, prompting some sort of meaningful response, is much trickier. In 2012 J-Lab surveyed 278 digital news start-ups whose responses made clear that they are desperately seeking more authoritative methods to measure engagement. "Better tools can be built, online publishers need to be trained to use them, and site supporters—from funders to advertisers—should require better measures of engagement and impact," Schaffer and Polgreen write (2012:35). I often encountered this sentiment during my visits to newsrooms. "I need to find better tools to watch and understand what people are responding to," said Amelia Newcomb, foreign editor of the *Christian Science Monitor* (pers. comm.). In this chapter I consider different ways news organizations are measuring the effectiveness of their engagement efforts—and, in some cases, how they convert that engagement into revenue.

SO MANY METRICS, SO LITTLE CONSENSUS

Chartbeat. Omniture. Geckoboard. SocialFlow. These are some of the more ubiquitous analytical services by which newsrooms monitor their web, mobile, and social media metrics, with real-time results often displayed on monitors for all employees to see.

Many newsrooms draw from the same usual suspects to measure digital and social reach: page views, unique visitors, re-tweets, shares, comments. But *Philly.com*, Internet home to the *Philadelphia Inquirer* and *Philadelphia Daily News*, was one of the earliest news outlets to develop its own "engagement index" incorporating seven components: frequency of clicks, duration of visit, "recency" of return visits, loyalty, direct visitors, interaction, and participation. Comments and shares make up only a small part of *Philly.com*'s index. "A lot of our users don't comment or share stories," said Chris Meares, senior data analyst for *Philly.com*. "But we have people—45 percent—[who] come back more than once a day, and those people are very engaged" (Beckett 2010).

Digital analytics provide unprecedented insights into how readers experience the news. After reading a story today, do readers come back tomorrow? How long do they visit? And do they interact with the content? "We actually know what people are reading for the first time ever," said David Clark Scott, online director at the *Christian Science Monitor*. "I now can tell exactly how many people are reading a story at a given moment. I can see that in real time, and that changes how I approach the story" (pers. comm.).

Still, "there's no one metric to rule them all," said Matt Thompson, an editorial product manager at NPR. "Just think about how different experiences are becoming" (pers. comm.). With a niche project like, say, the NPR science desk's initiative on global health, success might be measured in part by looking at the quality and quantity of comments from the specialized community of researchers in that area. That's a different metric altogether from the latest Arbitron ratings or podcast downloads for *Wait Wait . . . Don't Tell Me!* or *Fresh Air*.

At MLive newspapers across Michigan, reporters get daily "dashboard" reports with the site's top headlines as measured by page views, Facebook referrals, and other reader behavior trends. Editors get the same reports three times daily. The reports are "an instant critique," said John Hiner, MLive's vice president of content. "It used to be that your responsibility was pleasing your editor. Now, [reporters'] work is being instantly evaluated by an audience" (pers. comm.). Managers are aware of each reporter's page views per post, as well as their degree of interaction with online commenters, among other web metrics. "We do find that the more engaged a reporter is, the more engaged their users are," said Colleen Stone, MLive's statewide director of digital operations (pers. comm.).

Stone said MLive also closely tracks readers' actions, including comments and social media shares. But another key metric is time spent on the site: "How many one-and-dones do we have, and how many people are sticking around?" Time spent on site, however, is becoming an increasingly skewed metric as more readers get in the habit of quickly scanning the news on their mobile devices.

David Ho, mobile editor of the *Wall Street Journal*, agrees that metrics are particularly difficult to gauge with smartphones and tablets. "It's tricky how you measure the session," Ho said. "Does your session break when someone multitasks?" And if a story includes other elements, such as slide shows, videos, or interactive elements, how do you measure the overall success of that story? "A story isn't just a story, it's an experience," Ho said. "There are so many different elements to it" (pers. comm.).

Return visits are the driving measure of engagement at the *Christian Science Monitor*, where editors define a loyal reader as someone who visits their site at least nine times per month. To distinguish levels of reader commitment, *Monitor* editors often refer to a funnel, with casual web visitors at the larger end of the funnel and subscribers to the weekly magazine at the tip. "We want to find ways of engaging people all the way up that funnel," said Marshall Ingwerson, the *Monitor*'s current editor. "The first step is just to get someone to come back—the return visitor" (pers. comm.). The Investigative News Network, a consortium of nonprofit news organizations, developed a similar funnel that begins with site visitors, then progresses to brand recognitions, social media followers, e-mail subscribers, commenters, contributors, and, finally, financial contributors and members (Osder and Campwala 2012).

In mid-2011 Chicago Public Media (WBEZ-FM) began to systematically tally its numbers in five areas of engagement: station partnerships and collaborations; audience commenting online; audience-generated content (including call-ins, uploads, and e-mails); sharing of stories through social media and e-mail; and attendance at events (Richardson 2011). To gauge audience commenting, for instance, the station created the WBEZ Consume:Converse Ratio, which compares story page views to the number of times audience members shared their views publicly. Initial monthly results showed that the ratio was roughly four hundred page views for every audience comment. But what exactly does that mean? "The data doesn't tell us much right now, but I think over time it will," said Daniel Ash, WBEZ's vice president of strategic communications. Ash said the new engagement metrics would become more meaningful to WBEZ when the station is able to make monthly and annual comparisons.

Ash acknowledged, however, that WBEZ's new metrics still didn't reveal much about what types of stories "get hot" with radio listeners and online readers (pers. comm.). Along those lines an experiment by NPR Digital Services found that fans who follow the network on Facebook were most likely to share a locally focused story if it fell into one of nine categories, including "place explainers," "curiosity stimulators," "provocative controversies," and "awe-inspiring visuals" (Athas and Gorman 2012). Previous NPR research had shown that elements of emotion and positivity caused Facebook fans to share stories and that story headlines were an extremely important factor in deciding whether to share.

PAGE VIEWS: THE EVER-PRESENT METRIC

Whatever metrics newsrooms devise to measure engagement, the statistics inevitably will be considered in tandem with page views—the sheer volume of clicks. Digital display advertising has long been dictated by the cost per mille, the rate paid by advertisers for every one thousand views. There is no similar industry standard to measure and monetize engagement: "Despite an overwhelming number of available metrics, page views still dominate" (Stroud 2014).

"We're in a culture here where page views influence a lot," said Ray Brewer, sports editor of the *Las Vegas Sun*. "The bottom line is, we want to please our readers and please our bosses." Brewer said page views help guide his decisions about how best to deploy a staff of three sports-writers. The *Sun* sports desk, thinned by layoffs in recent years, has narrowed its main areas of coverage to fighting (UFC and boxing); the University of Nevada, Las Vegas; and local high school sports. "We've tried to go cover every ball that's bouncing in southern Nevada," Brewer said. "Not only was it not possible, we didn't have the manpower. So now we're going to only cover the balls that bounce the highest. We've got to pick our spots" (pers. comm.).

A growing chorus of journalists and media critics warns that focus-ing too much on page views can lead to news decisions that pander to the lowest common denominator. In August 2013 the satirical news site *The Onion* lampooned Meredith Artley, *CNN.com*'s managing edi-tor, for the site's decision to lead its home page with a story about Miley Cyrus's lewd antics at the Video Music Awards (Roderick 2013). Even Tony Haile, CEO of Chartbeat, railed against "the obsession with pageviews" in a guest post for *paidContent*, a site covering the busi-ness of digital news.[1] Haile argues that page views merely measure a story's provocativeness and do not indicate whether a piece can hold an audience:

> What matters is building an audience who knows who you are, likes what you do and most importantly comes back to you again and again. Your commercial team isn't selling Mercedes on that random spike of pageviews from Lithuania (an audience who will never return), they are selling a loyal returning audi-ence and the growth of that audience will be the test of sustain-ability and success. (Haile 2013)[2]

Several months after Haile's *paidContent* post, Haile and Chartbeat unveiled a redesigned dashboard that allows publishers to monitor their site visitors according to segments—new, returning, and loyal. "For a long time now, I have been somewhat frustrated by the way we as an industry have been chasing traffic," Haile told *TechCrunch* in an interview. "We've been buying traffic, using linkbait headlines, throwing in slideshows, all because it's driving more traffic, more traffic, more traffic. But the real goal is not to build traffic, it's to build an audience" (Ha 2013).

Allison Linn, a senior economics reporter for *NBC News Digital*, couldn't agree more. "To some people, *engagement* is just a code word for *traffic*," Linn said. "We want to build a loyal readership. We don't think the drive-bys matter as much" (pers. comm.). However, earning those return visits from loyal readers can be a calculated gamble based on editorial intuition, even in a world with infinite metrics. When I visited the *Daily Post* in North Wales, the newspaper's head of audience engagement, Helen Harper, hosted a real-time "Ask the Expert" online chat with a local university lecturer about early childhood parenting techniques. I asked Alison Gow, the paper's editor, what results she was expecting from the parenting chat. Gow said she wasn't concerned about the quantity of page views but hoped the chat would draw a high-quality audience inclined to return to the *Daily Post* for future coverage about parenting issues. "It's a small audience, but it's massively engaged," Gow said. "So from an advertiser perspective, I'm not getting the whole of the site here, but what I am getting is a whole bunch of people who actually really care" (pers. comm.).

Upworthy, the news aggregation site whose tantalizing headlines and visuals aim to make content go viral, announced a new metric in 2014 called "attention minutes" to better measure audience engagement. According to *Nieman Journalism Lab*, "the goal is to blend traditional eyeball-counting metrics with figures that more accurately measure engagement, or how much the audience actually likes the content that they're making" (O'Donovan 2014).

Editors of hyperlocal news sites say another important metric is perhaps the most old-fashioned one of all: word of mouth. "I live online, but it's still probably the metric that matters the most: Are people talking about you?" said Tracy Record, editor of the *West Seattle Blog* (pers. comm.). Paul Bass, editor of the *New Haven (CT) Independent*, said he's skeptical of any algorithm that purports to measure online engagement. "It's all fake, in my opinion," Bass said, likening web analytics to runaway pinball scores. "You've got to live somewhere and do the work. Everything else is just pinball" (pers. comm.).[3]

THE "HEALTHY TENSION"
BETWEEN REACH AND QUALITY

The *Christian Science Monitor*'s John Yemma freely acknowledges that the struggle to attract page views while still producing insightful journalism contributed to a "healthy tension" in his newsroom when he was editor from 2008 to 2014. That tension, Yemma said, probably will never go away. Since dropping its daily print edition in 2009, the *Monitor* has emphasized multipliers—list stories and quizzes that tempt readers to click on multiple pages—while also using techniques to draw more clicks through search engine optimization, or SEO. "You need reach, but you need quality," Yemma said. "You've got to be careful not to just celebrate traffic numbers" (pers. comm.).

Yet even as Yemma told me this, a silver bell with a black handle rested atop a cubicle partition in the *Monitor* newsroom, waiting to be rung by a web staffer each day at the moment when the website hits one million page views. Eight months earlier, on February 22, 2012, the bell rang more often than usual when the *Monitor* surpassed four million daily page views for the first time. The next day an editor sent Yemma an e-mail complaining about the ever-present bell, saying it made some of the paper's journalists feel cheap.[4] The bell ringing would continue, but Yemma acknowledged the apprehension. "SEO has its downsides, if you're only going to be about chasing trends," Yemma said. "But it depends on how much you're investing in that, and whether you can at least include a modicum of your brand promise." By design, he said, the *Monitor*'s list stories don't highlight the ten hottest places to pick up dates this weekend or the ten best celebrity hairdos. More common headlines are "Ralph Waldo Emerson: 12 Quotes on His Birthday" or "4 Ways US Can Boost Cyber Security."

Scott, the *Monitor*'s online director, said the bell ringing is somewhat of a newsroom joke, but it does carry symbolic significance. "It's a reminder of reach," he said. "And frankly, for us, more page views means more jobs saved" (pers. comm.).

MONETIZING ENGAGEMENT

Journalists often cringe at the word *monetize* because they regard their profession as a sacred public service, not a campaign to sell widgets. But in an era when downsized newsrooms are asked to do more work with fewer resources, efforts to engage readers must at least partly be measured according to their return on investment. "There are a lot of people we are engaging with that I doubt we can monetize," said Frank Blethen, publisher of the *Seattle Times*, singling out two types of readers in particular: Online commenters and visitors to sports blogs. "We've got our baseball guys, our football guys all spending this time blogging away, costing us a lot of money, and there's no monetization," Blethen said.

The *Times* tried to capture some of this lost value in the spring of 2013 when it introduced a metered paywall, which allows online visitors to view a limited number of articles for free before requiring a subscription (Boardman 2013). Blethen said his paper's plans for digital subscriptions were inspired in part by the success of the *New York Times*, which introduced a metered paywall in March 2011 (Lee 2012). "The *New York Times* did the industry a wonderful favor by getting out there in front of this," Blethen said. "You always wonder if a local marketplace like ours, a regional marketplace, can translate the way the *New York Times* readership does. People always talk about the *Wall Street Journal* and the wonderful job they've done with paid subscriptions, completely ignoring the fact that 95 percent were expense-account paid. It's not really apples to oranges" (pers. comm.).

Adopting a paywall can fundamentally change the way a newsroom approaches engagement. In April 2013 the *Telegraph* became the United Kingdom's first general interest newspaper to adopt a metered paywall (Greenslade 2013), allowing twenty free views a month before requiring users to sign up for a one-month trial subscription. Three months later, when I visited the *Telegraph* in London, Kate Day, then the social media and engagement editor, told me the paywall had forced a shift in the newsroom's culture of engagement. "What has changed is that just getting volume and no loyalty is no longer as valuable," Day said. Instead, she said, the *Telegraph* was more closely tracking metrics that help explain what gets people to click through and subscribe—for instance, the last page visited by users before they sign up for a subscription. "It's great marketing if you have a story go viral, but we're not pushing for volume in the way that, say, *Huffington Post* might be in their social accounts," Day said. "We're much more pushing for interaction and engagement with people, and trying to build loyalty at every step."

Overall traffic figures still matter, Day said. But as the statistics come in, page views and unique visitors are viewed "hand in hand" with new subscribers. And on social media channels, she said, the *Telegraph* strives not just to extend the reach of its stories but also to nudge readers to subscribe. "I see social, really, as the bridge between taking people from the outside world, general browsers, and trying to convert them into subscribers," Day said. On the *Telegraph* site itself reader engagement tools like polls and comments are designed to keep subscribers coming back. "It's a useful way to keep [subscribers] feeling as though they're getting value from the site," Day said. "Because if each time they're interacting in some way, spending a little bit longer, that will encourage them to subscribe again next month" (pers. comm.).

The quest to instill reader loyalty was a recurring theme during my visits to news organizations. Maintaining a base of engaged, loyal readers—not just fickle drive-by traffic—is a matter of business survival at a time when the news industry is beginning to rely less on mass advertising and more on individual consumers as a primary source of revenue (see Christensen, Skok, and Allworth 2012; Doctor 2012; Coscarelli 2012). Page views, re-tweets, and Facebook likes can serve as a useful barometer of overall reader interest. But for paywalled news sites—even those with a metered paywall like the *Telegraph*—the ultimate sign of engagement is when readers pull out their credit cards to subscribe.[5]

At advertising-driven sites that offer all content for free, volume remains a key element of the engagement equation. At *NBCNews. com* (formerly *MSNBC.com*), which attracts more than one billion page views per month, its managing editor's idea of engagement is filling readers' information needs with a steady flow of concise, timely, original stories. "What matters to the reader ultimately is, did you give them something new today?" Michael Wann said. During his first year as managing editor, Wann said, traffic doubled on the site's U.S. News section, while costs fell by 40 percent. His recipe? Getting reporters to write more quick-hit stories with an original angle and a crisp headline, reducing the site's reliance on wire services.

Wann said he doubted that *NBCNews.com* would add paywalls anytime soon, if ever. He acknowledged that rates for digital display ads were falling, but said *NBC News* was expanding its portfolio of digital advertising products to include more emphasis on video ads and customized campaigns that go beyond the standard banner ads (pers. comm.).

Regional and local news organizations also are betting on the free click-fueled model. Six months after MLive Media Group cut staff, reduced print delivery, and adopted a webcentric "hub" workflow, John Hiner, the chain's vice president of content, told me that *MLive* was seeing double-digit increases in its audience compared to the previous year, although he declined to be more specific.[6] He also said the new system was producing more page views, unique visitors, and page views per post (pers. comm.). In December 2013 an executive from *MLive*'s parent company, Advance Publications, sent employees a year-end letter delivering good news: most of the chain's retooled newsrooms, he said, "are rapidly increasing their digital revenue and approaching the point where digital ad revenue growth will be larger than print ad revenue declines" (Edmonds 2013).

In addition to *MLive* I visited several newsrooms pursuing the free page view–driven model, including those of the *Christian Science Monitor* and Digital First Media newspapers in Connecticut and Michigan. Critics have branded this model "hamster-wheel" journalism, since its commercial success depends largely on constantly producing enough content to draw a high volume of clicks. Dean Starkman, an editor at *Columbia Journalism Review*, argues that the real problem behind the free model followed by Advance and Digital First "isn't *merely* that it has failed to prove it can support quality journalism. The problem is, it is designed for the opposite. Digital first? Absolutely. But this version? No, thanks" (Starkman 2012).

Debates pitting paywalls against page views often gloss over the perspective that each strategy can succeed if it earns the attention of an engaged, loyal audience. The *New York Times*, *Telegraph*, and other outlets that have seen success with metered paywalls deserve credit for engaging their subscribers to the point they are willing to pay.[7] But Yemma, the architect of the *Monitor*'s transformation from a daily print newspaper to a web-first newsroom, disputes the idea that courting page views amounts to hamster-wheel journalism. "We will always have arguments, and should have arguments, within the world of journalism and within our specific newsroom over whether seeking greater reach means that you're somehow sacrificing quality. I think it's really reductionist, I think it's oversimplifying, to call that hamster journalism or to act as though newspapers have never been about reach." For much of the twentieth century, he said, newspapers widened their popular appeal through classified ads, coupons, sports coverage, comics, and other features that helped subsidize coverage of statehouses and city halls.

Before the *Monitor* abandoned its daily print edition in 2009 and went web first, Yemma said, it was often called "the best newspaper that nobody's ever read." "We've developed a web strategy which is helping to spread *Monitor* journalism more widely," Yemma said, adding, "which is good for us, because it's bringing more people into contact with our brand." He continued:

> There have always been people in the world of journalism who have been critical of sensationalism. And, listen, the *Monitor* was founded not to be sensationalistic. And so I understand the impulse and the desire not to go too far down that road. But I also think it's looking at the world in too stark a contrast to think that by writing short, fast, in-the-moment pieces, you have totally sacrificed quality. I think news organizations have always done short, fast, in-the-moment pieces. (pers. comm.)

At the same time, to maintain their credibility as a public trust, news organizations must recognize when to disregard metrics and simply investigate a story that nobody else will tell. "If it's important to our public-service mission," Kathy Best, editor of the *Seattle Times*, said, "we don't care about page views" (pers. comm.).

BEYOND PAYWALLS AND PAGE VIEWS

Regardless of the business model, an engaged news organization creates value by demonstrating relevance to its audience. "If people are interacting with the content, I think it's valuable," said Dan Gilgoff, cofounder of *CNN.com*'s *Belief Blog*. "In my mind the goals of the business model and the goals of journalism sync up in a meaningful way" (pers. comm.). And if news outlets show advertisers and sponsors that they can deliver a valuable audience, the potential to monetize that engagement extends far beyond paywalls and page views. Traditional media and digital news start-ups alike increasingly are turning to supplementary revenue streams to support their journalism, including custom advertising campaigns, corporate sponsorships, live events, and services. "It's not necessarily just enough to support the business just through the editorial content," said John Cook, cofounder of *GeekWire*. "You have to have five or six mini businesses connected to your editorial business" (Wolf 2013). *GeekWire*, founded in 2011, became profitable within two years, propelled by a business model that incorporates digital advertising, events, sponsorships, memberships, a jobs board, a service provider directory, and even a partnership that equips small start-ups with health insurance.

In a similar vein the *New York Times*'s new president and CEO, Mark Thompson, told *New York Magazine* in a 2013 interview that the paper was developing a "growing suite of paid products" to evolve beyond advertising and draw more revenue from the full "engagement curve" of *Times* readers, ranging from paid subscribers to people who click a single link (Hagan 2013). Ken Doctor, an industry analyst, is encouraged by the growing interest shown by the *Times* and other news organizations in diversifying their revenue streams: "We're finally moving beyond sales of omnibus subscriptions only—*take 'em or leave 'em*—to a world of delivering the best, timely content to the right reader at the right time and being paid for it" (Doctor 2013).

As I have explored here, the *Christian Science Monitor* boosted page views and web advertising dollars through such techniques as search engine optimization and multiplier quizzes and stories. But the *Monitor's* business model also includes a weekly print newsmagazine (also available in digital form), syndication, subscriptions to a daily news briefing, and its longtime Monitor Breakfast conversation series in Washington, D.C. Yemma reports that the *Monitor's* fiscal year ending April 30, 2012, was the "best we've done financially since 1963," although that result was partly achieved through lower staff costs. Still, Yemma said, the *Monitor* has cut in half its annual subsidy from the Church of Christ, Scientist, and is aiming to break even by 2017 (2012a).

About a year after *Quartz* was launched in 2012, the global business site sought to create value by improving the commenting experience for its readers. *Quartz* created an annotations system that allows registered users to submit comments; once approved by editors, the comments appear next to individual paragraphs in the margins of stories, instead of in a free-for-all at the bottom, the most common arrangement. And each time a reader clicks on an individual paragraph's comment box, a message informs that a corporate sponsor is presenting these cleaner, more civil, annotations: "Instead of monetizing the content, *Quartz* is monetizing the act of commenting" (Sternberg 2013). Meanwhile the nonprofit *ProPublica* announced plans in 2014 to monetize the data used in its investigations through the ProPublica Data Store, charging journalists an initial rate of $200 and academics $2,000 "for datasets that are the result of significant expenditures of our time and effort" (Klein and Grochowski Jones 2014).[8]

For established niche sites with passionate followings, deepening the relationship with core readers can present an opportunity to generate more revenue. A dozen years after it began during the Florida recount of the 2000 U.S. presidential election, the left-leaning political blog *Talking Points Memo* introduced a membership service called *TPM Prime* in 2012. For $50 a year subscribers receive access to ad-free articles, live chats with editors and reporters, members-only message boards, long-form pieces, and a "new to you" feature showing what stories have been published since you last checked the site. *TPM Prime* "treats readers as though they are special and gives them added benefits in addition to the regular free news content, while a paywall or traditional subscription simply charges everyone the same amount for the same content" (Ingram 2012).

News outlets with large social media followings can convert attention from those platforms into revenue as well. The *Denver Post*, owned by Digital First Media, capitalized on the popularity of the new Broncos quarterback Peyton Manning through its Facebook Fandemonium contest, which offered the *Post*'s Facebook fans the chance to win club-level tickets and autographed footballs if they followed sponsors on Facebook and signed up for e-mail lists. "It's driving more likes to us, it's driving more traffic for our websites, and it's selling ads," said Steve Buttry, former digital transformation editor at Digital First Media. "Win, win, win. It's where engagement and monetization come together" (pers. comm.). According to a summary published by the International News Media Association in 2013, the Fandemonium campaign produced nearly 72,000 new Facebook fans and more than 90,000 e-mail database entries for participating sponsors throughout the 2012 Broncos season while adding more than 33,000 fans to the *Post*'s own following on Facebook. "What newspapers and broadcasters, magazines—all traditional media—have always sold our business customers is the attention of a trusted audience," Buttry said. "Engagement increases attention, and it increases trust. . . . I think, more and more, rather than just selling eyeballs, we need to be selling product for businesses and getting more meaningful experiences than just, 'Hey, here's a thousand eyeballs, how much will you give me for them?'"[9]

Nonprofit news organizations are similarly searching for entrepreneurial ways to convert engagement into revenue. As Meghann Farnsworth of the Center for Investigative Reporting explained, attracting an engaged audience on social media channels can help boost the bottom line in other ways: "If we continue to get likes on Facebook and we suddenly have a large amount, we can then go to sponsors or donors and say, 'Hey, look at all these people who are engaged with us. Help us do this more. Donate to us'" (pers. comm.). When industry groups and community organizations invite top editors from the *Texas Tribune* to speak at private functions, the *Tribune* usually asks for an honorarium in the form of a donation. "There are ways that you can create revenue streams out of the work that we do that aren't worthy of a wince or anything to be ashamed of," said Evan Smith, the *Tribune*'s CEO. "I think, rather, it's an attempt to figure out, where are the opportunities for us to attach dollars to the work that we do, to enable us to do the work that we do?" (pers. comm.).

Clayton Christensen, a Harvard Business School professor, and his coauthors argue that as news organizations continue to search for ways to convert engagement into revenue, "they should ask whether their organization is doing such an outstanding job of satisfying consumers' needs that consumers will pay for their content" (Christensen, Skok, and Allworth 2012:12). This mantra also should be ever present in the minds of individual journalists. While it may be uncomfortable for reporters to think about the commercial value of their work, the profession's changing business model requires filling a need for the audience in a much more direct way than ever before.

A fifteen-second ESPN commercial called "Room Service" captures this idea more succinctly than perhaps anything else I encountered while researching and writing this book. The 2012 video, which promotes the network's Sunday *NFL Countdown* program, is set on an island resort. Adam Schefter and Chris Mortensen, reporters cast as bellhops, wheel a room-service cart up to a guest's room. When the guest—a New England Patriots fan—answers the door, Mortensen pulls away a silver food dome to unveil the main course: a handwritten note informing the guest that the star receiver Wes Welker "is doubtful for today's game." Schefter extends his palm toward the guest for a tip, noting that he and Mortensen "haven't even put it on Twitter yet." The guest obliges, pulling a wadded bill from his robe pocket. Schefter accepts, and the information transaction is complete.

The commercial is a joke, but behind the humor is an unmistakable message: Fill a need for your audience, and the money will follow. There is no shame in journalists' creating value that audiences will pay for.

MEASURING AND MONETIZING
ENGAGEMENT: COMMON ELEMENTS
OF PROACTIVE APPROACHES

When legacy media dominated the news landscape, newspapers, broadcasters, and the mass advertisers who supported them were content to measure audiences with the latest figures from the Audit Bureau of Circulations or ratings from Nielsen and Arbitron.[10] Even today these traditional metrics still hold significant weight. But as the journalism industry becomes more dependent on revenue from individual consumers instead of advertisers, it is becoming critically important for any news organization to directly measure how well it is engaging its audiences and to understand how those efforts contribute to the bottom line. Newsrooms that proactively measure and monetize engagement follow a number of common practices:

• *They define success.* News organizations are understandably clamoring for better ways to measure engagement (Schaffer and Polgreen 2012). But instead of waiting for that elusive catchall audience metric, newsrooms should take the initiative to define and measure their own success. *Philly.com*'s Engagement Index, WBEZ-FM's Consume:Converse Ratio, KTVK-3TV's Social Media Scorecards, and Upworthy's attention minutes all are examples of newsrooms' developing their own systems to track engagement. Their systems may not be perfect, but they reflect a focused institutional mission and establish a baseline for success.

• *They identify metrics that reflect their mission.* Whatever indicators a news organization monitors, the most important metrics should be tied to its ultimate financial mission. For regional news organizations like the *Seattle Times* or the *Boston Globe*, time spent on site is a telling metric, because people who live in a given area are more inclined to bookmark a news site's home page to stay abreast of the latest news, sports, weather, and traffic. However, readers have a different relationship with national and international news organizations like the *Christian Science Monitor*, where return visits and depth of visit are the biggest metrics. Yemma explained that each time a *Monitor* visitor returns to the site, "they're coming back into engagement with us, and if they do that, the more times they do that per month, the more they seem to have an affinity with our brand," which can lead to deeper forms of engagement. Adding a paywall, meanwhile, can change the benchmarks for success even further—when the *Telegraph* installed a metered paywall, it began to focus less on page views and more on metrics that shed light on what types of stories get readers to subscribe.

• *They make sure the newsroom understands how engagement fuels financial survival.* At the *Daily Post* in North Wales, I asked the paper's new head of audience engagement, Helen Harper, about how her role contributes to her employer's financial success. "Your average journalist, that probably doesn't cross their minds, to be perfectly honest," Harper said. She explained that she does work directly with the advertising department on special supplements. But aside from that, she said, "personally, I'm thinking more about engagement, getting people to be active in conversations online and get involved with the paper" (pers. comm.). I often encountered this sentiment during my newsroom visits, and it's understandable, given the long history of separation of journalistic and business operations. But at a time when building digital loyalty is becoming so intrinsic to news organizations' financial survival, it is crucial that journalists begin to better understand the commercial relevance of their work—and buy in to the idea that successful engagement can help pay for more journalism.

• *They back up digital initiatives with training.* Asking newsroom employees to fundamentally change the way they approach their jobs is no small undertaking. Dan Owen, executive editor for digital at the *Daily Post*, said appropriate training is essential if employers want journalists to rearrange their workflow around digital platforms and social media. Under the *Daily Post*'s "Newsroom 3.0" reorganization, Owen said, journalists have been trained to tell stories in real time on the breaking news blog, write more web stories, and shoot videos and photos with mobile devices, among other new responsibilities. "We're responsible for making sure that people have those skill sets," Owen said. "It's all very well for us to sit here and have this idealistic world of how we'd like things to operate, but unless we are giving people the skills in order to be able to fulfill the roles in the way that we want them to, then it's pretty much pie in the sky" (pers. comm.). Indeed a 2013 survey of more than one thousand U.S. journalists found that more than two-thirds of the respondents wanted more training to improve their digital skills (Willnat and Weaver 2014:23).

• *They stay flexible.* In an era of constant innovation the benchmarks for success often change. "What success looks like in engagement is continually evolving," concludes a report by the University of Missouri's Reynolds Journalism Institute. "Once you've figured out Twitter, the world will be on to something else. When you've made inroads with a specific group of people in your community, you'll be starting over with another" (Mayer and Stern 2011:2). When crafting an engagement strategy, news organizations need to select meaningful metrics, track them closely, and, when necessary, adjust them. "Newsrooms need to embrace the kind of number crunching more common to marketers," argues Raju Narisetti, a News Corporation executive (2013). They also must build in the ability to adapt quickly and embrace shifting definitions of success.

Conclusion

After decades of delivering disengaged one-way messages to mass audiences, journalists are directly engaging their readers, viewers, listeners, and—especially—digital users like never before. To be effective engaged journalism must actively consider the needs of an audience and wholeheartedly embrace constant interaction with that audience. When executed well, engagement can improve a newsroom's journalism, deepen audience loyalty, and generate revenue.

While visiting more than two dozen news organizations and conducting more than one hundred interviews between May 2012 and July 2013, I encountered an extensive array of audience engagement strategies that were, at their core, driven by five common principles: connecting with audiences in person; digitally interacting with audiences at every step; serving niche audiences; empowering audiences to satisfy their own curiosity; and measuring effectiveness and capturing value. These guiding principles, which I have described at length here, can provide a framework for news organizations as they work to develop strategies for practicing engaged journalism.

I also learned that while engaged journalism can enrich a news organization's relationship with its audience, it brings trade-offs as journalists adjust their traditional work routines. The most common challenge voiced by the journalists I interviewed was the perpetual balancing act between basic newsgathering and an ever-growing list of additional digital duties. "We're still struggling between the traditional and the digital," said Emily Olson, managing editor of the *Register Citizen* in Torrington, Connecticut (pers. comm.). The *Register Citizen* has been a celebrated pioneer in audience engagement for Digital First Media, going so far as to open its offices to the public with the Open Newsroom. But with just four reporters and two editors for the daily paper, Olson told me she works sixty to seventy hours a week and wishes she had still more time to work with young reporters. "We've all taken on more," said Olson, who would later become the newspaper's community editor. "I still have a lot of hope that things are going to work, but I'm tired." Olson is not alone. In 2013 Indiana University researchers conducted online interviews with 1,080 U.S. journalists and found that nearly 60 percent thought that their profession is headed in the wrong direction, citing, among other factors, the downsizing of newsrooms and hasty reporting (Willnat and Weaver 2014:3). Also, as *CNN.com*'s Dan Gilgoff warned, news outlets should make sure that their digital engagement initiatives do not replace original watchdog reporting but remain supplementary to it (pers. comm.).

Despite the pitfalls, most journalists I interviewed for this book have come to approach audience engagement as not only a necessity but also an opportunity to reinvigorate their careers and bring more relevance to their work. I sought out these journalists precisely because they are tackling these challenges with energy and optimism, realizing that they can no longer afford to take their audience's attention for granted. "If you do a story and nobody says anything, does it matter?" asked Suki Dardarian, then managing editor of the *Seattle Times* and now senior managing editor and vice president of the *Star Tribune* in Minneapolis (pers. comm.). *NBCNews.com*'s Allison Linn said constantly interacting with readers infuses her work with a heightened sense of purpose. "From my perspective, as a person who wants to be in journalism for the next thirty years, I want people to see value in what I write," Linn said (pers. comm.).

Journalists who once felt content to mostly ignore the preferences of their audience may resent the rise of feel-good events, impassioned blog debates, and interactive news quizzes, considering them an unwelcome diversion from hard news. But where's the harm in those efforts if they manage to make journalism more relevant to audiences while also generating revenue that helps keep news organizations in business? Engagement is no threat to watchdog journalism; indeed, it can be its lifeblood.

Still, done well, engaged journalism is hard work. Every victory journalists might have in engaging their audience is quickly tempered by the somewhat sobering realization that they must find ways to maintain that success. On the morning of November 1, 2012, Dave Scott, the *Christian Science Monitor*'s online director, gave the other editors a detailed breakdown of a record-setting October with more than fifty million page views, a milestone achieved in large part through the popularity of reader quizzes tied to current events. "Good work, everybody!" Scott said. Minutes later, barely ten hours into the new month, Marshall Ingwerson, the managing editor, asked Scott: "How are we doing in November?" Engaged journalism is an odyssey that never truly ends.

NOTES

PREFACE

1. More than a decade later the Crown Hill Neighborhood Association published a detailed chronology on its website that captured the store's prominent role in shaping the neighborhood (Madden and Jacobsen 2010).
2. Indeed, this was a deliberate decision. In writing my story I chose to refer to the better-known Ballard neighborhood instead of the much smaller Crown Hill, because I thought Ballard would be a more recognizable reference point for readers scattered across the Puget Sound region. However, by failing to mention Crown Hill at all, I alienated the readers who were most passionate about this story.
3. The neighborhood association's chronology later noted that Crown Hill residents "had mixed feelings" about the QFC takeover and "many were slow to embrace the change" (Madden and Jacobsen 2010). My story failed to reflect that sentiment.
4. Many of these reader interactions occurred on now-defunct *Dallas Morning News* blog platforms called *From the Scene* and *Capitol Letters*, which were billed as "Digital Extras" in promo boxes that appeared next to my stories in the printed newspaper. The term *Digital Extra* has since been phased out by the *News*, whose journalists increasingly have embraced social media, beat blogging, and other forms of reader engagement as part of their essential *regular* duties—not extra ones.
5. Best was managing editor when I interviewed her in June 2012. She was promoted to editor in September 2013.

6. In addition to their web and mobile offerings, many newspapers also offer electronic editions of each day's printed edition, distributed as PDFs with links to supplementary material. I did not closely examine e-editions for this book, which focuses on more direct forms of reader engagement, including face-to-face interaction, social media, and web and mobile platforms.

7. Journalists these days are more mobile than ever; keeping up with their job changes as this book went to press became a daunting task. Thus it seemed only sensible not to try, so I have provided journalists' titles as of the time I interviewed them. The exceptions I have made are for top editors who have moved on or retired, and digital editors who have gone on to big promotions, demonstrating that embracing digital journalism can lead to new career opportunities. Suki Dardarian and Kathy Best are good examples. Both held the title of managing editor when I interviewed them in June 2012. In September 2013 Best was promoted to editor, and in April 2014 Dardarian became senior managing editor and vice president of the *Minneapolis Star Tribune*.

8. I spent nine months tracking the early days of the *Texas Tribune* while reporting and writing an article for *Columbia Journalism Review* in 2009 and 2010. In August 2013, well after I had completed most of the research for this book, I began work as a Texas Tribune Fellow, funded by a grant from the Knight Foundation, as described in further detail in the acknowledgments.

INTRODUCTION: WHY ENGAGEMENT MATTERS

1. Some prominent and respected online journalism scholars intentionally avoid using the term *audience* because they believe it implies an antiquated view of the public as passive recipients rather than active contributors to the news ecosystem. These scholars instead refer to news consumers as "the former audience" (Gillmor 2004) or "the people formerly known as the audience" (Rosen 2006). I recognize and accept the value of that distinction. However, a growing body of research (Peck and Malthouse 2011; Singer et al. 2011; Napoli 2011; Osder and Campwala 2012; Schaffer and Polgreen 2012) recognizes that digital news audiences carry an expectation of participation and interactivity. I hope this book adds to that body of literature, and I use the cleaner term *audience* in that spirit.

2. Yemma stepped down as editor in 2014, though he continues to write for the *Monitor* as editor-at-large.

3. An illustration of the term's murkiness is Napoli's compilation of a table containing twenty definitions of *engagement* from 2006 and 2007 alone (2011:96–98).

4. A recent longitudinal study by Groves and Brown-Smith (2013) skillfully applies Napoli's model to document and assess various engagement strategies at the

Christian Science Monitor. The study also provides an excellent literature review of contemporary scholarship on engagement.

5. The company has sold its chain of mostly southern newspapers, a group of television and radio stations, and the *Boston Globe.* The News Media Group's holdings today include the *International New York Times* (formerly the *International Herald Tribune*) and the flagship paper.

6. In mid-2013 Boardman left Seattle to become dean of Temple University's School of Media and Communication.

7. Engaged journalism, as practiced in 2014 and beyond, builds (and improves) upon the tradition of the civic journalism and public journalism experiments of the 1990s. Since 2004 an important succession of works that explore the rising power of media consumers has documented this transition (Gillmor 2004; Jenkins 2006; Shirky 2008; Gillmor 2010; Peck and Malthouse 2011; Singer et. al 2011; Grueskin, Seave, and Graves 2011; Christensen, Skok, and Allworth 2012; C. W. Anderson 2013; Kennedy 2013a).

8. Among the more prolific and reliable journalism blogs chronicling these transformations on a daily basis are those at the websites www.niemanlab.org, www.gigaom.com, www.poynter.org, www.journalism.co.uk, www.cjr.org, www .digiday.com, and www.mashable.com.

1. FACE-TO-FACE ENGAGEMENT: HOW NEWS ORGANIZATIONS BUILD DIGITAL LOYALTY AND GENERATE REVENUE THROUGH THE "ORIGINAL PLATFORM"

1. This chapter is adapted from a conference paper originally presented at the International Symposium on Online Journalism in Austin, Texas (Batsell 2013). The chapter includes additional fieldwork that was not included in the conference paper.

2. In 2013 Flores returned to the *Seattle Times* as an assistant managing editor.

3. A series of critical blog posts in February 2014 prompted *Tribune* editors to announce a series of policy changes aimed at increasing transparency.

4. O'Shea's regrets about not devoting enough attention to business matters were similarly reflected by a majority of his peers surveyed in an extensive Pew Research Center study, which compiled responses from ninety-three nonprofit news organizations (Mitchell et al. 2013). The study found that 54 percent of responding organizations considered business, advertising, and fund-raising to be the area of greatest staffing need, compared with 39 percent who said editorial employees were the top need.

5. In chapter 5, I more closely examine how news organizations are measuring engagement.

2. NEWS AS CONVERSATION: NOT JUST INFORMING
BUT INVOLVING THE AUDIENCE

1. The Aurora experience would later inform the CNN *Belief Blog*'s news coverage when another tragedy occurred in December 2012. This time a mass shooting at an elementary school in Newtown, Connecticut, left twenty children and six staff members dead, prompting *Belief Blog* readers once again to openly question, defend, and debate the presence of God (Gilgoff and Marrapodi 2012).

2. Whether someone would recommend a product to a friend is, in fact, the chief factor that determines a brand's net promoter score—enthusiastic users who promote the brand to others, minus its passive consumers and its detractors—one of the most influential measures of customer loyalty in American business (see Reichheld 2003).

3. When I visited North Wales in July 2013, Gow was the *Daily Post*'s editor. Six months later, the paper's parent company, Trinity Mirror, promoted her to lead a digital innovation team for the British chain's regional newsrooms.

4. The hockey championship game lasted late into Saturday night. Ciokajlo later told me that, because of printing deadlines, the hockey game would not have made it into the Sunday paper even before the digitally focused overhaul that came along with the *Gazette*'s switch to MLive Media Group. But he said the *Gazette* learned from the readers' outcry and later made "serious accommodations" to hold print deadlines for some late-night Saturday college football games.

5. The Newsroom 3.0 campaign has since been rolled out across the United Kingdom by the *Daily Post*'s corporate parent, Trinity Mirror (McAthy 2013).

6. I wrote about the *Tribune*'s Kickstarter campaign for my fellowship blog, *News-Biz.org*.

7. To be fair, in the aftermath of the Boston bombings, reporting blunders also found their way into print media—the *New York Post* printed a photo on its cover of two men who had no connection to the attacks.

8. Also, in February 2012, when the *Press* posted a reader's photo of a confusing and hard-to-read school speed limit sign, the post received 101 likes, 114 shares, and 155 comments—which, newsroom staffers told me, prompted the city to change the sign.

9. When editors analyzed web traffic and social media patterns in the thick of the congressional race, they noticed that Fenster's @5thDistrictCT Twitter feed was generating @-mentions at twice the rate of the *Register*'s main Twitter handle (Buttry 2012).

10. *Monitor* readers can still post comments on Facebook, although Lane Brown, the social media manager, said she isn't shy about deleting them when readers are uncivil or off point. "The gauge we use is, is it moving the discussion along?" she

said. "We just want anybody who looks at it to say, okay, they're having a conversation" (pers. comm.).

11. I elaborate on my visits to newsrooms in the United Kingdom (the *Daily Post* in North Wales and the *Telegraph* in London) in greater detail on my *Texas Tribune* Fellowship blog, *News-Biz.org*.

12. Day was the *Telegraph*'s social media and engagement editor when I interviewed her in 2013.

3. MINING NICHE COMMUNITIES: SERVING TOPICAL AND HYPERLOCAL AUDIENCES THROUGH DIGITAL AND MOBILE PLATFORMS

1. *Vertical* is a marketing term that has crossed over into digital journalism as the news business has become more entrepreneurial. Steve Blank, the author, Stanford professor, and retired entrepreneur, defines a vertical market as "customers who identify themselves in a narrow industry or group of companies." Horizontal markets, in contrast, cut across a series of vertical markets (Blank 2009). Blank's definition describes how the term *vertical* is commonly used within the business world; the news industry applies the concept to identify communities of interest (topical or geographical) whose specialized information needs extend beyond what mass media outlets can provide.

2. Dana Chinn, an analytics expert and lecturer at USC's Annenberg School of Journalism, outlined the Lear Project's "verbs of engagement" during a presentation at the Online News Association conference in Atlanta in October 2013.

3. This chapter is an expansion of that article.

4. Alfano pointed out that the real-time scoring system also is available on the *SportsDayHS* website, where it is even more popular with users.

5. Curley, now editor of the *Orange County Register*, had a controversial four-year tenure as editor of *Greenspun Interactive*, the online arm of the *Sun*'s parent company. His audience-focused approach to digital journalism very much lives on at the paper, but his tenure included some expensive missteps, including the abrupt cancellation of a video and television initiative called 702.tv after just four months (see Kingsley 2010, 2012).

6. For more on the *Chicago News Cooperative*'s experience, see chapter 1.

7. Allbritton Communications does not publicly disclose specific financial results, and the percentage of revenue that comes from *Politico*'s weekday print edition is not known. But in mid-2013, when it was not yet seven years old, *Politico* was in full-fledged expansion mode with more than fifty active job openings, nineteen of which were for positions at *Politico Pro*.

8. The other major factor APME cited in selecting the *Times* for the innovation award was its Pulitzer-winning breaking news coverage of the Lakewood police shootings, described in more detail in chapter 2.

4. SEARCH, EXPLORE, PLAY: DRAWING READERS INTO JOURNALISM THROUGH INTERACTIVE EXPERIENCES

1. Participating news organizations included the Center for Public Integrity, Global Integrity, and Public Radio International. See the full project at http://www.stateintegrity.org.
2. Editors shared these internal statistics when I visited the *Monitor* newsroom in Boston in early November 2012.
3. Yemma shared these details when he visited my Digital Journalism class as a guest speaker on February 23, 2012.
4. The series, "On Shaky Ground," was a finalist for the 2012 Pulitzer Prize in local reporting and won the Scripps Howard National Journalism Award for public service.

5. SUSTAINING ENGAGED JOURNALISM: MEASURING AND MONETIZING THE AUDIENCE RELATIONSHIP

1. In 2012 *Gigaom* acquired *paidContent* and moved its media coverage to *Gigaom* in late 2013.
2. Chartbeat's prevailing metric is "concurrent visitors," which measures the total number of people actively visiting a site at any given moment.
3. In 2013 the Bill and Melinda Gates Foundation and the John S. and James L. Knight Foundation announced a $3.25 million project at the University of Southern California's Norman Lear Center to track media impact and develop "new ways to measure what matters" (Cieply 2013).
4. Yemma read this e-mail aloud to my Digital Journalism class without identifying the author.
5. Even if readers do not subscribe, emerging forms of digital advertising—such as programmatic buying and native advertising—depend on a news organization's ability to demonstrate evidence of relateionships with specific types of consumers (see Debelov 2014; Waldman 2014).
6. For more background on the controversial restructuring implemented by *MLive*'s parent company, Advance Publications, please see chapter 2. A more detailed

description of the Advance newsroom workflow is outlined in a memo leaked to the media insider blog *JimRomenesko.com* (Romenesko 2012).

7. By late 2013 the metered paywall—modeled by the *New York Times* and subsequently adopted by the *Telegraph* (London), *Washington Post*, *Seattle Times*, and others—was widely considered to be more effective than the all-or-nothing paywalls adopted and later abandoned by the likes of the *San Francisco Chronicle* and the *Dallas Morning News* (see Chittum 2013b; Indvik 2013).

8. *ProPublica* data sets for commercial use are subject to separately negotiated pricing.

9. In late 2014, Facebook announced it would ban businesses from using "artifical incentives" to boost likes (see Wilson 2014). The new policy highlights how efforts to monetize social media are constantly shifting. However, the *Denver Post* still deserves credit for this early experiment to convert Facebook attention into revenue.

10. The Audit Bureau of Circulations, founded in 1914, changed its name to the Alliance for Audited Media in 2012 to reflect a wider emphasis on digital analytics.

REFERENCES

Agogliati, M. 2011. "New Hartford Resident Fighting Legal Battle over His Farm Stand." *Register Citizen*, February 24. Retrieved June 24, 2013, from http://register citizen.com/articles/2011/02/24/news/doc4d65ef3ac8546561512009.txt.

Alexander, A. 2009. "The Post's 'Salon' Plan: A Public Relations Disaster." *Omblog* (blog), *Washington Post*, July 2. Retrieved June 5, 2013, from http://voices.washing tonpost.com/ombudsman-blog/2009/07/wps_salon_plan_a_public_relati.html.

Allen, M. and D. Victor. 2012. "Join ProPublica's Patient Harm Community." *Pro-Publica*, May 21. Retrieved July 28, 2013, from http://www.propublica.org/get involved/item/join-propublicas-patient-harm-community.

Alvarado, A. 2011. "California Watch and the Business of Coloring Books." *California Watch*, April 12. Retrieved September 15, 2013, from http://california watch.org/dailyreport/california-watch-and-business-coloringbooks-9775.

Anderson, C. 2006. *The Long Tail: Why the Future of Business Is Selling Less of More*. New York: Hyperion.

Anderson, C. W. 2012. "What's the Best Model for a Digital News Business?" *Columbia Journalism Review*, September–October. Retrieved March 6, 2014, from http://www.cjr.org/cover_story/digital_news_business.php.

———. 2013. *Rebuilding the News: Metropolitan Journalism in the Digital Age*. Philadelphia: Temple University Press.

Anderson, C. W., E. Bell, and C. Shirky. 2012. *Post-Industrial Journalism: Adapting to the Present*. New York: Tow Center for Digital Journalism, Columbia Journalism School. Retrieved June 5, 2013, from http://towcenter.org/research/post-industrial-journalism/.

Anderson, R. 2013. "Steve Kelley, Seattle Times Sports Columnist, Leaving 'To Do Something Else' After 31 Years." *Seattle Weekly*, January 4. Retrieved July 30, 2013, from http://www.seattleweekly.com/news/thedailyweekly/928621-129/seattletimes.

Applebome, P. 2010. "Walk in, Grab a Muffin and Watch a Newspaper Reinvent Itself." *New York Times*, December 15. Retrieved June 25, 2013, from http://www.nytimes.com/2010/12/16/nyregion/16towns.html?_r=1&.

Armbrester, P. 2013. "31 Things You Can Make Out of Cereal Boxes." *BuzzFeed*, August 7. Retrieved March 4, 2014, from http://www.buzzfeed.com/pippa/cereal-box-diys-50cb.

Athas, E. and T. Gorman. 2012. "What Kinds of Local Stories Drive Engagement? The Results of an NPR Facebook Experiment." *Nieman Journalism Lab*, November 27. Retrieved November 27, 2012, from http://www.niemanlab.org/2012/11/what-kinds-of-local-stories-drive-engagement-the-results-of-an-npr-facebook-experiment/.

Axon, S. 2010. "Local FOX Station Makes Hilarious Social Media Parody." *Mashable*, October 24. Retrieved June 1, 2013, from http://mashable.com/2010/10/24/fox-social-media-parody-video/.

Banchero, S. and D. Belkin. 2012. "Chicago News Cooperative to Halt Operations." *Wall Street Journal*, February 17. Retrieved June 6, 2013, from http://online.wsj.com/article/SB10001424052970204880404577230102181259464.html.

Baran, S. J. and D. K. Davis. 2009. *Mass Communication Theory: Foundations, Ferment, and Future*. 5th ed. Boston: Wadsworth Cengage Learning.

Batsell, J. 1998. "QFC Chain Buys Art's, Low-Cost Ballard Grocery." *Seattle Times*, June 20. Retrieved June 1, 2013, from http://community.seattletimes.nwsource.com/archive/?date=19980620&slug=2757043.

——. 2010. "Lone Star Trailblazer: Will the Texas Tribune Transform Texas Journalism?" *Columbia Journalism Review* July–August, 39–43.

——. 2012. "Friday Night Bytes: In Texas, High School Football Is the Killer App." *Columbia Journalism Review*, January–February, 39–41.

——. 2013. "The 'Original Platform': How Newsrooms Build Digital Loyalty and Generate Revenue Through Face-to-Face Engagement." *#ISOJ: The Official Research Journal of the International Symposium on Online Journalism* 3 (2): 274–89.

BBC (British Broadcasting Corporation). 2008. "We Want Your Ad-Hoc 'Reckon.'" *That Mitchell and Webb Look*, March 20, ser. 2, episode 5. London. Retrieved June 1, 2013, from http://www.bbc.co.uk/comedy/thatmitchellandwebbsite/watch/series2.shtml.

Beaujon, A. 2013. "Paton: 'Bad CEOs and Worse Editors' Are Trying to 'Kill Our Future.' *Poynter Institute*, June 21. Retrieved June 21, 2013, from http://www.poynter .org/latest-news/mediawire/216570/paton-bad-ceos-and-worse-editors-are-trying -to-kill-our-future/.

Beaumont, C. 2009. "New York Plane Crash: Twitter Breaks the News, Again." *Telegraph* (London), January 16. Retrieved July 27, 2013, from http://www.telegraph .co.uk/technology/twitter/4269765/New-York-plane-crash-Twitter-breaks-the -news-again.html.

Beckett, L. 2010. "Getting Beyond Just Pageviews: Philly.com's Seven-Part Equation for Measuring Online Engagement." *Nieman Journalism Lab*, October 26. Retrieved July 20, 2012, from http://www.niemanlab.org/2010/10/getting -beyond-just-pageviews-philly-coms-seven-part-equation-for-measuring-online -engagement/.

Bell. E. 2012. "Journalism by Numbers." *Columbia Journalism Review*, September–October, 48–49.

Benton, J. 2013. "With Gay Marriage Sure to Spark Emotional Responses, The Washington Post and New York Times Try Structuring Comments." *Nieman Journalism Lab*, June 26. Retrieved July 31, 2013, from http://www.niemanlab.org/2013/06 /with-gay-marriage-sure-to-spark-emotional-responses-the-washington-post -and-new-york-times-try-structuring-comments/.

Benzing, J. 2011. "On the Front Lines." *American Journalism Review*, March–April. Retrieved June 7, 2013, from http://www.ajr.org/article.asp?id=5079.

Bernier, N. 2012. "Public Schools Explorer: Behind the Scenes." *Texas Tribune*, July 17. Retrieved September 6, 2013, from https://www.texastribune.org/2012/07/17 /public-schools-explorer-behind-the-scenes/.

Bidgood, J. 2013. "Body of Missing Student at Brown Is Discovered." *New York Times*, April 25. Retrieved July 27, 2013, from http://www.nytimes.com/2013/04/26/us /sunil-tripathi-student-at-brown-is-found-dead.html.

Blank, S. 2009. "Vertical vs. Horizontal Markets." ECorner: Stanford University's Entrepreneurship Corner, November 11. Retrieved May 13, 2014, from http:// ecorner.stanford.edu/authorMaterialInfo.html?mid=2324.

Boardman, D. 2010. "Times Launches Husky Football App." *Seattle Times*, August 24. Retrieved August 8, 2013, from http://seattletimes.com/html/huskies /2012712297_huskyapp25.html.

———. 2013. "Digital Subscriptions Needed to Support Quality Journalism." *Seattle Times*, February 23. Retrieved September 25, 2013, from http://seattletimes.com /html/localnews/2020414873_boardmancolumnxml.html.

Branch, J. 2012. "Snow Fall: The Avalanche at Tunnel Creek." *New York Times*, December 20. Retrieved July 27, 2013, from http://www.nytimes.com/projects/2012 /snow-fall/.

Brendle, R. 2012. "My Take: This Is Where God Was in Aurora." *CNN Belief Blog*, July 28. Retrieved July 13, 2013, from http://religion.blogs.cnn.com/2012/07/28/my-take-this-is-where-god-was-in-aurora/.

Briggs, M. 2011. *Entrepreneurial Journalism: How to Build What's Next for News.* Washington, DC: CQ Press.

Brinkley, D. 2012. *Cronkite.* New York: HarperCollins.

Brown, B. 2010. "Brené Brown: The Power of Vulnerability." TED.com, December. Retrieved February 19, 2014, from http://www.ted.com/talks/brene_brown_on_vulnerability.html.

———. 2012. *Daring Greatly: How the Courage to Be Vulnerable Transforms the Way We Live, Love, Parent, and Lead.* New York: Gotham Books.

Buttry, S. 2011. "What Does 'Community Engagement' Mean?" *Buttry Diary* (blog), June 3. Retrieved June 5, 2013, from http://stevebuttry.wordpress.com/2011/06/03/what-does-community-engagement-mean/.

———. 2012. "Don't Be Selfish on Twitter; Tweeting Useful Information Is Good Business." *Buttry Diary* (blog), September 5. Retrieved July 30, 2013, from http://stevebuttry.wordpress.com/2012/09/05/dont-be-selfish-on-twitter-tweeting-useful-information-is-good-business/.

Caplan, J. 2012. "How Startup Sites Can Take Advantage of Emerging Revenue Streams." *Poynter Institute*, May 10. Retrieved June 7, 2013, from http://www.poynter.org/how-tos/leadership-management/entrepreneurial/173455/live-chat-today-how-startup-sites-can-take-advantage-of-emerging-revenue-streams/.

Carr, D. 2009. "News Erupts, and So Does a Web Debut." *New York Times*, November 8. Retrieved August 13, 2013, from http://www.nytimes.com/2009/11/09/business/media/09carr.html.

———. 2010. "Why Twitter Will Endure." *New York Times*, January 1. Retrieved August 24, 2013, from http://www.nytimescom/2010/01/03/weekinreview/03carr.html?pagewanted=all&_r=0.

———. 2011. "News Trends Tilt Toward Niche Sites." *New York Times*, September 11. Retrieved March 14, 2013, from www.nytimes.com/2011/09/12/business/media/news-consumption-tilts-toward-niche-sites.html.

———. 2013. "Guns, Maps and Data That Disturb." *New York Times*, January 13. Retrieved January 14, 2013, from http://www.nytimes.com/2013/01/14/business/media/guns-maps-and-disturbing-data.html.

Carr, N. 2008. "The Great Unbundling: Newspapers & the Net." *Encyclopedia Britannica Blog*, April 7. Retrieved August 10, 2013, from http://www.britannica.com/blogs/2008/04/the-great-unbundling-newspapers-the-net/.

Carvin, A. 2013. "ISOJ: Full Transcript of NPR's Andy Carvin Keynote Speech on Social Media, Journalism and Media Literacy." *Knight Center for Journalism in the Americas* (blog), April 19. Retrieved July 14, 2013, from https://knightcenter.utexas

.edu/blog/00–13644-isoj-full-transcript-npr's-andy-carvin-keynote-speech
-social-media-journalism-and-medi.

Charity, A. 1995. *Doing Public Journalism*. New York: Guilford.

Chittum, R. 2012. "Journal Register, Future-of-News Star, Is Bankrupt Again." *Columbia Journalism Review*, September 6. Retrieved June 19, 2013, from http://www
.cjr.org/the_audit/journal_register_future-of-new.php?page=all.

———. 2013a. "The Advance Publications Name Game." *Columbia Journalism Review*,
June 19. Retrieved June 19, 2013, from http://www.cjr.org/the_audit/the
_oregonian_readies_the_guil.php?page=all.

———. 2013b. "Lessons from the Dallas Morning News's Failed Paywall." *Columbia
Journalism Review*, October 2. Retrieved October 3, 2013, from http://www.cjr
.org/the_audit/the_dallas_morning_news_drops.php.

Christensen, C. M. 1997. *The Innovator's Dilemma: When New Technologies Cause
Great Firms to Fail*. Boston: Harvard Business School Press.

Christensen, C. M., D. Skok, and J. Allworth. 2012. "Breaking News: Mastering the
Art of Disruptive Innovation in Journalism." *Nieman Reports* 66 (3): 6–20.

Cieply, M. 2013. "Center Will Offer New Tools for Measuring the Impact of Media
Beyond Numbers." *New York Times*, April 28. Retrieved October 13, 2013, from
http://www.nytimes.com/2013/04/29/business/media/center-to-offer-tools
-for-gauging-impact-of-media.html.

Coscarelli, J. 2012. "The New York Times Is Now Supported by Readers, Not Advertising." *New York Magazine*, July 26. Retrieved June 5, 2013, from http://nymag
.com/daily/intelligencer/2012/07/new-york-times-supported-by-readers-not
-advertisers.html.

Coutts, S. and J. LaFleur. 2011. "Some States Still Leave Low-Income Students Behind;
Others Make Surprising Gains." *ProPublica*, June 30. Retrieved September 8,
2013, from http://www.propublica.org/article/opportunity-gap-schools-data.

Cox, A. 2010. "Home and Away: The Fallen in Afghanistan." *Afghanistan Crossroads*
(blog), *CNN.com*, May 28. Retrieved September 6, 2013, from http://afghanistan
.blogs.cnn.com/2010/05/28/home-and-away-the-fallen-in-afghanistan/.

Curley, R. 2009. "UFC: Las Vegas' Major-League Sports Franchise." *RobCurley.com*
(blog), August 3. Retrieved August 28, 2013, from http://robcurleycom/2009
/08/03/ufc/.

Davis, K. 2013. "News Nonprofits Must Balance Capacity, Growth of New Revenue."
Knight Blog: The Blog of the John S. and James L. Knight Foundation, November 14.
Retrieved March 2, 2014, from http://www.knightfoundation.org/blogs/knight
blog/2013/11/14/news-nonprofits-must-balance-capacity-growth-new-revenue/.

Debelov, A. 2014. "Advertising's New Addiction: Programmatic Buying." *VentureBeat*,
August 29. Retrieved September 7, 2014, from http://venturebeat.com/2014/08
/29/advertisings-new-addiction-programmatic-buying/.

DeFleur, M. L. 2010. *Mass Communication Theories: Explaining Origins, Processes, and Effects*. Boston: Allyn & Bacon.

Denton, F. and E. Thorson. 1995. "Civic Journalism: Does It Work?" *Pew Center for Civic Journalism*. Retrieved June 7, 2013, from http://www.pewcenter.org/doingcj/research/r_doesit.html.

DeRienzo, M. 2011. "What the Newsroom Cafe Has Taught Us About Improving Local Journalism." *Register Citizen Newsroom Cafe* (blog), September 13. Retrieved June 25, 2013, from http://newsroomcafe.wordpress.com/2011/09/13/the-newsroom-cafes-first-six-months-its-not-about-the-coffee/.

Doctor, K. 2012. "The Newsonomics of Majority Reader Revenue." *Nieman Journalism Lab*, May 31. Retrieved June 5, 2013, from http://www.niemanlab.org/2012/05/the-newsonomics-of-majority-reader-revenue/.

———. 2013. "The Newsonomics of 10 Ways We'll Judge 2014." *Nieman Journalism Lab*, October 10. Retrieved October 10, 2013, from http://www.niemanlab.org/2013/10/the-newsonomics-of-10-ways-well-judge-2014/.

Douthat, R. 2013. "How the Post Was Lost." *New York Times*, August 10. Retrieved August 10, 2013, from www.nytimes.com/2013/08/11/opinion/sunday/douthat-how-the-post-was-lost.html.

Drake, M. 2012. "Two Lake Orion Teens in Critical Condition After Oakland Township Car Crash." *Oakland Press* (Pontiac, MI), August 14. Retrieved May 10, 2014, from http://www.theoaklandpress.com/general-news/20120814/two-lake-orion-teens-in-critical-condition-after-oakland-township-car-crash.

Driscoll, M. 2012. "'Preschool Gems': 25 Funny Quotes from Preschoolers." *Christian Science Monitor*, August 15. Retrieved September 10, 2013, from http://www.csmonitor.com/Books/2012/0815/Preschool-Gems-25-funny-quotes-from-preschoolers/Illusion-vs.-reality.

Edmonds, R. 2013. "Advance Local President: 'Signs of Success Are Everywhere.'" *Poynter Institute*, December 19. Retrieved March 5, 2014, from http://www.poynter.org/latest-news/mediawire/233637advance-local-president-signs-of-success-are-everywhere/.

Elliott, J. 2012. "Revealed: The Dark Money Group Attacking Sen. Sherrod Brown." *ProPublica*, September 7. Retrieved September 7, 2013, from http://www.propublica.org/article/revealed-the-dark-money-group-attacking-sen-sherrod-brown.

Ellis, J. 2013a. "Politico Pro Grows to 1,000 Subscribing Orgs, Moves into Print." *Nieman Journalism Lab*, March 12. Retrieved February 23, 2014, from http://www.niemanlab.org/2013/03/politico-pro-grows-to-1000-subscribing-orgs-moves-into-print/.

———. 2013b. "What Makes the Texas Tribune's Event Business So Successful?" *Nieman Journalism Lab*, September 27. Retrieved August 8, 2013, from

http://www.niemanlab.org/2013/09/what-makes-the-texas-tribunes-event
-business-so-successful//.

———. 2014. "Q&A: John Yemma on Managing the Christian Science Monitor's
Leap from Print to Digital." *Nieman Journalism Lab*, January 17. Retrieved January 19, 2014, from http://www.niemanlab.org/2014/01/qa-john-yemma-on
-managing-the-christian-science-monitors-leap-from-print-to-digital/.

eMarketer. 2013. "Mobile Growth Pushes Facebook to Become No. 2 US Digital Ad
Seller." December 19. Retrieved March 3, 2014, from http://www.emarketer.com
/Article/Mobile-Growth-Pushes-Facebook-Become-No-2-US-Digital-Ad-Seller
/1010469.

Farhi, P. 2012. "Marcus Brauchli to Step Down as Editor of the Washington Post." *Washington Post*, November 13. Retrieved June 24, 2013, from http://www.washing
tonpost.com/lifestyle/style/marcus-brauchli-to-step-down-as-editor-of-the
-washington-post/2012/11/13/952698e0-2daf-11e2-a99d-5c4203af7b7a_story
.html.

Friedman, A. 2013. "Making Politics and Policy News Sexy: How the Texas Tribune
Raked in $23K from the Grateful Viewers of Its Legislative Livestream." *Colum-
bia Journalism Review*, June 27. Retrieved July 26, 2013, from http://www.cjr.org
/realtalk/texas_tribune_ftw.php?page=all.

Gans, H. 1979. *Deciding What's News: A Study of CBS Evening News, NBC Nightly
News, Newsweek and Time.* New York: Pantheon.

Garber, M. 2014. "Sit Back, Relax, and Read That Long Story—on Your Phone."
Atlantic, January 21. Retrieved March 3, 2014, from http://www.theatlantic
.com/technology/archive/2014/01/sit-back-relax-and-read-that-long-story-on
-your-phone/283205/.

Gaylord, C. 2012. "How Heinrich Rudolf Hertz Revealed the Invisible World."
Christian Science Monitor, February 22. Retrieved September 10, 2013, from
http://www.csmonitor.com/Innovation/Horizons/2012/0222/How-Heinrich
-Rudolf-Hertz-revealed-the-invisible-world.

Gibbs, R. 2012. "T-Squared: QRANK's Final Answer." *Texas Tribune*, September
3. Retrieved September 15, 2013, from http://www.texastribune.org/2012
/09/03/t-squared-farewell-qrank-news-quiz-game/.

Gilbert, G. 2008. "Citizen Journalism Will Shape the New Face of the Oakland
Press." *Oakland Press*, December 14. Retrieved July 28, 2013, from http://www.the
oaklandpress.com/articles/2008/12/14/opinion/doc4944876017642127238243.txt.

Gilgoff, D. 2012a. "Where Was God in Aurora Massacre?" *CNN Belief Blog*, July 24.
Retrieved July 13, 2013, from http://religion.blogs.cnn.com/2012/07/24/where
-was-god-in-aurora-massacre/.

———. 2012b. "'Where Was God in Aurora?' Comments Show Internet
as Church for Atheists." *CNN Belief Blog*, August 1. Retrieved July 13,

2013, from http://religion.blogs.cnn.com/2012/08/01/where-was-god-in-aurora -comments-show-internet-as-church-for-atheists/.

———. 2012c. "My Take: 5 Things I Learned Editing the Belief Blog." *CNN Belief Blog*, December 31. Retrieved August 2, 2013, from http://religion.blogs.cnn .com/2012/12/31/my-take-5-things-i-learned-editing-the-belief-blog/.

Gilgoff, D. and E. Marrapodi. 2012. "Massacre of Children Leaves Many Asking, 'Where's God?'" *CNN Belief Blog*, December 14. Retrieved July 13, 2013, from http://religion.blogs.cnn.com/2012/12/14/massacre-of-children-leaves-many -asking-wheres-god/.

Gillmor, D. 2004. *We the Media: Grassroots Journalism by the People, for the People.* Sebastopol, CA: O'Reilly Media.

———. 2010. *Mediactive*. San Francisco: Creative Commons.

Glasser, T. L. 1999. *The Idea of Public Journalism*. New York: Guilford.

Goldhill, O. 2013. "Mobile Advertising to Double This Year." *Telegraph* (London), June 25. Retrieved July 12, 2013, from http://www.telegraph.co.uk/technology /mobile-phones/10141492/Mobile-advertising-to-double-this-year.html.

Green, C. 2013. "Interactivity Is Essential to Online News." *Sojournalist* (blog), July 21. Retrieved September 12, 2013, from http://cynthiagreenblog.wordpress. com/2013/07/21/interactivity-is-essential-to-online-news/.

Greenslade, R. 2013. "Telegraph to Put Up Metered Paywall." *Guardian* (Manchester), March 26. Retrieved September 25, 2013, from http://www.theguardian.com /media/greenslade/2013/mar/26/telegraph-paywall.

Grissom, B. 2013. "T-Squared: Why We Unpublished Our Prisoner Database." *Texas Tribune*, July 22. Retrieved October 13, 2013, from http://www.texastribune .org/2013/07/22/tdcj-data-errors/.

Groves, J. and C. Brown-Smith. 2011. "Stopping the Presses: A Longitudinal Case Study of the Christian Science Monitor Transition from Print Daily to Web Always." *#ISOJ: The Official Research Journal of the International Symposium on Online Journalism* 1 (2). Retrieved June 19, 2013, from https://online.journalism. utexas.edu/2011/papers/GrovesBrown2011.pdf.

———. 2013. "40 Million Page Views Is Not Enough: An Examination of the Christian Science Monitor's Evolution from SEO to Engagement." *#ISOJ: The Official Research Journal of the International Symposium on Online Journalism* 3(2): 6–25.

Grueskin, B., A. Seave, and L. Graves. 2011. *The Story So Far: What We Know About the Business of Digital Journalism*. New York: Columbia Journalism School. Retrieved June 6, 2013, from http://www.cjr.org/the_business_of_digital_journalism /the_story_so_far_what_we_know.php/.

Guzman, M. 2012. "Join Us in Honoring June A. Almquist Award Winner Tracy Record." *SPJ Western Washington*, May 8. Retrieved August 16, 2013,

from http://www.spjwash.org/2012/05/join-us-in-honoring-june-a-almquist
-award-winner-tracy-record/.

———. 2013. "After Boston, Still Learning." *Quill*, May–June 2013, 22–25.

Ha, A. 2013. "Chartbeat Looks Beyond Clicks with Redesigned Publisher Analytics." *TechCrunch*, December 3. Retrieved March 5, 2014, from http://techcrunch.
com/2013/12/03/chartbeat-publishing-redesign/.

Hagan, J. 2013. "The Suit in the Newsroom." *New York*, August 23. Retrieved
October 10, 2013, from http://nymag.com/news/intelligencer/new-york
-times-mark-thompson-2013-9/.

Haik, C. 2012. "Say What? Breaking Down the Social Reaction to the Convention
Speeches." *Ask the Post* (blog), *Washington Post*, August 30. Retrieved July 26,
2013, from http://www.washingtonpost.com/blogs/ask-the-post/post/say
-what-breaking-down-the-social-reaction-to-the-convention-speeches/2012/08
/30/70c1b5f0-f247-11e1-adc6-87dfa8eff430_blog.html.

Haile, T. 2013. "Cargo Cults or the Wright Brothers? Metrics Can Improve Newsrooms but Only If the Culture Is Ready." *paidContent*, September 8. Retrieved
September 21, 2013, from http://paidcontent.org/2013/09/08/cargo-cults-or
-the-wright-brothers-metrics-can-improve-newsrooms-but-only-if-the-culture
-is-ready/.

Hajela, D. 2013. "InsideClimate News Snags Pulitzer for Coverage of Oil Pipeline
Issue." *Huffington Post*, April 16. Retrieved August 12, 2013, from http://www
.huffingtonpost.com/2013/04/16/insideclimate-news-pulitzer_n_3089684.html.

Hall, D. 2012. "A Brand New Off Air Series Is HERE!" *Beyond the Mic* (blog),
WBEZ91.5, September 18. Retrieved June 7, 2013, from http://www.wbez.org
/blogs/beyond-mic/2012-09/brand-new-air-series-here-102492.

Hamilton, R. and R. Gibbs. 2013. "T-Squared: The 2013 Session Scramble." *Texas
Tribune*, May 13. Retrieved September 15, 2013, from http://www.texastribune
.org/2013/05/13/t-squared-2013-session-scramble-starts/.

Harris, J. 2008. "Shifting Influence: From Institution to Individual." *Nieman Reports*,
summer 2008. Retrieved August 12, 2013, from http://www.nieman.harvard
.edu/reports/article/100014/Shifting-Influence-From-Institution-to-Individual
.aspx.

Haughney, C. 2012. "Newspaper Publisher Journal Register Files for Bankruptcy and
Plans for a Sale." *Media Decoder* (blog), *New York Times*, September 5. Retrieved
June 7, 2013, from http://mediadecoder.blogs.nytimes.com/2012/09/05
/newspaper-publisher-journal-register-files-for-bankruptcy-and-plans-for-a
-sale/.

———. 2013. "After Pinpointing Gun Owners, Paper Is a Target." *New York Times*,
January 6. Retrieved January 7, 2013, from http://www.nytimes.com/2013/01/07
/nyregion/after-pinpointing-gun-owners-journal-news-is-a-target.html.

Henley, J. 2013. "Firestorm: The Story of the Brushfire at Dunalley." *Guardian* (Manchester), May 22. Retrieved July 27, 2013, from http://www.guardian.co.uk/world/interactive/2013/may/26/firestorm-bushfire-dunalley-holmes-family.

Hiltzik, M. 2014. "Media Upheaval Is Bad News." *Los Angeles Times*, February 2, B1, B7.

Hoogland, J. 2011. "New Company, MLive Media Group, Formed to Carry Booth Newspapers and MLive.com into Next Era of News Media." *MLive*, November 2. Retrieved July 26, 2013, from http://www.mlive.com/news/index.ssf/2011/11/new_company_mlive_media_group.html.

Horowitz, B. 2014. "Can-Do vs. Can't-Do Culture." *Re/code*, January 1. Retrieved February 19, 2014, from http://recode.net/2014/01/01/can-do-vs-cant-do-culture/.

Indvik, L. 2013. "Washington Post to Go Behind Metered Paywall This Summer." *Mashable*, March 18. Retrieved October 3, 2013, from http://mashable.com/2013/03/18/washington-post-paywall/.

Ingram, M. 2012. "Talking Points Memo and Why Membership Is Better Than a Paywall." *Gigaom*, October 3. Retrieved October 5, 2012, from http://gigaom.com/2012/10/03/talking-points-memo-and-why-membership-is-better-than-a-paywall/.

International News Media Association. 2013. "Hail Peyton: The Denver Broncos Facebook Fandemonium Contest." Retrieved October 1, 2013, from http://www.inma.org/modules/campaignArchive/index.cfm?action=detail&zyear=2013&id=E9CA3EDD-C4C6-4795-8CEA313B4431D7C4.

Jarvis, J. 2007. "New Rule: Cover What You Do Best. Link to the Rest." *Buzz Machine*, February 22. Retrieved August 3, 2013, from http://buzzmachine.com/2007/02/22/new-rule-cover-what-you-do-best-link-to-the-rest/.

Jenkins, H. 2006. *Convergence Culture: Where Old and New Media Collide*. New York: New York University Press.

Jones, A. 2011. "Layoff Notice Numbers Confirmed for Booth Newspapers' Transition to MLive Media Group." *MLive*, November 18. Retrieved August 3, 2013, from http://www.mlive.com/business/index.ssf/2011/11/layoff_numbers_confirmed_for_b.html.

Kaempffer, W. 2012. "Fallen Tree on New Haven Green Unearths Human Skeleton." *New Haven (CT) Register*, October 30. Retrieved July 26, 2013, from http://nhregister.com/articles/2012/10/30/news/new_haven/doc50903ff79c7d9176762389.txt.

Kang, J. C. 2013. "Crowd-Sourcing a Smear." *New York Times Magazine*, July 28, 36–42, 50–51.

Katz, J. and W. Andrews. 2013. "How Y'all, Youse and You Guys Talk." *New York Times*, December 21. Retrieved March 4, 2014, from http://www.nytimes.com/interactive/2013/12/20/sunday-review/dialect-quiz-map.html?_r=0.

Keefer, C. 2012. "Dana White Not Amused with Forrest Griffin's Post-Fight Antics." *Las Vegas Sun*, July 8. Retrieved August 14, 2013, from http://www.lasvegassun .com/news/2012/jul/08/dana-white-not-amused-forrest-griffins-post -fight-/.

Keep, P. 2012. "Answering Reader Questions About Sports Coverage, Puzzles, Comics, TV Listings." *MLive*, March 25. Retrieved July 26, 2013, from http://www .mlive.com/opinion/index.ssf/2012/03/answering_reader_questions_abo .html.

Kennedy, D. 2013a. *The Wired City: Reimagining Journalism and Civic Life in the Post-Newspaper Age.* Amherst: University of Massachusetts Press.

———. 2013b. "Tracing the Links Between Civic Engagement and the Revival of Local Journalism." *Nieman Journalism Lab*, June 4. Retrieved June 5, 2013, from http://www.niemanlab.org/2013/06/tracing-the-links-between-civic-engage ment-and-the-revival-of-local-journalism/.

Kingsley, A. 2010. "A Tale of Two Newsrooms." *Las Vegas CityLife*, January 28. Retrieved August 14, 2013, from http://archives.lasvegascitylife.com/articles /2010/01/28/news/local_news/iq_33923638.txt.

———. 2012. "Logging Off: As Internet Superstar Rob Curley Leaves Las Vegas, We Reflect on His Legacy at the Las Vegas Sun." *Las Vegas CityLife*, May 24. Retrieved August 14, 2013, from http://archives.lasvegascitylife.com/articles/2012/05/24 /news/local_news/iq_53698620.txt.

Kirchner, L. 2011. "John Paton's Big Bet." *Columbia Journalism Review*, July–August. Retrieved June 5, 2013, from http://www.cjr.org/feature/john_patons_big_bet .php?page=all.

Klein, S. and R. Grochowski Jones. 2014. "Introducing the ProPublica Data Store." *ProPublica*, February 26. Retrieved March 5, 2014, from http://www.propublica .org/article/introducing-the-propublica-data-store.

Klug, F. 2012. "Kalamazoo Mayor Bobby Hopewell: 'We Love Our Veterans' But, Like Other Organizations, Korean War Veterans Must Pay for Exclusive Use of Branson Park." *Kalamazoo (MI) Gazette*, July 17. Retrieved June 24, 2013, from http:// www.mlive.com/news/kalamazoo/index.ssf/2012/07/kalamazoo_mayor_bobby _hopewell_7.html.

Kristof, N. D. and S. WuDunn. 2009. *Half the Sky: Turning Oppression into Opportunity for Women Worldwide.* New York: Random House.

Lail, J. 2010. "The Seattle Times Wins APME's Innovator of the Year Award." *Associated Press Media Editors*, October 22. Retrieved August 24, 2013, from http:// www.apme.com/news/51325/The-Seattle-Times-Wins-APMEs-Innovator-of -the-Year-Award.htm.

Lee, E. 2012. "The New York Times Paywall Is Working Better Than Anyone Had Guessed." *Bloomberg Tech Blog*, December 20. Retrieved September 25, 2013, from

http://go.bloomberg.com/tech-blog/2012-12-20-the-new-york-times-paywall
-is-working-better-than-anyone-had-guessed/.

Levy, S. 2012. "The Rise of the Robot Reporter." *Wired*, May, 132–36.

Linn, A. 2011a. "Hey Middle Class, Tell Us About Yourselves." *TODAY Money*,
November 2. Retrieved July 28, 2013, from http://www.today.com/money/hey
-middle-class-tell-us-about-yourselves-1C7101070.

———. 2011b. "We Are the Median: Living on $50,000 a Year." *TODAY Money*,
December 5. Retrieved July 28, 2013, from http://www.today.com/money/we
-are-median-living-50-000-year-1B7879451.

Machin, D. and S. Niblock. 2010. "The New Breed of Business Journalism for Niche
Global News: The Case of Bloomberg News." *Journalism Studies*, November,
783–98.

Macleod, I. 2013. "Digital to Account for 25% of Total Media Ad Spend in 2013,
eMarketer Finds, with Mobile Up 95%." *Drum*, August 21. Retrieved August
24, 2103, from http://www.thedrum.com/news/2013/08/21/digital-account
-25-total-media-ad-spend-2013-emarketer-finds-mobile-95.

MacMillan, T. 2012. "City Offers Traffic-Calming Clues." *New Haven (CT)
Independent*, August 21. Retrieved July 14, 2013, from http://www.newhaven
independent.org/index.php/archives/entry/when_is_traffic_calming_coming
_to_my_street/.

MacMillan, T. and M. Bailey. 2012. "Skeletal Remains Found in Upended
Tree; Death Investigator Exhumes Skull." *New Haven (CT) Independent*, October 30. Retrieved July 26, 2013, from http://www.newhaven
independent.org/index.php/archives/entry/skeleton_found_in_upended_tree
_on_green/.

Madden, H. and C. Jacobsen. 2010. "How a Grocery Store Shaped a Neighborhood:
The Story of Art's Food Center." *Crown Hill (Seattle) Neighborhood Association*,
July 1. Retrieved June 1, 2013, from http://crownhillneighbors.org/wp/2010/07
/how-a-grocery-store-shaped-a-neighborhood-the-story-of-arts-food-center/.

Marshall, S. 2013. "Royal Baby Coverage: Facts and Figures from Digital News Outlets." *Journalism.co.uk*, July 26. Retrieved July 27, 2013,
from http://www.journalism.co.uk/news/royal-baby-coverage-facts-and-figures
-from-digital-news-outlets/s2/a553655/.

Martinez, Amy. 2011. "Tale of Lost Diamond Adds Glitter to Nordstom's Customer
Service." *Seattle Times*, May 11. Retrieved June 24, 2013, from http://seattle
times.com/html/businesstechnology/2015028167_nordstrom12.html.

Martinez, Anthony. 2012. "A Green Roofs Check-in." *WBEZ.org*, August 13.
Retrieved July 28, 2013, from http://www.wbez.org/series/curious-city
/green-roofs-check-101677.

Malthouse, E. C. and A. Peck. 2011. "Medill on Media Engagement: An Introduction." In *Medill on Media Engagement*. Edited by A. Peck and E. C. Malthouse, 3–19. Cresskill, NJ: Hampton Press.

Mayer, J. 2010. "So Long, 'Wizard of Oz' Journalism. Let's Make Margaritas!" *Reynolds Journalism Institute* (blog), September 15. Retrieved June 3, 2013, from http://www.rjionline.org/blog/so-long-wizard-oz-journalism-lets-make -margaritas.

———. 2011. "Three Kinds of Engagement: Outreach, Conversation, Collaboration." *Reynolds Journalism Institute* (blog), June 18. Retrieved June 5, 2013, from http:// rjionline.org/blog/three-kinds-engagement-outreach-conversation-collaboration.

———. 2012. "Community Engagement and Your News Organization." *Poynter Institute* (webinar), June 28. Retrieved June 28, 2012, from http://www.newsu.org /community-engagement-your-news-organization.

Mayer, J. and R. Stern. 2011. *A Resource for Newsrooms: Identifying and Measuring Audience Engagement Efforts.* Columbia, MO: Reynolds Journalism Institute.

Mazotte, N. 2013. "Spanning the Lines Between Journalism and Entertainment, Newsgames Growing in Brazil." *Knight Center for Journalism in the Americas* (blog), August 8. Retrieved September 15, 2013, from https://knight-center.utexas.edu/blog/00–14254-spanning-line-between-journalism-and -entertainment-newsgame-growing-brazil.

McAthy, R. 2012. "Open Journalism and 'Pop-up' Newsrooms at Digital First Media." *Journalism.co.uk*, June 29. Retrieved March 1, 2014, from http:// www.journalism.co.uk/news/talking-mobile-pop-up-newsrooms-with -digital-first-media/s2/a549728/.

———. 2013. "Trinity Mirror's 'Newsroom 3.0 Model' to Focus on Digital." *Journalism.co.uk*, February 7. Retrieved August 2, 2013, from http://www .journalism.co.uk/news/how-trinity-mirror-s-newsroom-3-0-model-will-switch -focus-from-print-to-multi-platform/s2/a552009/.

McDuling, J. 2013. "If You Won't Pay to Read the New York Times, Will You Pay to Play It?" *Quartz*, December 10. Retrieved March 4, 2014, from http://qz.com/156024 /if-you-wont-pay-to-read-the-new-york-times-will-you-pay-to-play-it/.

Meyer, R. 2014. "The New York Times' Most Popular Story of 2013 Was Not an Article." *Atlantic*, January 17. Retrieved March 4, 2014, from http://www.theatlantic .com/technology/archive/2014/01/-em-the-new-york-times-em-most-popular -story-of-2013-was-not-an-article/283167/.

Miller, M. 2008. "Ultimate Cash Machine." *Forbes*, April 17. Retrieved August 14, 2013, from http://www.forbes.com/forbes/2008/0505/080.html.

Mitchell, A., M. Jurkowitz, J. Holcomb, J. Enda, and M. Anderson. 2013. "Nonprofit Journalism: A Growing but Fragile Part of the U.S. News System." *Pew Research*

Journalism Project, June 10. Retrieved June 24, 2013, from http://www.journalism
.org/analysis_report/nonprofit_journalism.

Moos, J. 2011. "Pulitzer Prizes Change Breaking News Category to Emphasize 'Real-Time' Reporting." *Poynter Institute*, November 30. Retrieved July
27, 2013, from http://www.poynter.org/latest-news/mediawire/154546
/pulitzers-shift-to-all-digital-entry-format/.

Moses, L. 2014. "Capital N.Y. Is Rolling Out a Nearly $6,000 Annual Paywall."
Adweek, January 20. Retrieved March 3, 2014, from http://www.adweek.com
/news/press/capital-ny-rolling-out-nearly-6000-annual-paywall-155070.

Murphy, R., B. Grissom, and N. Seger. 2011. "Visualization: Executions on Perry's
Watch." *Texas Tribune*, September 2. Retrieved September 6, 2013, from http://
www.texastribune.org/library/data/perry-executions/.

Myers, S. 2012. "What the Future of News Looks Like in Alabama After Advance
Cuts Staff by 400." *Poynter Institute*, June 14. Retrieved June 7, 2013, from
http://www.poynter.org/latest-news/top-stories/177191/what-the-future-of
-news-looks-like-in-alabama-after-advance-cuts-staff-there-by-400/.

Napoli, P. M. 2011. *Audience Evolution: New Technologies and the Transformation of
Media Audiences*. New York: Columbia University Press.

Narisetti, R. 2013. "To Save Journalism, News Needs to Buy into Data." *Digiday*,
October 18. Retrieved March 5, 2014, from http://digiday.com/publishers/
data-save-journalism/.

Newton, E. 2012. "Eric Newton: Journalism Schools Aren't Changing Quickly
Enough." *Nieman Journalism Lab*, September 10. Retrieved June 14, 2013,
from http://www.niemanlab.org/2012/09/eric-newton-journalism-schools-arent
-changing-quickly-enough/.

New York Times. 2009. "News Blogs and Online Columns." Internal memo. Retrieved
July 30, 2013, from http://graphics8.nytimes.com/packages/pdf/ttnr/Blog
_standards.pdf.

O'Donovan, C. 2014. "You Won't Believe Upworthy's New Way of Measuring
Audience Engagement Until You Read It." *Nieman Journalism Lab*, February 6. Retrieved March 5, 2014, from http://www.niemanlab.org/2014/02
/upworthy-has-a-new-way-of-measuring-engagement/.

Olson, E. M. 2011. "Everyone's Welcome at the Newsroom Cafe." *Nieman Reports*,
summer 2011. Retrieved June 7, 2013, from http://www.nieman.harvard.edu
/reportsitem.aspx?id=102640.

Osder, E. and K. Campwala. 2012. *Audience Development and Distribution Strategies:
A Primer for Nonprofit News Organizations*. Encino, CA: Investigative News Network. Retrieved June 1, 2013, from http://www.investigativenewsnetwork.org
/sites/investigativenewsnetwork.org/files/INN-audience-development-white
paper.pdf.

Owen, L. H. 2013. "Politico Hits 1,000 Pro Subscriptions and Plans to Launch a Magazine." *paidContent*, March 12. Retrieved August 8, 2013, from http:// paidcontent.org/2013/03/12/politico-hits-1000-pro-subscriptions-and-plans -to-launch-a-magazine/.

Palmer, D., M. Oliver, and P. Allen. 2013. "Interactive: Challenge Your Musical Ear." *Telegraph* (London), June 13. Retrieved July 12, 2013, from http://www.tele- graph.co.uk/culture/music/10116919/Interactive-Challenge-your-musical-ear .html.

Patterson, T. E. 2013. *Informing the News: The Need for Knowledge-Based Journalism.* New York: Vintage Books.

Peck, A. and E. C. Malthouse. 2011. *Medill on Media Engagement.* Cresskill, NJ: Hampton Press.

Pecoskie, T. 2010. "Hyperlocal 'News Cafes' Are Taking the Czech News Scene by Storm." *Newspapers Canada*, May 13. Retrieved April 15, 2014, from http://www .newspaperscanada.ca/news/events/the-new-newsroom-how-hyperlocal -news-cafes-are-taking-the-czech-news-scene-storm.

Perry, D. 2004. "Civic Journalism: News as Transactional Pedagogy." *Education and Culture* 20 (2): 25–41.

Pew Center for Civic Journalism. Undated. "Doing Civic Journalism." Retrieved June 7, 2013, from http://www.pewcenter.org/doingcj/.

Pew Research Center. 2013. "2013 State of the News Media: The Challenges Inten- sify." Infographic. *Pew Research Center's Project for Excellence in Journalism.* Retrieved October 12, 2013, from http://stateofthemedia.org/2013/overview-5 /overview-infographic/.

Phelps, A. 2011. "For the Texas Tribune, 'Events Are Journalism'—and Money Mak- ers." *Nieman Journalism Lab*, July 25. Retrieved June 7, 2013, from http://www .niemanlab.org/2011/07/for-the-texas-tribune-events-are-journalism-and -money-makers/.

Poulson, D. 2010. "Try a Little Carp Humor to Woo More Traffic to Your Online News Site." *Society of Environmental Journalists*, October 15. Retrieved August 12, 2013, from http://www.sej.org/publications/journalismmedia/try-little -carp-humor-woo-more-traffic-your-online-news-site.

Prothero, S. 2012. "My Take: CNN Readers' 7 Answers to 'Where Was God in Aurora?'" *CNN Belief Blog*, July 26. Retrieved July 13, 2013, from http://religion.blogs.cnn .com/2012/07/26/my-take-cnn-readers-7-answers-to-where-was-god-in-aurora/.

Ramshaw, E. 2014. "T-Squared: Trib Transparency, Continued." *Texas Tri- bune*, February 28. Retrieved March 2, 2014, from http://www.texastribune .org/2014/02/28/t-squared-ethics-and-us/.

Reichheld, F. 2003. "The One Number You Need to Grow." *Harvard Business Review*, December, 46–54.

Reider, R. 2013. "Reider: Tough Times for Patch, Hyperlocal News." *USA Today*, August 15. Retrieved August 16, 2013, from http://www.usatoday.com/story/money/columnist/rieder/2013/08/14/aol-patch-hyperlocal-news-struggles/2652337/.

Richardson, B. 2011. "Measuring Community Engagement: A Case Study from Chicago Public Media." *Reynolds Journalism Institute* (blog), December 1. Retrieved July 25, 2012, from http://www.rjionline.org/blog/measuring-community-engagement-case-study-chicago-public-media.

Roderick, K. 2013. "The Onion Skewers a Familiar Name over CNN's Miley Cyrus Handling." *LA Observed*, August 26. Retrieved September 23, 2013, from http://www.laobserved.com/archive/2013/08/the_onion_skewers_a_famil.php.

Romenesko, J. 2004. "Columnist to Snide Critics: This Isn't a Dialogue, It's a Lecture." *Poynter Institute*, February 4. Retrieved May 5, 2014, from http://www.poynter.org/latest-news/mediawire/20869/columnist-to-snide-critics-this-isnt-a-dialogue-its-a-lecture/.

———. 2012. "Oregonian Memo Describes a Beat Reporter's Digital Day." *Jim Romenesko.com* (blog), September 5. Retrieved August 1, 2013, from http://jimromenesko.com/2012/09/05/oregonian-memo-describes-a-beat-reporters-digital-day/.

Rooney, B. 2013. "Smartphones Outsell Feature Phones." *Wall Street Journal*, August 14. Retrieved August 25, 2013, from http://blogs.wsj.com/digits/2013/08/14/smartphones-outsell-feature-phones-for-first-time/.

Root, J. 2012. "Liveblog: Rick Perry at the Texas Tribune Festival." *Texas Tribune*, September 21. Retrieved September 21, 2012, from http://www.texastribune.org/texas-people/rick-perry/liveblog-rick-perry-texas-tribune-festival/.

Rosen, J. 2006. "The People Known Formerly as the Audience." *PressThink*, June 27. Retrieved June 1, 2013, from http://archive.pressthink.org/2006/06/27/ppl_frmr.html.

———. 2013a. "Mark Thompson, CEO of the New York Times, Misinforms Columbia B-School About the Meter." *PressThink*, June 3. Retrieved June 5, 2013, from http://pressthink.org/2013/06/mark-thompson-ceo-of-the-new-york-times-misinforms-columbia-b-school-about-the-meter/.

———. 2013b. "Old Testament and New Testament Journalism." *PressThink*, November 3. Retrieved November 4, 2013, from http://pressthink.org/2013/11/old-testament-and-new-testament-journalism/.

Rosenthal, B. M. 2012. "Day Cut Short: Seattle Schools' Weather Response Raises Questions." *Seattle Times*, January 17. Retrieved July 27, 2013, from http://seattletimes.com/html/education/2017263831_snowschools18m.html.

Rossignol, A. and R. Gleason. 2011. "Great Lakes Smackdown! Terrestrial Terror." *Great Lakes Echo* (Michigan State University), March 14. Retrieved September 15, 2013, from http://greatlakesecho.org/2011/03/14/great-lakes-smackdown-terrestrial-terror/.

Rothstein, B. 2012. "*Politico* Announces Changes in Gargantuan Memo." *Mediabistro's FishbowlDC*, November 30. Retrieved June 22, 2013, from http://www.media bistro.com/fishbowldc/politico-announces-changes-in-gargantuan-memo _b90564.

Roush, C. 2012. "The Business of Covering Tech at GeekWire." *Talking Biz News*, April 6. Retrieved June 7, 2013, from http://www.talkingbiznews.com/1 /the-business-of-covering-tech-at-geekwire/.

Santana, A. D. 2011. "Online Readers' Comments Represent New Opinion Pipeline." *Newspaper Research Journal* 32 (3): 66–80.

Sasseen, J., K. Olmstead, and A. Mitchell. 2013. "Digital: As Mobile Grows Rapidly, the Pressures on News Intensify." *Pew Research Center's Project for Excellence in Journalism*. Retrieved August 25, 2013, from http://stateofthemedia.org/2013 /digital-as-mobile-grows-rapidly-the-pressures-on-news-intensify/.

Schaffer, J. and E. Polgreen. 2012. *Engaging Audiences: Measuring Interactions, Engagement and Conversions*. Washington, DC: J-Lab. Retrieved June 1, 2013, from http://www.j-lab.org/publications/engaging-audiences.

Seattle Times. 2012. "Help Us Measure How Liquor Prices Have Changed." May 31. Retrieved September 6, 2013, from http://seattletimes.com/html/localpages /2018327065_seattle-liquor-price-changes.html.

Seattle Times Company. 2011. "Community News Partnership Survey." Results from internal survey, conducted March 14–23. Copy in the author's files.

Shedden, D. 2002. "Citizen/Public Journalism Bibliography." *Poynter Institute*, July 20. Retrieved June 7, 2013, from http://www.poynter.org/uncategorized/790 /citizen-public-journalism-bibliography/.

Shepherd, J. 2010. "109 Cats in Sweaters." *BuzzFeed*, October 7. Retrieved March 4, 2014, from http://www.buzzfeed.com/expresident/109-cats-in-sweaters.

Shields, M. 2014. "BuzzFeed's Peretti: Mobile Is a Better Ad Vehicle." *Adweek*, January 21. Retrieved March 3, 2014, from http://www.adweek.com/news /advertising-branding/buzzfeeds-peretti-mobile-better-ad-vehicle-155109.

Shirky, C. 2008. *Here Comes Everybody: The Power of Organizing Without Organizations*. New York: Penguin.

Shoemaker, P. J. and S. D. Reese. 1996. *Mediating the Message: Theories of Influences on Mass Media Content*. 2nd ed. New York: Longman.

Shoemaker, P. J. and T. P. Vos. 2009. *Gatekeeping Theory*. New York: Routledge.

Silverman, C. 2012. "Narisetti: 'The Promiscuity of Our Audiences Is Only Going to Dramatically Increase.'" *Poynter Institute*, July 13. Retrieved June 6, 2013, from http://www.poynter.org/latest-news/mediawire/180842/narisetti-the -promiscuity-of-our-audiences-is-only-going-to-dramatically-increase/.

Singer, J., A. Hermida, D. Domingo, A. Heinonen, S. Paulussen, T. Quandt, Z. Reich, and M. Vujnovic. 2011. *Participatory Journalism: Guarding Open Gates at Online Newspapers*. Oxford: Wiley-Blackwell.

Smith, E. 2013. "T-Squared: The Last 48 Hours and the Next Few Years." *Texas Tribune*, June 27. Retrieved July 26, 2013, from http://www.texas tribune.org/2013/06/27/t-squared-last-48-hours-and-next-few-years/.

———. 2014. "T-Squared: Lucky '13." *Texas Tribune*, January 6. Retrieved March 2, 2014, from http://www.texastribune.org/2014/01/06/t-squared-our-best-year-ever/.

Spivak, C. 2013. "Solving the Hyperlocal Puzzle." *American Journalism Review*, April–May, 12–17.

Starkman, D. 2012. "The Hamster Wheel vs. the Quality Imperative." *Columbia Journalism Review*, September 14. Retrieved June 19, 2013, from http://www.cjr.org/the_audit/jrc_low-quality_is_baked_into.php?page=all.

Stern, R. 2012. "Arizona Guardian Political News Site Bites the Dust." *Phoenix (AZ) New Times Blogs*, June 4. Retrieved August 13, 2013, from http://blogs.phoenix newtimes.com/valleyfever/2012/06/arizona_guardian_political_new.php.

Sternberg, J. 2013. "The Pageview's Days Are Numbered." *Digiday*, September 21. Retrieved September 21, 2013, from http://digiday.com/publishers/death-of-pageview/.

Stiles, M. and N. Babalola. 2010. "Texas Tribune Database Library Update." *Texas Tribune*, May 31. Retrieved September 3, 2013, from http://www.texastribune.org/texas-local-news/public-information-act/texas-tribune-database-library-update/.

Stiles, M., S. D'Otreppe, C. Groskoph, J. Bowers, and B. Boyer. 2013. "Fire Forecast." *NPR.org*, March 15. Retrieved September 6, 2013, from http://apps.npr.org/fire-forecast/.

Stroud, N. J. 2011. *Niche News: The Politics of News Choice*. Oxford: Oxford University Press.

———. 2013. *The Engaging News Project: Journalist Involvement in Comment Sections*. Austin: Annette Strauss Institute for Civic Live, University of Texas.

———. 2014. "News Engagement Workshop." *The Engaging News Project: News Engagement Workshop Report*, April 29. Austin: Annette Strauss Institute for Civic Live, University of Texas. Retrieved May 16, 2014, from http://engaging newsproject.org/workshop/.

Sullivan, M. 2012. "After an Outburst on Twitter, the Times Reinforces Its Social Media Guidelines." *Public Editor's Journal* (*New York Times* blog), October 17. Retrieved July 31, 2013, from http://publiceditor.blogs.nytimes.com/2012/10/17/after-an-outburst-on-twitter-the-times-reinforces-its-social-media-guidelines/.

Swicegood, T. 2013. "On the Records: Prisoner Database Back Online." *Texas Tribune*, July 30. Retrieved October 13, 2013, from http://www.texastribune.org/2013/07/30/prisoner-database-back-online/.

Thornton, T. 2013. "CNN's Jeff Zucker Talks Social Media, Considers Native Ads." *PBS Media Shift*, April 17. Retrieved July 13, 2013, from http://www.pbs.org/mediashift/2013/04/cnns-jeff-zucker-talks-social-media-considers-native-ads107.

Timmerman, L. 2011. "Techflash Duo, Todd Bishop and John Cook, Quit PSBJ to Start New Site, GeekWire." *Xconomy*, March 7. Retrieved August 11, 2013, from http://www.xconomy.com/seattle/2011/03/07/techflash-duo-todd-bishop-and-john-cook-quit-psbj-to-start-new-site-geekwire/.

Tuchman, G. 1978. *Making News: A Study in the Construction of Reality*. London: Free Press.

Waldman, S. 2014. "The Backstory on Native Advertising." *Columbia Journalism Review*, August 6. Retrieved September 7, 2014, from http://www.cjr.org/the_audit/the_backstory_on_native_advert.php?page=all.

Wemple, E. 2012. "No More TBD.com." *Erik Wemple* (*Washington Post* blog), August 15. Retrieved August 16, 2013, from http://www.washingtonpost.com/blogs/erik-wemple/post/no-more-tbdcom/2012/08/15/51846356-e705-11e1-936a-b801f1abab19_blog.html.

Weprin, A. 2010. "WebMediaBrands Acquires 10,000 Words Blog." *SocialTimes*, October 10. Retrieved September 15, 2013, from http://socialtimes.com/webmediabrands-acquires-10000-words-blog_b53643.

White, D. M. 1950. "The 'Gate Keeper': A Case Study in the Selection of News." *Journalism Quarterly* 27:383–90.

Wilkinson, E. J. 2012. "What Rapid Changes in U.S. Newsrooms in Past 30 Days Mean to Us All." *The Earl Blog*, June 19. Retrieved June 5, 2013, from http://www.inma.org/blogs/earl/post.cfm/what-rapid-changes-in-u-s-newspapers-in-past-30-days-mean-to-us-all.

Williams, K. 2013. "Man Rescued After Being Stuck in Mud in Rhyl." *Daily Post*, July 22. Retrieved October 13, 2013, from http://www.dailypost.co.uk/news/north-wales-news/man-rescued-after-being-stuck-5169171.

Willnat, L. and D. H. Weaver. 2014. *The American Journalist in the Digital Age: Key Findings*. Bloomington: School of Journalism, University of Indiana. Retrieved May 16, 2014, from http://AmericanJournalistSurvey.com.

Wilson, M. 2014. "Facebook Nixes 'Like-Gating'." *PR Daily*, August 11. Retrieved September 7, 2014, from http://www.prdaily.com/Main/Articles/Facebook_nixes_likegating_17079.aspx.

Wolf, J. 2013. "GeekWire Profitable After Only Two Years." *Journalism That Matters*, July 11. Retrieved August 10, 2013, from http://www.journalismthatmatters.net/geekwire_profitable_after_only_two_years.

Workman, K. 2012. "The Sweetest Thing: Davisburg Man Honors Wife for Coping with Health Crisis." *Oakland Press* (Pontiac, MI), February 14. Retrieved

July 29, 2013, from http://www.theoaklandpress.com/articles/2012/02/14/life
/doc4f39684bba722070092405.txt.

Yemma, J. 2012a. "How the Monitor Is Doing." *Upfront Blog (Christian Science
Monitor)*, May 1. Retrieved June 14, 2013, from http://www.csmonitor.com
/Commentary/editors-blog/2012/0501/How-the-Monitor-is-doing.

———. 2012b. "A Word About Comments on CSMonitor.com." *Upfront Blog (Christian Science Monitor)*, September 5. Retrieved July 30, 2013, from http://www
.csmonitor.com/Commentary/editors-blog/2012/0905/A-word-about-
comments-on-CSMonitor.com.

Zamora, A. 2012. "Crowdsourcing Campaign Spending: What We Learned from
Free the Files." *ProPublica*, December 12. Retrieved September 6, 2013, from
http://www.propublica.org/article/crowdsourcing-campaign-spending-what
-we-learned-from-free-the-files.

———. 2013. "ProPublica Crowdsourcing: Free the Files." Presentation at Investigative Reporters and Editors conference in San Antonio, Texas, June 21.
Retrieved June 12, 2013, from http://prezi.com/lz7oa5n_-tb9/propublica
-crowdsourcing-free-the-files/.

INDEX

accessibility, ethic of: and database publication, 105; and Open Newsroom Project (*Register Citizen*, CT), 33
Advance Publications: as digitally-centered organization, 51–52; engagement model of, xxi; and hub strategy, 31; layoffs at, 74; and qualities of good reporters, 74; reader-focused workflows at, 75; success of, 136
advertising: cost of, page views and, 130; declining revenue from, 5, 7, 19, 135; in era of traditional journalism, 3, 5; in event-related publications, 38; hyperlocal journalism and, 95; in interactive databases, 105, 125; on mobile devices, 100; social media traffic as selling point for, 140–41; traditional separation of journalism from, 25; website multipliers and, 114, 117, 125
advertising-driven sites: criticisms of, 136, 137; and journalist standards, 136, 137; loyalty as key to success of, 137; volume of traffic as metric of engagement for, 135–36
Alfano, Rich, 83, 86
Allbritton Communications, 79–80, 93, 153n7; and hyperlocal journalism, 94–95
Allworth, J., 49–50
Alvarado, Ashley, 122
American City Business Journals, events by, 21
American Journalism Review, 95, 96
Anderson, Chris, 11, 92
Anderson, Kevin, 101, 111
AOL, and hyperlocal journalism, 95

apps: crowd-powered, 85; *Dallas Morning News* high school football app, 83–85, *84*, 86, 103; as engagement strategy, xxii; feedback on, importance of reading, 99; by NPR, xxii, 108; revenue from, 86, 103; *Seattle Times* University of Washington football app, 85–86, 103

Arab Spring coverage by NPR, crowdsourcing in, 46

Arizona Guardian (Phoenix), 94

Arrieta, Romeo, 28

Artley, Meredith, 4, 43, 78, 131

Art Walk Central (*Morning Sun* [MI] event), 37–38

Ash, Daniel, 22, 31, 130

Associated Press Managing Editors (APME), xviii; Innovator of the Year award, xvii, 97

"attention minutes," as measurement of engagement, 132, 142

audience: active seeking of, 44–45, 46; vs. public, 12; as term, 150n1. *See also* hyperlocal audiences; niche audiences

audience, new: attracting with games, 119; attracting with multipliers, 114, 118

audience advocates/czars, benefits of appointing, 76

audience-centric mind-set, as key to engagement, 8

audience comments: *Christian Science Monitor's* disabling of, 68–70, 76–77, 152–53n10; correction of errors by, 68; as engagement tool, 135; journalists' views on, 69–70; management of, 66–68; monetizing of, 139; structured formats for, 71; time

and energy consumed by, as issue, 68–71, 76–77

audience engagement: audience photos and videos, use of, 63–64; characteristics of engaged users, 48; creation of through conversation, 48–50; limited, in traditional model of journalism, xiii–xv, xvi–xvii, 3–4; meeting audience needs as key to, xxiii, 10–11, 145; monetizing of, 138; multipliers and, 113–18; page views as measurement of, 127, 128, 130–32; social media as tool for, 9, 46–47; subscription models and, xxii–xxiii, 7–8, 134–35, 137. *See also* conversation with audience; empowering audiences to satisfy curiosity; engagement, by journalists; events and meetups; games and contests; loyalty of audience

Audience Evolution (Napoli), 7

audience interests: conversations with audience as means of monitoring, 44, 45; Internet tools for monitoring, 45; necessity of active seeking, 44–45, 46; twitter as tool for engaging, 42

audience trust: journalists as trusted filter of information and, 64–65, 66; monetizing of, 140

Aurora, CO, shootings, CNN *Belief Blog* coverage of, xix, 42–45

Austin American-Statesman, and crowdsourcing, 60

Austin Chronicle, events by, 23–24

avoiding information, empowering audience ability for, 57

Babalola, Niran, 105

events and meetups: advertising revenues from publications related to,
38; by American City Business Journals, 21; by *Austin Chronicle*, 23–24;
benefits to news organizations
from, 18–19, 26; career counseling
events, 36; by *Chicago News Cooperative*, 26; in civic journalism tradition, 18, 20–21, 39–40; and creation
of engagement, 9, 10; criticisms of,
24–25; customer service model for,
39; by *Dallas Morning News*, 37; as
entrepreneurial opportunity, 21, 40;
failures to engage audience with, 26;
fees for, 17, 21, 22, 23; garage sales
as, 31; by *GeekWire*, 17–18, *18*, 23,
29–30, 37, 40; increasing use of, 138;
as journalism, 25; and loyalty, creation of, 10, 18, 21, 22, 24, 28, 29–30,
41; by magazines, 21; measuring
success of, 37–39, 41; by *Morning
Sun* (Mount Pleasant, MI), 37–38;
networking as draw for, 28, 29–30,
40; by *New York Times*, 22; by *Politico
Pro*, 29, 37, 40; popularity of, 21; by
Puget Sound Business Journal, 21, 39;
range of event types, 19, 21–22, 41;
reporters' and editors' involvement
in, 29, 40–41; as revenue source for
news organizations, 18–19, 21, 23,
24–25, 26–27; by *San Francisco Public
Press*, 22–23; by *Seattle Times*, 36;
and sense of community, building of, 18–19, 23, 30; as source of
intangible good will, 38, 41; by *Texas
Monthly*, 25; by *Texas Tribune*, 19,
23–24, 25, 27–29, 40; by *Washington
Post*, 24–25, 37; by WBEZ-FM (Chicago), 21–22; by *West Seattle Blog*,
31; "you-have-to-be-there" vibe and,

27–29, 40. *See also* corporate sponsors for events and meetups
evolution of journalism, from lecture to
conversation, xv
experience, delivery of, creation of
loyalty through, 12

Facebook: creating targeted groups
on, 61; and crowdsourcing, 59, 61;
engagement rates, calculation of,
xix; Fandemonium contest (*Denver
Post*), 140; fan groups on, 85; games
and contests on, 38, 121; interaction
with readers on, 70; and measurement of engagement, 135; and
microaudiences, creation of, 66;
monitoring and measuring activity on, 126–27; posting audience
photos and videos on, 63; revenue
generated on, 121; and shallow *vs.*
authentic engagement, 12; sharing
of games on, 118; sharing of stories,
motives for, 130
face-to-face engagement with audiences, 17–41; book clubs and,
37; effective, common elements
of, 39–41; as guiding principle
of engagement, 10, 145; importance of, as underappreciated, 37;
informational handouts and, 36–37;
measuring impact of, 37–39, 41;
Open Newsroom Project (*Register
Citizen*, CT) and, xx, 32–36, *33*. *See
also* events and meetups
Farnsworth, Meghann, 6, 117, 140
Fenster, Jordan, 66, 152n9
Fire Forecast App (NPR), xxii, 108
First Amendment Award (Society of
Professional Journalists), xvi
flexibility, value of in digital age, 144

Hufman, Matt, xxi, 49, 67
hyperlocal audiences: *vs.* subject-
focused niche audiences, 82; tactics
for attracting, 96. *See also* niche
audiences
hyperlocal journalism: and audience
loyalty, xiii–xiv; and measures
of engagement, 132; new outlets
devoted to, xiv; partnering of with
other news outlets, xiv, xvii–xviii,
97–98; partnering with other outlets, xv–xvi; profitability of, 11, 98;
successes and failures in, 94–97. *See
also* niche journalism

Informing the News (Patterson), 3
Ingwerson, Marshall, 88, 114, 129
The Innovator's Dilemma (Christensen),
26–27
in-person connections. *See* events and
meetups; face-to-face engagement
with audiences
InsideClimate News, 89
interaction with audience at every
step, 42–78; as guiding principle of
engaged journalism, 10, 145; real
time engagement, as daily habit,
50–53. *See also* blogging; conversation with audience; face-to-face
engagement with audiences; social
media
interactive content, 104–25; ease of
navigation and, 57; as method of
creating engagement, 9; revenue
from, 125; simplicity, importance of,
124; successful, common elements
of, 123–25. *See also* games and contests; interactive databases
interactive databases: and audience
engagement, xviii, 11, 104–5; chica-

gocrime.org crime databases, 106;
crowdsourcing of, 109–11; errors in,
as issue, 112; ethic of transparency
and, 106, 110, 113; funding of, 107;
increasing use of, 106–7; as journalism, 106, 112–13, 124; and judgment,
need to exercise, 112–13; monetizing of, 139; necessity of promoting, 111–12; at NPR, xxii, 108; at
ProPublica, xxii; range of data useful
for, 107; refreshing, importance of,
124; revenue from, 105, 125; of *Texas
Tribune*, 104–5, 107, 109, 113, 125;
usability, importance of, 107–8
international news organizations, and
measurements of engagement,
142–43
Investigative News Network, 129
It's News to Me (TV game show), 123

Jacobson-Hines, Julie, 61
Jarvis, Jeff, 64
Jenkins, Joe, 100–101
JimRomenesko.com, 74
journalism: goals of, and goals of business model, 138; quality of *vs.* page
views, as unresolvable tension,
133; role of in age of social media,
49–50; traditional separation from
business side of news organizations,
25, 39. *See also* traditional model of
journalism; watchdog journalism
journalistic standards: advertising-
driven sites and, 136, 137; engagement and, 146
journalists: and audience comments,
views on, 69–70, 143; and economic
value of work, focus on, 141, 143;
and events, involvement in, 29,
40–41; good, qualities of, 74;

story leads and tips, audience submission of: audience loyalty and, 30; at events, 40; during live chat news meetings, 50; open newsrooms and, 32, 33; on Twitter, 73, 90

Stroud, Natalie Jomini, 91

subscribing, as form of engagement, 80

subscription models: and changes in approach to engagement, 134–35, 143; and engagement, necessity of, 7–8, 135, 137; at London *Telegraph*, 134–35, 137; metered paywalls, 134, 135, 137, 143; at *New York Times*, 134, 137; at *Politico Pro*, xxii; at *Seattle Times*, 7–8, 134; at *Telegraph* (London), xxiii; at *TPM Prime*, 139–40; at *Wall Street Journal*, 134

subscriptions, increasing revenue from, 5, 7

Sullivan, Margaret, 73

Summer Bash party (*GeekWire*), 17–18, 18, 29–30

Superstorm Sandy, skeletons unearthed by, coverage of, xxii, 53–54

Supreme Court, U.S., same-sex marriage ruling by, 71

surveys. *See* polls and surveys

survival of media outlets: necessity of engagement for, xvi, 4, 5, 8, 146; watchdog function and, 4–5

tablets. *See* mobile devices

Talking Points Memo, 139–40

targeting of content, as method of engagement, 9. *See also* hyperlocal journalism; niche journalism

Taylor, Jaycee, 34

TBD.com, 94–95

TechCrunch, 21, 87, 131

Telegraph (London): games by, 118–19, 124; subscription model of, xxiii, 134–35, 137, 143

Telegraph Media Group: engagement model of, xxii–xxiii; and journalists' engagement, rewarding of, 77–78; and mobile device revenue, 101; subscription model of, 7

television news: era of network dominance in, 58; social media as ahead of, 58

10000Words.net, 122

Texas Education Agency, online databases, 107, 108

Texas Monthly, events held by, 25

Texas Prison Inmates databases, errors in, 113

Texas Tribune: criticisms of events held by, 25; diversification of revenue sources at, 141; engagement of audience by, xviii; events held by, 19, 23–24, 25, 27–29, 40; games and contests by, 119–20, 122–23, 124–25; live Davis filibuster coverage, 56–57; as niche journalism, 88–89, 93–94; online databases of, 104–5, 107, 109, 113, 125; revenue, viewer empowerment and, 57; and *Texas Weekly*, purchase of, 81

Texas Tribune Festival, xviii, 24, 25; "you-have-to-be-there" vibe of, 27–29, 40

Texas Weekly, 81, 88–89, 102–3

Thompson, Mark, 125, 138

Thompson, Matt, 128

Tinsley, Clarice, 1, 2

topical niches. *See* niche audiences; niche journalism

town square, newspapers as, partnerships with hyperlocal blogs and, 97

CPSIA information can be obtained at www.ICGtesting.com
Printed in the USA
BVOW08*2133080915

416992BV00001B/1/P